IMPROVING OUTCOMES FOR STUDENTS WITH OR AT RISK FOR READING DISABILITIES

EDUCATION IN A COMPETITIVE AND GLOBALIZING WORLD

Additional books in this series can be found on Nova's website under the Series tab.

Additional e-books in this series can be found on Nova's website under the e-book tab.

EDUCATION IN A COMPETITIVE AND GLOBALIZING WORLD

IMPROVING OUTCOMES FOR STUDENTS WITH OR AT RISK FOR READING DISABILITIES

KATRINA PETRONE
EDITOR

nova publishers

New York

Library of Congress Cataloging-in-Publication Data

ISBN: 978-1-63321-168-1

Published by Nova Science Publishers, Inc. † New York

CONTENTS

PREFACE

Reading difficulties present serious and potentially lifelong challenges. Children who do not read well are more likely to be retained a grade in school, drop out of high school, become teen parents, or enter the juvenile justice system. Thus, preventing reading difficulties early in children's school careers has potential long-term benefits to the individual as well as society. This book describes what has been learned regarding the improvement of reading outcomes for children with or at risk for reading disabilities through research funded by the National Center for Education Research and National Center for Special Education Research. The synthesis describes contributions to the knowledge base produced by IES-funded research across four focal areas: assessment, basic cognitive and linguistic processes, intervention, and professional development. This book also offers specific recommendations to help educators identify students in need of intervention and implement evidence-based interventions to promote their reading achievement. It also describes how to carry out each recommendation, including how to address potential roadblocks in implementing them.

Chapter 1 - In this report, the authors review the results of the first eight years of IES-funded research that focused on ways to prevent and remediate reading difficulties in students with or at risk for reading disabilities. Supporting investigations on assessment, cognitive and linguistic processes of reading, effective interventions, and teacher professional development, IES-funded research has made substantive contributions to answering some of the most pressing research questions in reading. These projects have elucidated ways to identify and help children who may struggle with reading before the problems become entrenched. IES research has also identified critical component skills that support proficient reading, found ways to assess these skills, and developed and tested interventions for children at risk of developing reading disabilities, including children with who are deaf or hard of hearing or who have intellectual disabilities. Importantly, IES-funded research has funded projects that investigate ways to bring effective interventions into our nation's classrooms. This includes designing professional development training that increases teachers' knowledge about literacy and deepens their understanding of how to teach reading effectively to all students, including students who are struggling to learn to read.

Chapter 2 - In the primary grades students with reading difficulties may need intervention to prevent future reading failure. This guide offers specific recommendations to help educators identify students in need of intervention and implement evidence-based interventions to promote their reading achievement. It also describes how to carry out each recommendation, including how to address potential roadblocks in implementing them.

The authors, are a small group with expertise in various dimensions of this topic. Several of us are also experts in research methodology. The recommendations in this guide reflect not only the author's expertise and experience but the findings of rigorous studies of interventions to promote reading achievement.

Each recommendation received a rating that describes the strength of the research evidence that has shown its effectiveness. These ratings—"strong," "moderate," or "low"—are defined as:

Strong refers to consistent and generalizable evidence that a program causes better outcomes.

Moderate refers to evidence from studies that allow strong causal conclusions but cannot be generalized with assurance to the population on which a recommendation is focused (perhaps because the findings have not been widely replicated) or to evidence from studies that are generalizable but have more causal ambiguity than offered by experimental designs (such as statistical models of correlational data or group comparison designs for which equivalence of the groups at pretest is uncertain).

Low refers to expert opinion based on reasonable extrapolations from research and theory on other topics and evidence from studies that do not meet the standards for moderate or strong evidence.

Table 1 details the criteria used to determine the level of evidence for each recommendation. For questions about what works best, high-quality experimental and quasi-experimental studies, such as those meeting the criteria of the What Works Clearinghouse (www.whatworks.ed.gov), have a privileged position. The evidence considered in developing and rating these recommendations included experimental research on providing differentiated instruction in a general education classroom and rigorous evaluations of intensive reading interventions. The authors also examined studies on the technical adequacy of batteries of screening measures.

In: Improving Outcomes for Students …   ISBN: 978-1-63321-168-1
Editor: Katrina Petrone   © 2014 Nova Science Publishers, Inc.

Chapter 1

IMPROVING READING OUTCOMES FOR STUDENTS WITH OR AT RISK FOR READING DISABILITIES: A SYNTHESIS OF THE CONTRIBUTIONS FROM THE INSTITUTE OF EDUCATION SCIENCES RESEARCH CENTERS[*]

*Carol M. Connor, Paul A. Alberto, Donald L. Compton
and Rollanda E. O'Connor*

EXECUTIVE SUMMARY

Improving Reading Outcomes for Students with or at Risk for Reading Disabilities: A Synthesis of the Contributions from the Institute of Education Sciences Research Centers

Reading difficulties present serious and potentially lifelong challenges. Children who do not read well are more likely to be retained a grade in school, drop out of high school, become teen parents, or enter the juvenile justice

---

[*] This is an edited, reformatted and augmented version of a report, NCSER 2014-3000, prepared under contract for the National Center for Special Education Research, dated February 2014.

system. Thus, preventing reading difficulties early in children's school careers has potential long-term benefits to the individual as well as society.[1] In this report, we review the results of the first eight years of IES-funded research that focused on ways to prevent and remediate reading difficulties in students with or at risk for reading disabilities. Supporting investigations on assessment, cognitive and linguistic processes of reading, effective interventions, and teacher professional development, IES-funded research has made substantive contributions to answering some of the most pressing research questions in reading. These projects have elucidated ways to identify and help children who may struggle with reading before the problems become entrenched. IES research has also identified critical component skills that support proficient reading, found ways to assess these skills, and developed and tested interventions for children at risk of developing reading disabilities, including children with who are deaf or hard of hearing or who have intellectual disabilities. Importantly, IES-funded research has funded projects that investigate ways to bring effective interventions into our nation's classrooms. This includes designing professional development training that increases teachers' knowledge about literacy and deepens their understanding of how to teach reading effectively to all students, including students who are struggling to learn to read.

I. Assessment

Enactment of the No Child Left Behind Act (NCLB; 2002) along with the reauthorization of the Individuals with Disabilities Education Act (IDEA, 2004), significantly changed the assessment landscape for all students in public schools and in particular those who are at risk for poor reading outcomes. One of the more significant provisions of NCLB was the requirement that states adopt standards and conduct annual assessments to gauge school districts' progress in improving students' academic achievement. States were similarly required to test and report the progress of the various subgroups of students, including English learners and students with disabilities. In addition, states were responsible for holding schools accountable for documenting Adequate Yearly Progress (AYP) of these subgroups based on the state assessments. As a result, states needed to know how to identify students who struggle with reading using fair and valid assessments.

IES-funded research has provided knowledge on the following important guiding principles for reading assessment:

- Screening all students' reading skills (i.e., universal screening) at the beginning of the school year, especially in the early grades, and then using assessments to monitor their progress can be a valid and efficient way to: (1) identify children who are at risk for poor reading outcomes and (2) guide the decision making process, for example, through a Response to Intervention (RtI) approach, for determining whether an intervention is improving a student's reading skills.
- Reading assessments can be tailored to a wider range of diverse learners to support accurate calculation of Adequate Yearly Progress (AYP) and to identify failing schools.

II. Basic Cognitive and Linguistic Processes Support Reading Skills and Can be Improved through Intervention

IES supports basic research to understand the underlying processes and mechanisms of reading. By applying cognitive and developmental perspectives to reading, this interdisciplinary research has studied the cognitive and linguistic skills that distinguish children with typical reading skills from children with or at risk for reading disabilities and examined the extent to which those skills are changeable through targeted interventions and the points of the developmental trajectory that may be most amenable to change.

IES-funded researchers identified important targets for intervention based on the cognitive and linguistic skills children bring to the classroom.

- Malleable linguistic processes such as oral language skills and vocabulary contribute to children's reading performance.
- Several important cognitive processes such as working memory, grasp of the principles of conservation and seriation, and abstract and inferential reasoning are critical for students' reading success.
- Although the same sets of linguistic and cognitive skills are involved in learning to read, children bring unique constellations of these skills to the classroom with important implications for instruction.

III. Intervention, Including Reading Instruction for Children with Low Incidence Disabilities

IES has funded rigorous, causal research that identifies the types of interventions that improve students' reading outcomes, along with the optimal timing for delivering these interventions and the likely effects of improved instructional intensity for students with different profiles of component skills. This work builds on the foundation set over the last two decades by reading researchers.

- Increasing the intensity of interventions in kindergarten and first grade can prevent reading difficulties for many students.
- Fluency interventions that focus on repeated reading of text, opportunities to practice reading in the classroom, and reading a range of texts can generally improve students' fluency and comprehension.
- Language outcomes for many preschool children at risk for language disabilities can improve if they are provided extensive opportunities to hear and use complex oral language.
- Peer-assisted or cooperative learning is a promising method to increase the intensity of instruction for students and improving their reading outcomes.
- Interventions that are differentiated to target an individual student's profile of component skills are effective in improving students' reading development.

Children who have intellectual disabilities or who are deaf or hard of hearing face serious challenges when they are learning to read. For example, children who are deaf or hard of hearing cannot easily access the auditory aspects of reading, such as phonological awareness and letter-sound associations. Children with intellectual disabilities face cognitive challenges that impact their reading progress. At the same time, children with disabilities are being served in the general education classroom.

IES-funded research has moved the field forward in practical ways with newly developed and promising instructional interventions for children with low incidence disabilities.

- The developmental sequence of learning to read and reading theories, such as the *Simple View of Reading*, which inform effective instruction for typical readers, also hold for students with low incidence disabilities, including children with mild and moderate intellectual disabilities and children who are deaf or hard of hearing. This means that effective interventions can be developed based on this research, and implemented to improve achievement.

V. Supporting Effective Teachers and Effective Teaching of Reading

We cannot bring research into the classroom and improve students' reading skills if we cannot effectively support teachers' efforts to use efficacious or evidence-based interventions and instructional strategies. The No Child Left Behind Act specifically called for students to have highly qualified teachers. In the past, teacher quality was defined in terms of academic degree or years of experience. However, these teacher characteristics are rarely associated with gains in student achievement.[2]

IES-funded research has identified ways to support teachers' implementation of evidence-based reading instruction and interventions.

- Developing teachers' specialized knowledge and supporting consistent long-term implementation of evidence-based instructional practices can improve delivery of complex, evidence-based instruction and interventions.
- Combining multiple professional development strategies, including coaching, linking student assessment data to instruction, using technology, and participating in communities of practice, can support teachers' learning and implementation of research-based reading instruction.

Summary

For this research synthesis, we examined peer-reviewed journal articles and chapters that were products of IES funded research projects that focused on improving reading for children with or at risk for reading disabilities. We reviewed research from grants that were initially awarded from 2002 through 2008 through the National Center for Education Research and the National Center for Special Education Research. Based on this review, we found that these research projects have extended our knowledge about how to help students with or at risk for reading disabilities. We have learned more about how to prevent reading difficulties through valid and reliable assessments.

Such assessments can accurately identify students who need additional instruction. Other research projects have developed and tested interventions that are targeted, intensive, and based on rigorous evaluations so that schools can support learning to read for all students. Through IES-funded research, we are gaining a better understanding of the components of reading comprehension and how underlying cognitive and linguistic processes operate in a coordinated fashion to support reading. This research has also helped to illuminate how children bring different and developing profiles of skills to the classroom with implications for assessment and instruction. Additionally, IES-funded research is improving reading instruction for children who are deaf or hard of hearing, who have intellectual disabilities, or other low incidence disabilities. Finally, IES-funded research has helped to provide new knowledge on ways for bringing research-based assessment and instructional practices into the classroom by identifying and testing ways to improve the effectiveness of teachers and their practice.

The research centers in IES continue to support rigorous research that will enable schools to implement effective instructional practices and interventions to help all students become better readers.

Preamble from the Institute of Education Sciences

In 1999, the National Research Council published a report on the state of education research in the United States. The panel concluded,

> One striking fact is that the complex world of education—unlike defense, health care, or industrial production—does not rest on a strong research base. In no other field are personal experience and ideology so frequently relied on to make policy choices, and in no other field is the research base so inadequate and little used.
>
> National Research Council (1999, p. 1)

Three years later with the passage of the Education Sciences Reform Act of 2002, Congress established the Institute of Education Sciences (IES) and charged it with supporting rigorous, scientifically valid research that is relevant to education practice and policy. To meet this charge, IES established long-term programs of research that focused on topics of importance to education practitioners and leaders (e.g., reading, teacher quality, education systems), clearly specified methodological requirements for projects, and established a scientific peer review system for reviewing grant proposals.

Since 2002, IES' National Center for Education Research has funded a broad range of work targeted toward providing solutions to the education problems in our nation. In 2006, IES' National Center for Special Education Research began funding a comprehensive program of special education research designed to expand the knowledge and understanding of infants, toddlers and children with or at risk for disabilities. In both IES Centers, the funds are provided for exploratory research, development of education interventions, development and validation of measurement instruments, and evaluation of the impact of interventions. Exploratory research examines the relations between education outcomes and malleable factors (i.e., factors that can be changed, such as child behaviors, teacher practices, school management strategies), as well as the mediators and moderators of those relations. Exploratory research can inform the development of new education interventions or identify those interventions that are associated with better education outcomes and should be rigorously evaluated. Development and innovation projects are intended to create potent and robust interventions that may be effective for improving education outcomes. Development research is important because we have not yet solved old problems (e.g., closing achievement gaps), and we continue to face new challenges and opportunities (e.g., integrating new technologies into education systems). In addition to developing interventions, IES supports research to develop and validate measurement instruments, including screening tools, progress monitoring instruments, measures of child outcomes, and assessments of teachers' and administrators' knowledge and skills.

A critical component of IES research has been rigorous evaluation of the impact of programs, practices, and policies on education outcomes. Education has always produced new ideas, new innovations, and new approaches, but as in any field, new may not always be better. Historically education research has not rigorously tested whether programs and policies actually produce positive effects on education outcomes. The research enterprise has not provided education leaders and practitioners with scientifically valid information on which interventions appear to be effective in achieving their intended goals, which need more work to become more potent or more robust, and which appear ineffective and should perhaps be discarded. Since its inception, IES has been committed to supporting rigorous experimental and quasi-experimental evaluations to answer the questions of what works, for whom under what conditions; and why something does or does not work. This document is an effort to stock of what we have learned thus far.

IES Research Syntheses

As part of our assessment of the work that IES is doing, we are asking panels of eminent scholars to review peer-reviewed journal articles and book chapters that are products of IES-funded research grants in a specific area (e.g., reading, early childhood). These papers include empirical studies as well as theoretical pieces. The task for each panel of scholars is to synthesize what we have learned from IES-funded research on their topic and to summarize the results for a general audience that includes policymakers and other stakeholders. The syntheses are not intended to be typical research reviews, which provides a grand overview of research in a field. Rather, the task is to look across the research projects that IES has funded to determine what has been learned and where empirical and theoretical progress has been made as a result of IES funding, and to provide suggestions for further research in order to improve education in our country.

The first step involved in producing an IES research synthesis is to select a topic. Topics are determined by IES staff members who review the overall research portfolio to identify topics that include multiple projects that have been completed and from which peer-reviewed articles and book chapters have already been published. A panel chair is selected who is a nationally recognized researcher in the topic area. Next, IES staff works with the chair to identify a small number of panelists to co-author the research synthesis. These are people the chair believes are nationally recognized experts in the topic area, and are, in many cases, themselves recipients of IES grants. IES identifies the research grants that are relevant to the topic and gathers the peer-reviewed journal articles and book chapters that were produced under these grants relevant to the topic being reviewed. IES staff consults with grantees when appropriate in order to ascertain the relevance of the funded project to the topic of the synthesis and to confirm that all peer-reviewed articles emerging from these projects are included. The panel meets several times, either in person or via conference calls, to discuss the focus of the synthesis and to identify organizing questions or themes.

The panel is given a relatively short deadline of 4 to 6 months to produce a draft document. Under the broad question of what has been learned from IES-supported research, the panel reviews the published research and organizes the synthesis under topics or questions that reflect the work that has been published. The panel may also include non-IES research in the synthesis, to provide the background or context for the IES-sponsored research or to describe the work on which IES research builds. The expert panel interacts with and receives feedback from IES staff during the development of the research synthesis. However, the panel uses their collective expertise to determine the foci of the written report, and the synthesis reflects the panel members' expert judgment as to the strength of the evidence presented in the published work and the contribution of the reviewed articles and book chapters to the synthesis topic. The panel members are the authors of the synthesis and thus responsible for the final product.

Before the research synthesis can be published, it is subjected to rigorous external peer review through the IES Standards and Review Office, which is responsible for independent review of IES publications. The panel then responds to the peer-reviewer comments and makes appropriate revisions.

This focus of the present synthesis reflects the Institute's emphasis on research on programs, practices, and policies intended to improve reading outcomes for children with or at risk for reading disabilities. IES-funded projects whose primary emphasis was improving the reading skills of children with typical reading abilities were not included in the studies selected for review. IES has funded research on improving reading outcomes since 2002 through the National Center for Education Research (NCER) and since 2006 through the National Center for Special Education Research (NCSER). NCER funds reading research through multiple topics, including Reading and Writing, Interventions for Struggling Adolescent and Adult Readers and Writers, Cognition and Student Learning, and Teacher Quality. NCSER funds reading research primarily under the Reading, Writing, and Language Development, Cognition and Student Learning in Special Education topics.

In reading this synthesis, readers should remember that it is not intended to be an overview of the existing research on improving reading for children with or at risk for reading disabilities. Panel members were only asked to review those published articles or book chapters that had emerged from IES-funded projects. Specifically, the panel was asked to review articles from peer-reviewed journals and book chapters from funded projects that were published or in press as of December 2011 (thus some articles that were in press in 2011 will have published dates in 2012 or 2013). Thus, there is a great deal of ongoing research that is not represented in this synthesis because some grants are not yet at the stage in the research process where findings are in and summarized for publication. Note also that reports of IES-funded research that have not been subjected to the peer-review process in publication are not included in this review. Appendix A lists the projects and publications that were reviewed for this synthesis.

Given panel members were only asked to review those peer-reviewed articles and book chapters that emerged from IES-funded projects available at the time this synthesis was written, there likely are peer-reviewed articles or book chapters emerging from ongoing IES-funded research relevant to the synthesis topic. IES plans to include those articles and book chapters in future updates of this synthesis.

Context and Organization of This Report

Reading difficulties and disabilities present serious and potentially lifelong challenges. Children who do not read well are more likely to be retained a grade in school, drop out of high school, become a teen parent, or enter the juvenile justice system.[3] Building on the extant research and seminal studies including the National Reading Panel and the National Early Literacy Panel reports,[4] research supported by the Institute of Education Sciences (IES) has expanded our understanding of ways to identify and help children who are at risk for reading disabilities. This body of work has also contributed to the identification of critical component skills that support proficient reading (e.g., phonological awareness, word knowledge, working memory), better ways to assess these skills, and more effective interventions for children at risk of developing reading difficulties, including children who are deaf or have intellectual disabilities.[5] Research funded by IES has investigated ways to bring these efficacious interventions into our nation's classrooms by developing and evaluating professional development training that increases teachers' knowledge about literacy and how to teach reading effectively to all students, including students who are struggling to learn how to read. This is important because the most recent National Assessment of Educational Progress[6] reports that by fourth grade, one-third of our students are failing to attain basic reading skills. In this synthesis, we, the panel convened by IES, connect the building blocks of assessment, cognitive and linguistic components of reading, effective interventions, and teacher professional development to show how IES-funded research is contributing to solutions for improving reading and preventing reading difficulties.

Based on our initial reading of the papers, and following an initial in-person meeting to discuss the articles that we read, we organized the contributions into four broad categories with component research questions:

I. **Assessment**: What have we learned about effective identification and assessment of students who have or are at risk for reading difficulties or disabilities?

II. **Basic Cognitive and Linguistic Processes**: What are the basic cognitive and linguistic processes that support successful reading and how can these skills be improved for students who have or who are at risk for reading disabilities?

III. **Intervention**: How do we make reading instruction more effective for students who have or are at risk for developing reading disabilities? How do we teach reading to students with low incidence disabilities?

IV. **Professional Development**: How do we bring research-based instructional practices to the classroom?

These categories emerged directly from the articles that we read and reflect the areas in which we believe that IES-supported research has made contributions to advancing our understanding of how to improve reading outcomes for students with or at risk for reading disabilities. For each question, the panel synthesized the available research findings and highlighted key contributions.

Scope of the Research Synthesis

For this research synthesis, we examined 111 peer-reviewed journal articles and book chapters that were products of 48 research projects focused on improving reading for children with or at risk for reading disabilities funded by IES with initial awards (i.e., first year of funding) from 2002 through 2008.[7] These papers included both empirical studies as well as theoretical pieces. (Appendix A provides a list of all of the projects and publications included in our review.) Our task was to synthesize what has been learned thus far through IES research grant activities focused on improving reading for children with or at risk for disabilities. This is not a typical synthesis intended to provide a grand overview of research in a field, nor is it a meta-analysis that quantitatively synthesizes a specific body of work. Rather, our task was to look across the range of projects that IES has funded in this area to determine what has been learned, where progress has been made as a result of IES funding, and to provide suggestions for further research in improving reading skills of children with or at risk for reading disabilities.

I. ASSESSMENT: WHAT HAVE WE LEARNED ABOUT EFFECTIVE IDENTIFICATION AND ASSESSMENT OF STUDENTS WHO HAVE OR ARE AT RISK FOR READING DIFFICULTIES OR DISABILITIES?

Enactment of the No Child Left Behind Act (NCLB, 2002) along with the reauthorization of the Individuals with Disabilities Education Act (IDEA, 2004) substantially changed the assessment landscape for all students in public schools. In particular, assessment for those who are at elevated risk for poor reading outcomes, including students with limited English proficiency, students from minority racial or ethnic groups, students with disabilities, and students from low- income families, was brought to the forefront. The shift in focus to include all students in accountability testing has led to increased scrutiny of state assessments from an accessibility standpoint. An accessible and valid assessment is one that evaluates the targeted knowledge and skills of all students, including students whose characteristics create challenges for accurate measurement using traditional assessments.[8] Implicit within this definition of accessibility is the presumption that the assessments are valid measures of performance for students with very different skills and challenges. The Standards for Educational and Psychological Testing[9] calls for testing professionals to investigate the validity of the intended score interpretation for all students, with special rules for students with disabilities because tests can be less valid and reliable when used for students with limited English proficiency or students with disabilities. As a result, IES has made significant investments into research exploring the psychometric properties of alternative or accommodated assessments of reading to explore ways to ensure testing validity when assessing children who are at significant risk for very poor reading outcomes.

Results from IES-sponsored research examining reading assessment questions related to NCLB and IDEA contributes to the evidence base showing that universal screening and progress monitoring assessments can work for identifying students in need of early reading intervention and for making instructional decisions. A broad range of assessments and accommodations are also being developed and evaluated for use with a wider range of diverse learners. Below we present the following contributions from IES-funded research through 2011 in the area of assessment including: (1) the use of universal screening to identify students at risk for poor reading outcomes who are eligible for early reading intervention; (2) methods for quantifying actual or potential response to research-based intervention (i.e., progress monitoring); (3) valid assessments for English learners; and (4) evaluation of testing accommodations for students with learning disabilities or other disabilities.

Universal Screening

Background. The success of early intervening service models such as RtI hinge on an accurate determination of which students are at risk for reading disabilities, according to several professional organizations.[10] RtI uses a process where students who fail to respond to instruction, based on assessment results, receive increasingly intensive interventions, moving from Tier 1 (general education) to Tier 2 (typically small group instruction) to Tier 3 (individual instruction). Correct identification of students at risk for reading disability in preschool through first grade can trigger early reading intervention prior to the onset of significant problems, which in turn can place students on the path of adequate reading development. Universal screening is a principal means of identifying students as being at risk for reading difficulties.[11] In both research and practice, it usually involves measures of early literacy and foundational reading skills, including phonemic awareness, letter naming fluency, concepts about print, word reading, and oral language ability, including vocabulary. Frequently a score cut-point is established where children with scores falling below the cut-point are considered at risk for reading difficulties and hence in need of additional intervention.[12]

Predicting which preliterate children are at risk for developing reading disabilities has proven problematic.[13] Initial differences among preschool and kindergarten children associated with family literacy practices may diminish with formal instruction,[14] however, once children begin reading instruction, the screening measures expand to include skills that are more closely aligned to reading[15] and measurement precision increases with age as intra-child stability increases.[16] The vast majority of studies examining preschool and kindergarten screening tools have identified too many children who do not develop reading problems (false positive cases),[17] with estimates ranging from 20 percent to 60 percent.[18] At the same time, children who do develop reading problems are missed (false negatives cases), with percentages ranging from 10 percent to 50 percent.[19] However, expanding the screening battery beyond measures of phonological processing, alphabetic knowledge, general language ability, and print concepts has yielded limited improvements in predictive utility.[20]

Because accurately assessing reading improves as children experience more reading instruction, other reading researchers argue that screening should occur at the beginning of first grade rather than in preschool and kindergarten.[21] Despite the benefits of waiting, the accuracy of determining risk among first graders remains relatively low, with false negative rates approaching minimally acceptable levels; unfortunately, false positive rates fall well outside the acceptable range,[22] yielding unmanageable risk pools for an RtI framework. More optimistically, these false positive rates may reflect children's response to the instruction they receive.

Contributions from IES-Supported Research

Contribution 1. Screening all students' reading skills (i.e., universal screening) at the beginning of the school year, especially in the early grades, can be a valid and efficient way to identify students who are at risk for poor reading outcomes. Several IES-funded researchers are examining the use of universal screening for young children. In general, the IES investment exploring applied issues related to screening for eligibility for intervening services among preschool through first grade children has resulted in important increases in the knowledge base and furthered our understanding of universal screening procedures.

In an attempt to improve the screening accuracy of preliterate children IES-funded researchers are further developing, evaluating, and refining two screening measures, Individual Growth and Development Indicators (IGDI) and Get Ready to Read!. Both the IGDI[23] and Get Ready to Read![24] measurement systems were designed to screen preschool children to identify those at elevated risk for poor reading outcomes. The Get Ready to Read! screening tool is a 20-item task that measures print knowledge and phonological awareness whereas the IGDI system contains a number of tasks designed to measure a more diverse array of developmental domains from birth to 8 years. As such, the Get Ready to Read! assessment is more focused on reading and therefore potentially more sensitive to the identification of early literacy problems. The IGDI system also differs from Get Ready to Read! in that it is designed to allow skills to be monitored across time and allow the use of estimated growth rates to identify the need for and monitor response to early intervention.

In an IES-supported study, Wilson and Lonigan (2009) administered the Get Ready to Read! and IGDI screening tools to preschoolers. Get Ready to Read! and IGDI measures were used to classify children identified as at risk on a diagnostic measure of early reading skill administered 3 months later. In general, both the Get Ready to Read! and IGDI systems showed promise as early screening tools with Get Ready to Read! out-performing IGDI on predicting overall emergent literacy skill, although neither reached the level of accuracy recommended by Jenkins (2003).

As well as supporting research examining screening young children, IES has invested in exploring basic measurement issues surrounding universal screening procedures in first grade. In a series of studies supported by IES as well as NICHD and OSEP, Compton et al. (2006, 2010, 2012)[25] explored ways of improving screening batteries to (a) increase the overall classification rates, (b) decrease the number of false positive cases, (c) improve the efficiency of universal screening procedures, and (d) accelerate the movement of the most at-risk readers to more intensive levels of intervention services. In the initial NICHD supported study of classification models, based on an evaluation of 206 first-grade children followed through the end of second grade, Compton et al. (2006) reported that a multivariate screening battery containing measures of phonological awareness, rapid naming, oral vocabulary, and word identification fluency skills produced classification accuracies (sensitivity of .90 and specificity of .83) consistent with the recommendation of Jenkins (2003). In an IES-supported follow-up study of 355 first grade children followed through the end of second grade, Compton et al. (2010) replicated the initial model developed in the 2006 study. Measures designed to directly assess (progress monitoring) or forecast (dynamic assessment) children's response to classroom instruction added significantly to prediction accuracy by reducing the rate of false positives. Models adding progress monitoring measures to the base multivariate screening battery developed in the 2006 study significantly increased classification accuracy (sensitivity of .90 and specificity of .91).

As part of the 2010 study, Compton et al. extended the screening literature by examining the use of a two-step screening procedure, hoping that it might yield an efficient overall screening system that would accurately classify students. In the two-step procedure, all children are administered a single, brief measure, and only children who score within the risk range on that initial measure complete the longer screening battery. A measure of phonemic decoding efficiency eliminated the greatest number of true negatives (40% of the sample) from screening. Phonemic decoding efficiency significantly outperformed measures of sight word efficiency, word identification, and word attack in reducing the sample to be screened further. The researchers therefore recommended the use of a two-step gated procedure where all students are tested and then only those falling below a cut-point receive a longer battery of assessments, as a means to increase the efficiency of one-step universal screening procedures.

Finally, Compton and colleagues (2012) working with first-grade children determined to be unresponsive to general education who were enrolled in a small group intervention found that Tier 2 response data may not be necessary to accurately predict a group of children for whom Tier 2 interventions were unlikely to be effective. Rather, by using local norms on first-grade word identification fluency growth and linking those norms to distal outcomes of reading disability at the end of second grade, the team was able to accurately predict students who did and did not respond to the intervention. This suggests that students can be identified accurately for Tier 3 intervention without participating in (and failing to benefit from) Tier 2 interventions.

Future Directions. Results of the preschool studies are encouraging and suggest that we may be able to apply universal screening for reading disability risk to preschool children. More work is warranted at this age level to meet the screening accuracy defined by Jenkins (2003). As children move into formal reading instruction (i.e., first grade), results from these funded projects indicate that we can achieve classification accuracy levels that exceed those recommended through the use of two-stage multivariate screening batteries, however more work is still needed to continue to optimize these systems across larger and more diverse samples of children.

Progress Monitoring

Background. A cornerstone of alternative approaches to learning disabilities identification, outlined in the reauthorization of IDEA (2004), is the provision requiring the measurement of children's outcome gains in response to scientific, research-based intervention. Progress monitoring assessments allow us to gauge students' progress. For example, within RtI models, progress-monitoring assessment results are used to make a series of decisions that move students between more and less intensive levels of intervention. Given the importance of these decisions within an RtI framework, validity and measurement issues associated with progress monitoring procedures need to be explored. IES has funded studies to further develop, evaluate the psychometrics, and explore the predictive utility of various progress monitoring measures that can be used to accurately judge children's response to research-based interventions.

Two progress monitoring measures are frequently used for indexing and monitoring first-grade reading development: Word Identification Fluency[26] and Nonsense Word Fluency.[27] These measures were developed to be sensitive to early reading development skills. With Word Identification Fluency, students have one minute to read isolated high-frequency words presented in a list containing 50 words. With Nonsense Word Fluency, the child is presented with a single page of 50 consonant-vowel-consonant or vowel-consonant pseudo-words. Fuchs et al. (2004) compared the predictive validity of Nonsense Word Fluency in 151 at-risk first-grade children who were monitored for 20 weeks (including fall and spring semesters) using alternate forms of Word Identification Fluency and Nonsense Word Fluency. In the spring of first-grade children received standardized measures of decoding, word identification, passage fluency, and reading comprehension. Overall, results favored Word Identification Fluency over Nonsense Word Fluency as a predictor of end of year reading skill.

Contributions from IES-Supported Research

Contribution 2. Using assessments to monitor students' progress can be a valid and efficient way to guide the decision making process –for example, through a Response to Intervention (RtI) approach-for determining whether an intervention is improving a student's reading skills. Given the advantage of Word Identification Fluency over Nonsense Word Fluency as a first- grade progress monitoring measure, Zumeta, Compton, and Fuchs (2012) examined whether sampling procedures for developing Word Identification Fluency lists might have an effect on growth parameter estimates and the correlation between student outcome growth estimates and their future reading skills. Three samples of students were drawn from an overall pool: a representative sample which reflected the distribution of readers in the study, and included low, average, and high achieving students, a second sample that included all students with low reading achievement, and a third sample with high/average achievement. Word Identification Fluency data were collected weekly for 15 weeks using two different lists, broad lists and narrow lists. Broad lists were developed by sampling words from 500 high-frequency words, whereas narrow lists were created by sampling from the 133 words from Dolch preprimer, primer, and first-grade word lists. Overall, narrow sampling was found to be better for screening the representative group and the high/average subgroup. Broad sampling was superior for screening the low-achieving subgroup and for progress monitoring across groups. Evidence continues to mount indicating that Word Identification Fluency is well suited as a screening and progress-monitoring mechanism that can be used to make accurate decisions regarding children's movement within a tiered RtI model.

Dynamic assessment has been used to determine whether interventions are working and, potentially, as an alternative to actually putting children through long and potentially ineffective interventions. In such a model, dynamic assessment is used as a very short and focused session of instruction that is intended to gauge whether a particular intervention strategy actually helps a particular student.[28] In three IES-funded studies[29] researchers used 45 minute dynamic assessments to index students' potential to benefit from kindergarten phonological awareness, first grade decoding, and second grade listening comprehension instruction, respectively.

Bridges and Catts (2011) developed and examined the predictive validity of a dynamic assessment screening of phonological awareness in two samples of children who were administered the dynamic assessment in the beginning of kindergarten and standardized measures of reading achievement at the conclusion of the school year. In the first sample the predictive utility of dynamic assessment was compared to a static version of the same screening assessment, where no feedback or support was provided. Results provided initial evidence of the promise of dynamic assessment to forecast future reading ability in young developing readers more accurately than static measures. In the second sample (N=96), the predictive utility of dynamic assessment was compared to Dynamic Indicators of Basic Early Literacy Skills (DIBELS) Initial Sound Fluency, a commonly used screening measure. Findings revealed that dynamic assessment predicted kindergarteners' end of year reading skills over and above what was measured by the Initial Sound Fluency alone.

In a study of first grade students, Fuchs and colleagues (2011) examined the predictive validity of dynamic assessment of decoding skill learning. Students were assessed in the fall on an array of instruments that were given with the aim of forecasting students' responsiveness to early reading instruction. Factor analysis indicated that dynamic assessment loaded on a factor that included language ability and IQ and was distinct from factors representing speeded alphabetic knowledge and task oriented behavior. Multilevel modeling indicated that dynamic assessment significantly predicted future end-of-first-grade reading performance. Results support the construct and the predictive utility of dynamic assessment and reveal that dynamic assessment may have value as part of a first grade test battery to identify young children with severe learning needs who require the most intensive treatment in RtI frameworks.

Elleman et al. (2011) explored a listening comprehension dynamic assessment intended to tap students' inference making skills. The researchers hypothesized that such skills might be predictive of future reading comprehension performance. The dynamic portion of the assessment taught children to be "reading detectives" by using text clues to solve what was happening in the story. The dynamic assessment was administered to second-grade children along with standardized measures of reading comprehension. Results showed that students who had lower dynamic assessment scores also had generally lower reading comprehension scores. Plus, the dynamic assessment measure predicted reading comprehension skills even after considering students' vocabulary and word identification skills. In addition, results suggested that dynamic assessment may be more effective than the standardized measures of reading comprehension at identifying the different profiles of literacy skills found among young students.

Another research team supported by IES[30] has begun to examine the use of the Individual Growth and Development Indicators (IGDI) progress monitoring system combined with a web-based decision making tool to guide teachers and other service providers through a decision-making process for early intervention. Results suggest that linking the progress monitoring data to a web-based decision making system may improve practitioners' ability to implement effective early childhood intervention with at-risk children.

Future Directions. In the area of progress monitoring, IES-funded projects have further developed and evaluated the psychometrics and explored the predictive utility of various progress monitoring measures that can be used to more accurately judge children's response to research-based interventions. This research has revealed that Word Identification Fluency is a strong progress-monitoring tool that can be used to make more accurate decisions regarding children's need for more or less intensive interventions. However the research suggests that item sampling issues must be considered when developing new forms of Word Identification Fluency. The use of dynamic assessment within RtI models is a new and potentially exciting line of research currently supported by IES. Dynamic assessment has the potential advantage of indexing response to intervention without actually putting children through long, costly interventions that may not meet their individual needs. Given increased use of multi-tier systems in schools to prevent early reading problems in children more work on assessment systems designed to quantify actual response or predict potential response progress of children to validated instruction may promote more effective instruction for students who are at risk or have reading disabilities by helping to ensure they are receiving individualized intervention at the intensity and RtI tier they need to progress.

Assessment for English Learners

Background. Many children who are English learners are at serious risk for reading disabilities but present specific challenges with regard to assessment and identification of disabilities versus differences. Moreover, NCLB requires that state assessment data of students who are English learners be disaggregated and that schools document Adequate Yearly Progress (AYP) of English learners. IDEA and its regulations include the Child Find mandate that requires school districts to identify, locate, and evaluate all children with disabilities, regardless of the severity of their disabilities. The Child Find mandate applies to all children who reside within a state, including children who attend private schools and public schools, highly mobile children, migrant children, homeless children, and children who are wards of the state. As the number of English learners in US schools increases, threats to the validity of assessing and properly determining schools' AYP along with accurately identifying English learners who also have a disability in the Child Find Mandate remains high. IES has invested research funds to develop and evaluate alternative assessments for students with limited English proficiency to be used in estimating educational progress and identifying children with disabilities. A variety of linguistic and cultural factors affect assessment outcomes of English learners. The risk of misrepresenting educational progress and misclassifying English learners with disabilities increases as English skill proficiency decreases,[31] with improper identification of English learners potentially resulting in inappropriate instruction and violation of their rights protected under IDEA.

Contributions from IES-Supported Research

Contribution 3. New assessments for English learners indicate that reading comprehension can be assessed without overburdening word reading and oral language skills. With support from IES, Francis, Snow, and colleagues[32] designed and evaluated the Diagnostic Assessment of Reading

Comprehension for assessment of English learners in kindergarten through third grade. By minimizing the need for high levels of English oral proficiency or decoding ability, the Diagnostic Assessment of Reading Comprehension has the potential to accurately reflect the comprehension skills of English learners who are reading text in English. Students' performance is assessed on four central processes: remembering newly read text, making inferences within the text, accessing relevant background knowledge, and making inferences that require integrating background knowledge with the text (text memory, text inferencing, background knowledge, and knowledge integration). In a study of Spanish-speaking students in kindergarten through third grade,[33] the Diagnostic Assessment of Reading Comprehension was found to measure the four separate comprehension processes and scores on the Diagnostic Assessment of Reading Comprehension were less influenced by word reading skills compared to comprehension cloze tasks where students provide a missing word in a phrase, sentence or passage. Francis and colleagues (2006) compared the performance of third grade Spanish-speaking English learners on the Diagnostic Assessment of Reading Comprehension and a cloze task. Results suggest that the two measures were moderately correlated ($r= .61$) and influenced by different factors. As in the previous study, the Diagnostic Assessment of Reading Comprehension was less strongly related to word-level skills and more strongly related to measures of narrative language production and memory.

Future Directions. IES investment in the development and evaluation of alternative reading assessments for English learners represents an important line of inquiry at its early stages of development. As we move forward with accountability schemes that mandate assessment and disaggregation of progress data of all student groups, we will need continued research to inform the use of alternative reading assessments.

Assessment Accommodations for Students with Disabilities

Background. As a result of NCLB, a majority of school-age students with disabilities are now assessed in reading as part of large-scale standards-based reading assessments.[34] The challenge for test developers of large-scale reading assessments is to develop accessible tests that "measure only those student characteristics that are essential parts of the reading proficiency the test intends to measure, and not those characteristics that could be related to the student's disability".[35] Thus, a major research question is whether the scores obtained on an accommodated test have the same meaning as scores on a standardized administration of the test. A change in the way a test is administered to a student is usually designated as either a modification or an accommodation. A modification to a test administration procedure changes the measurement of the test construct and therefore the interpretation, which is not ideal. An accommodation, on the other hand, is a change in the test administration that does not change the test construct or the interpretation of the score, which is ideal. An important question asked of test accommodations is whether they level the playing field by providing differential boosts to students with disabilities. That is, students with disabilities show an increase in their score but students without disabilities do not. Differential boost favoring students with disabilities indicates that an accommodation is valid and does not change the meaning of the test results.

Contributions from IES-Supported Research

Contribution 4. Assessment accommodations can be made for students with disabilities that do not modify the construct being measured, and therefore represent a valid measure of this construct. To address a wide range of test accommodation issues for students with disabilities, IES provided support for the National Accessible Reading Assessment Project, a collaboration of three projects[36] intended to: (a) identify assumptions underlying test accessibility, (b) consider the characteristics of students with disabilities and how their abilities affect reading and performance on reading assessments, (c) generate possible ways to create fully accessible reading assessments, and (d) develop a set of accessibility principles and guidelines to guide the development of reading assessments. Results from the various projects are summarized in what follows.

One area of focus in the three IES-funded projects has been on examining the appropriate assignment of testing accommodations to students with disabilities and the accompanying impact these accommodations have on the interpretation of scores. A series of studies have examined the effects of various reading test accommodations on the performance of students with and without disabilities. Laitusis (2010) examined the impact of a read-aloud accommodation (i.e., students listen to the test) on the standardized test scores of a reading comprehension test, the Gates-McGinitie Reading Test, for typically developing students and students with reading disabilities at grades four and eight. Mean comprehension scores for the audio version of the test were higher at each grade level with differential boost at both grade levels reported on the audio version for the students with reading disabilities. Results suggest that an audio version of a reading comprehension test represents an accommodation, as opposed to a modification, for students with reading disabilities.

A study by Cook, Eignor, Steinberg, Sawaki, and Cline (2010) employed a multi-group confirmatory factor analysis of the Level 4 Gates-McGinitie Reading Test given with and without a read-aloud accommodation to typically developing students and students with reading disabilities. Results suggest that the Gates-McGinitie Reading Test measured the same underlying construct of comprehension in both groups. In a second study, Cook, et al. (2010) administered a fourth grade English-Language Arts assessment to four different groups: (a) students without disabilities taking the test under standard conditions; (b) students with learning disabilities who took the test under standard conditions; (c) students with learning disabilities who took the test with accommodations specified in their 504 plan or Individualized Education Program (IEP); (d) students with learning disabilities who took the test with a read-aloud accommodation/modification. Again, results suggest that the same underlying construct was being measured for typical students or students with learning disabilities whether given with or without accommodation. In a related study with fourth and eighth grade students who were blind or have visual impairments, Stone, Cook, Laitusis, and Cline (2010) demonstrated that using large print or Braille to present a standards-based English-language arts assessment to students with visual impairments served as valid accommodations. Results support the accessibility and validity of large print or Braille accommodations for students who are blind or have visual impairments.

Kato, Moen, and Thurlow (2009) examined performance differences between students with a range of disabilities and students without disabilities on the state reading assessment in third and fifth grade. While results indicated a lack of test bias, there were minor differences in item functioning across disability groups, suggesting that some test items are unfairly difficult for students with disabilities.

Abedi, Kao, Leon, Mastergeorge, Sullivan, Herman, and Pope (2010) examined the effects of assessing eighth grade students using reading comprehension passages that were presented in shorter segments to accommodate working memory deficits and fatigue in students with disabilities. Results indicated that segmenting did not differentially affect performance of students with or without disabilities and improved the overall reliability of the test for students with disabilities, suggesting a valid accommodation.

Dillon, O'Brien, Kato, Scharber, Kelly, Beaton, and Biggs (2009) developed a reading comprehension assessment that addresses students' interests and their sense of self-efficacy with the goal of making the assessment more accessible to fourth and eighth graders with a range of disabilities that affect their reading of typical large-scale comprehension tests. The goal was to examine whether improving the motivational characteristics of a large-scale reading assessment increased its accessibility for students with disabilities by making it more interesting to them. Results indicated that expository texts containing more interesting topics (e.g., literary texts about young people their own age working through daily challenges and life issues) were of higher interest to readers in both fourth- and eighth-grade, compared to texts topics that were less interesting. In particular, fourth graders were drawn to expository texts about animals; eighth graders were drawn to expository texts on unusual and sometimes gruesome topics. The results also indicate that creating motivating assessments using interesting passages was positively correlated with reading performance, especially for low-performing students at fourth grade and to some extent, students at grade eight, which indicates this is a valid accommodation.

Finally, Moen, Liu, Thurlow, Lekwa, Scullin, and Hausmann (2009) attempted to identify child characteristics of students for whom reading assessments tended to be less valid and reliable. Students who were less accurately measured tended to have globally slow processing, very poor decoding skills, and exceptional difficulty staying on task.

Future Directions. Results from these studies suggest that reading tests can be adapted to accommodate students with a range of disabilities and increase the accessibility of standardized measures of reading. Overall, studies suggest that a variety of accommodations are valid and can lead to a differential boost on reading assessments for students with disabilities compared to typically developing students.

Summary of Contributions for Research Question I: Assessment

Assessment issues associated with the enactment of NCLB and reauthorization of IDEA have put pressure on test developers to investigate the validity of assessment systems designed to estimate schools' AYP including all students, particularly those groups with longstanding achievement gaps and students with disabilities. Also critical, as part of IDEA, is the support of new ways of identifying students with learning disabilities, including RtI models. This means that valid and reliable assessments to monitor students' response to different scientifically-based interventions are needed. Meeting these challenges, IES has funded a number of assessment projects designed to investigate the validity of various assessment measures, and of accommodations to them, so that we are assessing students' reading skills accurately. Important lessons learned from these IES-funded projects include the following:

1. The science of universal screening is evolving to where it is possible to identify first grade students who may be at risk for developing reading disabilities and who may need reading interventions, and that this can be done precisely so that students who need intervention and those who do not are more accurately identified. At the same time, additional research is needed to develop assessments that can identify kindergarten and preschool students who may be at risk for learning disabilities.

2. In terms of monitoring response to research validated intervention, various progress monitoring tools have been shown to be sensitive to reading development growth as well as predictive of future reading difficulties. New dynamic assessment measures show promise in allowing intervention strategies to be tested quickly prior to implementing long term interventions and hence permitting interventions to be tailored to individual students.

3. In terms of students who are English learners, new reading comprehension measures have been developed that reduce word reading and oral language demands and tap more central comprehension processes so that students' comprehension skills are assessed more accurately.

4. Finally, multiple IES-funded studies have reported test accommodations that measure the same underlying construct in students with and without disabilities, with several demonstrating differential boost in the students with disabilities.

Although important advances have been made, continued research is warranted in each of these four assessment areas in order to continue the strong scientific advances made and further support the achievement of children at risk or with reading disabilities.

II. BASIC COGNITIVE AND LINGUISTIC PROCESSES: WHAT ARE THE BASIC COGNITIVE AND LINGUISTIC PROCESSES THAT SUPPORT SUCCESSFUL READING AND HOW CAN THESE SKILLS BE IMPROVED FOR STUDENTS WHO HAVE OR WHO ARE AT RISK FOR READING DISABILITIES?

A key contribution of IES funding has been to provide support for the application of basic research carried out by cognitive and developmental psychologists that have helped our understanding of the underlying processes and mechanisms of reading. This interdisciplinary research has endeavored to identify key components of reading, such as word knowledge and working memory; to test their contribution to students' reading comprehension, distinguishing between children with typical reading skills, and children with or at risk for reading disabilities; and, notably, the extent to which basic processes can be changed (i.e., are malleable) and therefore are potential targets for intervention. This work is important because, as Juel (1988) noted, it was not until researchers focused on the basic components of successful reading, and in this case decoding, that real progress was made in understanding how to prevent and remediate basic reading difficulties. This early work summarized by Adams (1990) and Torgesen et al. (1999) focused on the act of decoding and identified phonological awareness and grasp of the alphabetic principle as malleable sources of influence on young students' foundational reading skills. Research has also focused on the more complex skills required for reading comprehension including oral language skills, vocabulary, background and academic knowledge among others (Snow 2001).

Although for all children the same skills are involved in learning to read, each child brings a unique constellation of these skills to the classroom with implications for instruction. In this section, we describe underlying theories that have motivated the work on complex processes and the results of studies that have been informed by these theories. These studies have helped identify profiles of skills that children bring to the process of reading. Others have examined how multiple underlying components of reading work together to predict reading comprehension. Specifically, we describe IES-funded research in (1) cognitive processes and skills (e.g., enacted representations, the oddity principle, working memory), (2) linguistic processes and skills (e.g., word knowledge, use of non-mainstream English dialects), and (3) unique skill profiles that differentiate children who are typically developing readers versus children who have or are at risk for reading disabilities.

Enactive Representation; Oddity, Seriation, and Conservation; Working Memory; and Coherent Mental Representations and Higher Order Cognitive Processes

IES has funded research that begins with well established general cognitive theories of learning and seeks to understand whether changes in how children learn might lead to changes in their reading outcomes. These studies focused on the cognitive constructs of enactive representation, the oddity principle, working memory, and developing coherent mental representations, which are further explained below.

Contributions from IES-Supported Research

Contribution 5. Several basic cognitive processes, including working memory and abstract and inferential reasoning, have been found to be critical for students' reading success.

Enactive Representation

Background. Researchers Glenberg, Levin and Marley applied Piagetian principles[37] and theories offered by Bruner[38] to extend our understanding about cognitive development and how it relates to children's oral language and reading comprehension development. These researchers proposed that many children under 8 years of age cannot fully understand complex events, such as those described in story narratives, unless they can act them out. This is a process referred to as enactive representation. As children grow older and gain more experience, they are better able to understand such events without concrete representations like acting out stories because they can mentally process more abstract ideas.[39] For example, Glenberg and colleagues hypothesized that it should be easier for young children to read and retell instructions on how to build a block house if they were allowed to actually act out building the block house as they read. They suggested that such acts allowed children to develop internal images, index symbols (i.e., words) to objects, and create better understanding or more coherent mental representations of the text they were listening to or reading.

Contributions from IES-Supported Research

Glenberg and colleagues (2004) conducted 3 different experiments with first and second graders. Across these experiments, these researchers discovered that manipulating toys, watching toys being manipulated, and imagining the toys generally increased children's comprehension of the story when compared to the students in the control conditions. That is, they were better able to remember what they had read, even after some time had passed.

The researchers then explored whether they could replicate these results when the intervention was provided to small groups of children rather than individually.[40] In this experiment, first and second graders, Glenberg and colleagues found that children who had the opportunity to enact the stories and watch their group members enact stories were better able to recall the stories after time had passed than did the children in the re-reading condition.

Next, the researchers examined whether enacting stories with toys or watching someone enact stories would improve the listening comprehension skills of Native American students who were struggling readers.[41] Native American children are at high risk for developing reading disabilities because they frequently are learning English as a second language and are disproportionately more likely to live in poverty. Results were similar to those found for students with typical reading skills. Students who either manipulated or watched the researcher manipulate toys to enact stories were generally better able to recall details of the stories than were students who just listened to stories. Thus, enacting the stories and enacting complex language by creating concrete representations helped Native American students with reading difficulties better understand complex stories. Unfortunately, struggling readers in the treatment conditions were not able to generalize the idea of using their imagination instead of manipulatives to enact the stories, which the first and second graders who were typical readers in the treatment group were able to do.

Future Directions. The results from this set of IES-supported studies suggest that reading comprehension interventions that make abstract and complex stories more concrete by enacting them with toys or other visual imagery should support all students' reading and listening comprehension skills, including students with or at risk for reading disabilities.

Oddity, Seriation, and Conservation

Background. Pasnak and colleagues also relied on Piaget and cognitive theories to develop the hypothesis that improving children's ability to understand abstract principles, specifically oddity, seriation, and conservation, would lead to better general learning.[42] Young children who do not understand the oddity principle have difficulty finding an object that does not belong when the objects in a set are all different colors and the dimension of difference is shape or size. They focus on the color rather than the crucial information that is different. Children who do not grasp the seriation principle can put objects in size order but have difficulty figuring where an object goes in a series they have already constructed. Children use the wrong strategies or focus on the wrong aspect of the object (e.g., color rather than size) to decide where the extra object should go in the series. Conservation is the ability to understand that just because objects are physically rearranged or liquid is poured from a tall container to a short and wide container that the number of objects or the amount of liquid has not changed. Although most children have grasped these concepts by kindergarten, the researchers argued that children who have not mastered them may have more difficulty learning in the classroom.

Pasnak and colleagues created interventions that were designed to teach these abstract principles to kindergartners who had not already mastered them. For example, while playing a game in which a toy dinosaur would only eat the object that was different from three other objects, children learned to understand the oddity principle through repeated episodes of success and failure. These games are called learning sets.

Contributions from IES-Supported Research

Pasnak and colleagues, in a series of IES-funded experiments, moved their laboratory experiments into schools. In one study,[43] they conducted an experiment with kindergartners who had not mastered the abstract principles (i.e., oddity principle, seriation, conservation). Children who were taught the oddity principle, seriation, and conservation learning set intervention showed greater gains in learning all three principles than did children in numeracy, reading or art interventions. They also achieved stronger number and reading skills compared to the art group and their number skills generally equaled the kindergarteners who received the numeracy intervention. Plus, their reading skills equaled kindergarteners who received the reading intervention. These results are highly similar to those found in their other IES-funded studies.[44]

Future Directions. Learning these abstract principles appears to help children learn numbers and reading more generally although they were not the target of the intervention. The researchers offer a number of ideas for this finding. First, most instruction provided to typical kindergarteners assumes that they have grasped these abstract principles. Remember, the intervention was delivered only to children who had not mastered them. It is likely that instruction in numbers and basic reading rely implicitly on grasp of these principles. For example, to develop phonological awareness, children have to understand how phonemes (certainly an abstract principle to kindergartners) relate to each other, how changing one phoneme can change the word "pin" to "pan" and how reversing the order of phonemes also changes the word "tip" to "pit". Learning numbers also requires grasp of these abstract principles.

It appears that understanding the oddity principle, seriation, and conservation helps students better understand the reading and mathematics instruction they were receiving.

Working Memory

Background. There is compelling evidence from the cognitive literature that children who have difficulty comprehending what they read, frequently have less working memory capacity than do children who do not have difficulty.[45] Working memory is the ability to keep an idea (or a set of ideas) in mind while performing another task or remembering something else. For example, a typical working memory task involves reading a number of sentences that tell a story, recalling the story, and then remembering what the last word in each sentence was.

Working memory is considered one component of the executive system. Another is short term memory, which is the ability to remember phone numbers or the ability to recite a series of words or letters. These skills, along with others, are thought to represent basic cognitive abilities that generally impact reading as well as other academic skills, such as mathematics. Other cognitive skills include inhibition and updating. Inhibition is the ability to inhibit information that is no longer needed. Updating involves the ability to stop remembering one thing and begin to remember another.

Contributions from IES-Supported Research

Swanson and colleagues sought to better understand the relationship between cognitive factors and reading ability in a prospective study.[46] They tested the working memory, short term memory, inhibition and updating, processing speed, IQ, and reading skills (both decoding and comprehension) of students who ranged in age from 7 to 17 years. Based on reading scores, they identified four reading ability groups: low word reading and low comprehension with typical verbal IQ scores (reading disabilities); high word reading but low comprehension (comprehension deficits only) with typical verbal IQ scores; strong reading overall (skilled readers) with typical verbal IQ scores; and children who had low word reading, comprehensions, and verbal IQ scores (poor readers). Children with only comprehension deficits had stronger working memory skills than did children with reading disabilities. These students had stronger working memory skills compared to poor readers. Skilled readers had the strongest working memory skills among the groups. Results also indicated that working memory and short term memory may share some underlying components such as processing speed and updating. Indeed, individual differences in updating and short term memory predicted working memory skills consistently across the reading skill classifications. This is important because it supports the idea that stronger working memory skills are not a result of reading comprehension but are an independent cognitive skill. Swanson and colleagues also reported that the biggest difference in executive function for children with reading disabilities and low comprehension readers was that children classified as having reading disabilities had less storage capacity (i.e., less short term memory capacity) than did children classified as having only a comprehension deficit. This difference was principally a function of the phonological system (the ability to repeat nonsense words, for example).

In an IES-supported meta-analysis that reviewed almost 90 studies exploring the relationship between cognitive processes and reading ability, Swanson and colleagues (2009) observed that students and adults with reading disabilities performed more poorly on tests of working and short term memory than did typical readers, that these deficits persisted across the age groups, and that working and short term memory were not moderated by students' IQ or the severity of their reading disability. Moreover, stronger working memory and short term memory were both associated with reading skill. Students with stronger working memory skills tended to have stronger reading comprehension skills than did students with weaker working memory skills. In contrast, short term memory skills were more highly associated with students' decoding and word reading.

This is a particularly important finding: if working memory can be improved as a result of intervention (i.e., is malleable), then interventions might be developed to improve working memory and, in turn, improve reading. IES-supported researchers, Swanson and colleagues, pursued two potentially promising avenues to improve working memory and reading comprehension. First, they proposed that learning comprehension strategies, such as rehearsal, clustering, association and elaboration, might improve working memory and comprehension.[47] In two studies comparing the performance of 10-year-old students with and without reading disabilities (i.e., RD vs. typical readers), with the second study a randomized control trial where students were randomly assigned within RD and typical groups to an intervention or control condition, they hypothesized that children with reading disabilities would show greater improvement in working memory when they received strategy training than would typical readers because it would allow them to improve or to compensate more for their weaker working memory skills. The results revealed that children with reading disabilities did indeed improve their skills when they received strategy instruction compared to peers in the control condition but so did typical readers. Gains were greater for children who chose from a more stable set of strategies compared to children who chose a wide range of frequently less optimal strategies. Moreover, strategy instruction with fifth and sixth graders led to stronger working memory skills for both groups relative to a randomly assigned control group – not, as hypothesized, more for the reading disability group than the typical reading group. Thus, working memory does appear, at least in this study, to be somewhat malleable for children with reading disabilities – but not to the extent of bringing their working memory skills to the same level found for children who are typical readers – typical readers still had stronger working memory skills after the intervention. Thus, the researchers state, "the evidence is still not clear as to whether increases in working memory might have a direct influence on higher order skills such as reading comprehension" (p. 43).

In their IES-funded study, Swanson and O'Connor (2009) conjectured that improving children's fluency might improve or help compensate for weak working memory. Fluency is the ability to read rapidly with accuracy and appropriate prosody. The researchers cited three different theories that they wanted to test. The first theory was the Decoding Proficiency Hypothesis – that proficiency in word decoding is more important than working memory in explaining reading comprehension skills.[48] By improving fluency, the ability to understand text should improve regardless of working memory skills because working memory is a secondary system. Second are theories that suggest that dysfluent reading uses up working memory capacity and reduces resources for understanding what is read.[49] For example, the Compensatory Hypothesis states that improving fluency skills may help children compensate for weak working memory skills.[50] Thus dysfluent readers with weaker working memory may be especially responsive to fluency interventions compared to children with stronger working memory skills. The third theory, the Working Memory Resource Hypothesis, states that working memory is a basic cognitive process that will operate independently of fluency.[51] In this theory, working memory is unlikely to be very malleable and will operate independently of fluency to predict reading comprehension outcomes.

Setting out to test these hypotheses, Swanson and O'Connor conducted an experiment with second and fourth grade children with poor reading fluency to a control group (no intervention) or one of two fluency interventions – a repeated reading intervention or a continuous reading intervention. Based on assessment of children's working memory, fluency, and comprehension, results revealed that, in general, both fluency interventions resulted in stronger fluency skills compared to the control group for both grades. However, when reading comprehension outcomes were compared, students in the continuous reading fluency intervention made greater gains overall than did students in the repeated reading fluency intervention. Children in the latter intervention performed no better than did the students in the control condition. However, neither fluency training intervention led to stronger working memory skills. Moreover, fluency and working memory operated independently to predict reading comprehension outcomes. Thus, neither the Decoding Proficiency Hypothesis nor the Compensatory Hypothesis was supported. Instead, the third theory, the Working Memory Resource Hypothesis, was best supported by the results.

Future Directions. Taking these IES-funded studies altogether, the results have helped to extend our understanding of working memory as an important cognitive process that is weak for many children with reading difficulties and is particularly important for proficient reading comprehension. It reliably distinguishes between skilled and struggling readers. Strategy instruction, such as repeating important information, may strengthen working memory. On the other hand, fluency interventions do not appear to lead to improvements in working memory although they may improve reading comprehension and so may act to help students who struggle with reading compensate for weak working memory.

Coherent Mental Representations and Higher Order Cognitive Processes

Background. In the long run, the reason we read is to understand the text in front of us, and we may do this for pure enjoyment, to gain information and to learn. Van den Broek, Rapp, their colleagues, and others suggest that in order for students to comprehend and understand what they are reading, they must make coherent mental representations of the information or story in the text they are reading.[52] To understand a text, students have to make appropriate and meaningful connections among the ideas in the text and this requires higher order cognitive processing. Higher order skills include: making inferences by connecting ideas in the text or with their background knowledge, understanding cause and effect, thinking logically, and understanding how the text is organized. One of the challenges in trying to understand how students use their higher order cognitive processes is that these processes happen during reading; they are "online",[53] which make them difficult to assess. Most of the methods we use to measure comprehension ask students to read a passage and then answer questions. If they can answer the questions correctly then we assume they understood the text. But it is possible that students' online processes differ in important ways that may have implications for designing interventions to improve their comprehension processes and their ability to make sense of complex sentence structure.

Contributions from IES-Supported Research

One way to figure out how well students are coordinating their higher order processes is to use a method called eye tracking. To use eye tracking, the students read text on a computer and a special device records where their eyes focus (a fixation), how long they look at a word (duration) and whether they look backwards to re-read text (a regression). When van den Broek and colleagues (2009) compared the eye tracking patterns of skilled and struggling fourth, seventh, and ninth grade students while reading, they found that struggling readers made the same number of fixations as typical and skilled readers, but their fixation times were longer. Furthermore, although their rate of regressions (looking back to re-read text) was the same, the struggling readers were much less systematic with regard to what information they reread. For example, "instead of reading specific, informative segments, as proficient readers did, the struggling readers reread entire sections …often uninformative sections… before [continuing]" (p. 116). Thus the struggling readers in this sample were not reading substantially differently, but they were reading less efficiently and less strategically than their peers who were proficient readers.

Future Directions. As we design instruction and interventions to improve students' reading skills overall, both underlying, basic, and higher order cognitive processes and the effective and efficient coordination of these skills clearly deserve attention.

Word Knowledge, Dialects, and Fluency

Background. Linguistic processes are defined here as the cognitive processes involved in talking and listening. It is well documented that there are linguistic foundations for reading, particularly reading comprehension[54] but how to intervene is not well understood. Whereas over three decades of research has revealed that when students master the alphabetic principle they are better readers than those who do not and that these skills can be taught effectively,[55] skill at reading words fluently does not ensure proficient reading for understanding.[56] There is evidence that some children do not have the word knowledge and more formal oral language, including use of English syntax associated with School English,[57] needed to fully understand the more complex syntax and unfamiliar vocabulary that is characteristic of the academic texts they are expected to read.[58]

Contributions from IES-Supported Research

Contribution 6. Malleable linguistic processes, such as oral language skills and vocabulary, contribute to children's reading performance.

Word Knowledge: In a paper describing their IES-funded study, Tannenbaum, Torgesen, and Wagner (2006) suggest that word knowledge, which is frequently assessed using vocabulary tests, is multidimensional, incorporating vocabulary breadth, depth, and fluency. Vocabulary breadth is the number of words that children recognize and understand although their understanding of the word may be shallow. For example, a child may know that a rock is a large stone that is hard and rough or a type of music but not know that the verb rock means to move back and forth. Grasp of such multiple meanings represents the depth of children's word knowledge. When word knowledge is deep, children can use the words in their vocabulary flexibly and in a variety of situations, including different kinds of text. Word knowledge fluency, Tannebaum et al. suggest, represents the child's ability to rapidly access word meanings. These researchers found that for the third graders in their sample, students with strong word knowledge depth also accessed words more rapidly and accurately and that, it seemed, depth and fluency represented one skill. However, this depth/fluency skill was distinct from vocabulary breadth and both skills differentiated typical from struggling third grade readers. These researchers also found that vocabulary breadth and depth/fluency were independently associated with these third graders' reading comprehension skills; that, overall, students with greater breadth and depth/fluency also had stronger reading comprehension skills and that those with weaker vocabulary breadth and depth/fluency had weaker reading vocabulary skills. At the same time, over half of the variability in students' reading comprehension was explained by aspects of language that both types of word knowledge shared (i.e., shared variance). These results suggest that interventions that focus on word knowledge might be effective in improving reading comprehension, especially if the interventions focus on developing both breadth and depth/fluency of word knowledge.

Another IES-funded study that focused on word knowledge was conducted by Uccelli and Paez (2007) with young English learners. Uccelli and Paez asked whether the vocabulary skills of kindergarteners who spoke Spanish at home but English at school would be associated with their development of narrative skills (the skills required to tell a story that has a beginning, middle, and end as well as characters, a setting, and a plot). Other researchers have found that children with stronger narrative skills are generally more likely to develop stronger literacy skills.[59] Uccelli and Paez assessed 24 bilingual kindergartners' Spanish and English vocabulary breadth, as well as their narrative skills in both languages, and then examined these skills again when the children entered first grade. With only a few exceptions, most children's vocabulary scores in both languages were well below grade and age expectations. Children with weak narrative skills in Spanish also tended to have weak narrative skills in English. They found that the children's English vocabulary and narrative skills improved by first grade. However, their Spanish vocabulary skills generally did not improve although their Spanish narrative skills did. This was a concern because the researchers also found that kindergarteners with stronger Spanish vocabulary and narrative skills were more likely to produce better narratives in English in first grade than were kindergartners with weaker Spanish language skills. Thus, this study also highlights the importance of understanding how children's word knowledge and vocabulary across languages contributes to their reading comprehension in English and the potential role of these constructs as targets for intervention.

Dialects: When speakers from states in the North visit states in the South (and vice versa), they may notice that some speakers sound different. Speakers in the south are using a dialect called Southern Vernacular English. Another example of a dialect is African American Vernacular English, which is used by members of many Black communities in the United States.[60] Across the United States, many communities use dialects that are easily understood as English but have slightly different rules for grammar and pronunciation. These differences are important for two reasons. First, children who use these non-mainstream dialects are frequently misidentified as having language disabilities because markers of specific language impairment, such as leaving off the "is" in "he is running," are perfectly acceptable in African American Vernacular English[61] and other non-mainstream dialects.[62] Second, researchers have conjectured that the mismatch between non-mainstream dialects and the English used in schools and books might be one reason some children who use non-mainstream dialects have difficulty learning to read.[63] However, emerging research findings indicate that the association might be more complex.[64]

In an IES-funded study, Terry et al. (2010) argued that the mismatch between non-mainstream dialect and the more formal English used in school might not present the same challenge to all students; that it would depend on their linguistic flexibility or dialect awareness. To test this, they explored the association between first graders' dialectic differences, using Part 1 of the *Diagnostic Evaluation of Language Variation-Screening Assessment*, and the trajectory of growth in early literacy skills. Roughly half of the first graders were African American and half were White. All were from the geographical Southeastern United States and so used varying amounts of Southern Vernacular English or African American Vernacular English, which are fairly similar. They also considered the level of poverty at the students' schools. They found that children who used many features of non-mainstream dialect AND children who used very little non-mainstream dialect had stronger reading skills than did their peers who used moderate amounts of non-mainstream dialect. This inverted U-shaped association held whether students were African American or White and whether they attended a higher poverty school or not. Overall, students at higher poverty schools had lower reading scores regardless of their non- mainstream dialect use.

In a second study, again with first graders, Terry, Connor, Petscher, and Conlin (2012) found that most students who used non-mainstream dialect at the beginning of first grade used substantially more school English or mainstream English by the end of the year and this continued through second grade. Students who did not increase their use of school English displayed generally weaker reading skill growth compared to students who did increase their use of school English. Students who shifted to school English had generally stronger language skills than did students who did not shift. These researchers concluded that non-mainstream dialect use may not actually be why students struggle with reading. Rather, they suggested that students with weaker oral language skills are more likely to be confused by the differences in the dialect they speak and read at school and the dialect they use at home. For children with stronger language skills, this mismatch presents less of a challenge.

Fluency: Tilstra, McMaster, Van den Broek, Kendeou, and Rapp (2009) proposed an expanded version of the Simple View of Reading which asserts that decoding and oral language skills are sufficient to explain reading comprehension.[65] Describing fluency as the "ability to group words into meaningful grammatical units and to read quickly, effortlessly, and with expression" (p. 385), they argued that the *Simple View* may be more informative when fluency is considered in addition to decoding and oral language skills. They also conjectured that the associations among decoding, oral language skills, and fluency might contribute to students' reading comprehension in different ways, depending on students' grades and the kinds of reading they are expected to do. To examine these research questions, they evaluated fourth, seventh, and ninth grade students' reading and language skills using an extensive battery of assessments. Of these students, about one-third had reading difficulties. The researchers found that the measures assessed four different kinds of skills (i.e., constructs): (1) reading fluency; (2) depth of word knowledge, which these investigators call "verbal proficiency;" (3) oral language skills, which they called "listening comprehension;" and (4) decoding. The results from this IES-funded study showed that all four skills predicted students' reading comprehension but the importance of the skills in explaining why some students had strong reading comprehension and others weak differed by grade. For fourth graders, the most important predictor was decoding. In contrast, for seventh and ninth graders, oral language skills (i.e., listening comprehension) was the strongest predictor. These researchers pointed out that for students in middle and high school, the relation between oral language and reading comprehension appeared to become more reciprocal than it was for fourth graders. This means that strong reading comprehension appeared to contribute to improvements in students' oral language, which in turn, appeared to support stronger reading comprehension. Thus, if students had weak reading comprehension skills, then they were less likely to achieve stronger oral language skills and so continued to fall farther behind. These results have implications for skills included in screening and progress monitoring assessments for students at different ages. Later in this section, we discuss interventions that support students' fluency and reading comprehension development.

Future Directions. The integration of cognitive science and education is extending our understanding about the mechanisms and skills that support proficient reading with implications for developing new and effective interventions for students with or at risk of reading disabilities. In particular, fruitful lines of research in executive and linguistic processes and how to intervene to improve these skills for students with or at risk of reading disabilities are explicating new directions for improving reading achievement overall.

Unique Skill Profiles

Background. The rest of this section focuses on studies that examine a number of component skills, such as word knowledge, fluency, strategy use, and other cognitive processes, to see how they work separately and together to support proficient comprehension. These studies use what is called "person centered" statistics.[66] Rather than trying to find the general trend or mean achievement, person centered strategies work to identify different profiles of learners. For example, a group of first graders may have average decoding and vocabulary skills when the skills are considered together. However, some students will have strong decoding skills and weak vocabulary skills and others will have weak decoding skills but strong vocabulary skills. IES-funded studies and other studies reveal that there are different profiles (or clusters) of skills for preschoolers,[67] second and third graders,[68] and adolescents,[69] with implications for how to design more effective instruction and interventions.

Contributions from IES-Supported Research

Contribution 7. Although the same sets of cognitive and linguistic skills are involved in learning to read, children bring unique constellations of these skills to the classroom with important implications for instruction.

Profiles of Skills – Preschoolers: By assessing preschoolers who attended publicly funded preschools, such as Head Start, and who were at risk for developing academic difficulties, on a wide variety of oral language and code-related skills, Cabell, Justice, and colleagues (2010) were able to classify preschoolers into one of five different profiles. They tested oral language skills including vocabulary and understanding and using grammar, as well as code-related skills including knowing letters and sounds, name writing, rhyming, and print concepts (how to hold books, understanding that books are read from left to right, and so on). They found that the preschoolers' oral language skills were consistent within five profiles profiles; one profile had consistently above average oral language skills, three had fairly typical language skills, and one had very delayed language skills. What differed were preschoolers' code-related skills. The researchers conjectured that preschoolers' home and preschool experiences might have been responsible for the differences in code-related skills and that these skills appeared to develop unevenly for many children. When the researchers tested these preschoolers again when they were in kindergarten, they found that the profile to which a preschooler belonged predicted the progress they were going to make in reading by the end of kindergarten. Children who had strong code-related skills and either strong or typical language skills had stronger reading skills by the end of the school year than did children with weaker code-related skills. Taken together, these results show that even among preschoolers attending programs for children at risk of developing academic difficulties, there are important differences in their literacy skills and that the profile of skills predicts how well they will do in kindergarten.

Profiles of Skills – Elementary School Children: Do we find similar profiles once children begin formal schooling and when, arguably, reading instruction is more consistent than it is for preschoolers? The study by Pierce, Noam and colleagues (2007) explored the profiles of 140 second and third graders who attended urban schools and who were at risk for reading disabilities. They tested the students' oral language (vocabulary depth), decoding (phonological awareness, non-word decoding), fluency (both word and text), and reading comprehension, which translated into four groups of skills: decoding, vocabulary, fluency (efficiency), and text skills, respectively. When they conducted cluster analyses, they found that, for the second and third graders who were at risk for becoming poor readers, reading failure fell into one of four profiles: (1) weaker text skills; (2) relatively typical skills overall; (3) weaker efficiency skills; and (4) weak skills overall. Unlike the preschool sample where oral language skills were fairly consistent, for second and third graders who struggled with reading, oral language skills were inconsistent across profiles.

Profiles of Skills – Adolescents: Do profiles differ again for adolescents? Based on the views of practitioners and some early research, it was assumed that for adolescents who have reading difficulties, the greatest weaknesses occur in reading for understanding and that by the time students reached middle and high school decoding difficulties have been resolved. In their IES-funded study, Hock and colleagues (2009) challenged this conventional wisdom and hypothesized that, just like preschoolers and elementary school age children, adolescent readers would show different profiles of skills. What is interesting is that reading skills tended to fall into four types that were similar to those found for younger students: (a) decoding including word reading; (b) fluency (word and text); (c) vocabulary (breadth – depth was not assessed); and (d) comprehension (both when listening and when reading). The investigators then compared students in their sample who showed reading difficulties with those who did not. Students with reading difficulties were more likely to come from families living in poverty and to be enrolled in special education. In other ways, the two groups were almost the same. When the researchers examined the profiles of students with reading difficulties, they found that more than half of the students judged to have reading difficulties scored low on all components of reading, including decoding. A much smaller percentage of students fit the profile of conventional wisdom that decoding skills were fine and that the other comprehension related skills (fluency, vocabulary and comprehension) were weak. Moreover, the majority of all students tended to read slowly and not very accurately (i.e., weak fluency). Even students with adequate reading skills had difficulty with fluency.

Future Directions. It is evident from the findings across the age-groups (preschool, elementary, and high school) that students have different strengths and weaknesses and that students with or at risk for reading disabilities have weaker skills across the board -- decoding, word knowledge, oral language, and fluency. As we think about instruction and intervention, these results indicate that like preschool and elementary school-age students with reading difficulties, many adolescent readers continue to struggle with decoding, word reading skills, and fluency and that intervention tailored to fit each student's unique profile may be more effective in supporting improved reading skills than taking a "one-size-fits-all" approach or trusting to conventional wisdom.

Summary of Contributions for Research Question II: Basic Cognitive and Linguistic Processes

The IES-funded research described above, which examines cognitive and linguistic processes and how these comprise different profiles or clusters of skills from preschool through middle and high school, has extended our understanding and provided clear implications for designing effective reading instruction and interventions, particularly for students who are at risk or with reading disabilities.

Cognitive processes are important because some appear to be malleable. For example, if we improve kindergarteners' understanding of more abstract concepts, such as conservation (the ability to understand that the amount of water is the same even if the shape of the container is different), their reading skills will generally improve as well.

Linguistic processes are also important because they too appear to be malleable. For example, if we improve kindergarteners' vocabulary and fluency skills, their reading skills are likely to improve as well.

The third contribution is increasing recognition that although the same cognitive and linguistic skills are necessary for proficient reading for all children, each student brings a unique constellation of these skills to the classroom. These profiles may change as children receive effective instruction. Further, this may help to explain why instruction that is effective for one child might be ineffective for another child in the same classroom but who has a different profile of skills.

III. INTERVENTION: HOW DO WE MAKE READING INSTRUCTION MORE EFFECTIVE FOR STUDENTS WHO HAVE OR ARE AT RISK FOR DEVELOPING READING DISABILITIES? HOW DO WE TEACH READING TO STUDENTS WITH LOW INCIDENCE DISABILITIES?

The demands of reading change as children develop and progress through school.[70] In preschool and kindergarten, oral language sets the stage for reading comprehension and is a key area for intervention research.[71] In kindergarten and first grade, the skills that lead to decoding and word recognition (phonemic awareness, letter-sound knowledge, and quick recognition of high frequency words) take center stage. By second grade and through the elementary school years, gradual increases in reading rate and accuracy, vocabulary, and reading comprehension become principal instructional goals. By middle and high school years, students are expected to use reading as a tool for learning, finding, and using information.[72] Slow development along any of these dimensions can signal reading difficulties or reading disabilities.[73] In contrast, students with typical and more advanced reading skills may not need specific instruction on these components because they develop interactively and students can learn them more implicitly.[74] These developmental changes in how "reading" is defined influence how assessments and interventions are designed, and how learning is evaluated. Educators, policy makers, and researchers agree that reading instruction is crucial for improving the outcomes of students who are at risk for or have reading disabilities.[75] IES has funded research to help identify the types of interventions that can improve reading outcomes, along with the optimal timing for delivering these interventions, the training necessary for implementing these interventions in schools, and the likely effects of improved instructional intensity for students with different characteristics.

Prevention through Intensity of Instruction

Background. Because accumulating research has established that reading difficulties become more entrenched as students continue to experience difficulty learning to read well,[76] many researchers begin identifying students with low skill levels and intervening with them in kindergarten and first grade. Others begin even earlier to improve oral language skills of preschoolers because of the strong impact that early language may have on reading comprehension by the mid-elementary grades.[77] By teaching key literacy components such as oral language, phonological awareness, and letter knowledge near the beginning of students' formal schooling, early deficits may be remediated and the compounded problems created by chronically low reading achievement can be ameliorated.[78] Over the past decade, accumulating research, including research funded by IES, has demonstrated that early intervention is effective for many students with or at risk of reading disabilities and may even prevent reading disabilities.[79] The IES-funded studies discussed in this section have helped to advance our knowledge about effective intervention and the importance of using rigorous experimental designs in education research.

Contributions from IES-Supported Research

Contribution 8. Increasing the intensity of interventions in kindergarten and first grade may prevent reading difficulties for many students.

Denton and colleagues (2010) scaled-up a supplementary reading intervention designed to increase the intensity of intervention for first graders with or at risk of reading disabilities. Validated in earlier development and efficacy grants (funded by IES), their supplemental reading intervention, *Responsive Reading Instruction*, was used with first graders for whom whole-class instruction was ineffective. These students were assigned randomly to *Responsive Reading Instruction* or to typical school-designed interventions. *Responsive Reading Instruction* included word work, scaffolded reading, and rereading of decodable books (a phonics approach similar to the explicit instruction used by Vadasy and Sanders (2010) and Hagan-Burke et al. (2010)). This was along with supported writing, in which students took turns generating a sentence for all students in the group to write with teacher assistance. There were significant positive effects of *Responsive Reading Instruction* compared to typical school designed interventions on students' reading achievement in addition to generally better reading outcomes, 91 percent of students who received *Responsive Reading Instruction* achieved grade level expectations compared to only 79 percent of control students (grade level expectations were defined as within half a standard deviation of the national norms). The area that remained weakest for *Responsive Reading Instruction* and control students was oral reading fluency. The results of this study make an important contribution because the experiment occurred in real world conditions with levels of professional development and oversight likely to be available in many school districts. Moreover, students in *Responsive Reading Instruction* and control interventions received similar amounts of time in small groups, suggesting that intensity may be as much about the content of instruction as simply increasing intervention time.

English Learners: To extend our understanding about how phonics instruction in kindergarten might affect reading achievement for students who have reading difficulties and are English learners, Vadasy and Sanders (2010) randomly assigned students with reading difficulties to 18 weeks of one-to-one instruction or to a kindergarten-as-usual control. Half of the students in the study were English learners. Overall, children in the intervention group achieved higher scores than did children in the control group on nearly all measures. Students who were English learners in the treatment group outscored English learners in the control condition. However, they achieved lower scores compared to students who were not English learners and who received the intervention. The researchers also found that instruction in the general education classroom played a role in the results. For example, children made greater gains when they were in classrooms where a higher proportion of the time was spent teaching phonics. The study helps to show that including English learners in early interventions in reading can have positive effects on their reading. This finding is important because English learners have often been excluded from reading instruction until they reach some proficiency in English.

Behavior Problems: A second group of students often excluded from early interventions are those with behavioral problems. Students with or at risk of reading disabilities and behavior problems arguably may have more difficulty negotiating the complexities of the classroom environment. For example, they may experience less optimal learning environments because their outbursts disturb the classroom activity thus interfering with their learning and the learning of their classmates.[80] Previous research indicates that students with reading difficulties in first grade are more likely to demonstrate behavior problems in third grade and students with behavior problems in first grade are more likely to experience reading difficulties in third grade.[81] Thus learning environments that provide effective reading instruction and support for behavior may be particularly effective in mitigating the sequelae of reading disabilities.

In their IES-funded study, Hagan-Burke, Kwok, Zou, Johnson, Simmons, and Coyne (2010) examined the impact of instruction that takes advantage of current understandings on best practice for literacy instruction in kindergarten and how these practices might affect reading development for students with and without behavior problems. They defined these best practices as instruction that integrates phonemic awareness, the alphabetic principal, and decoding, and is explicit, systematic, and code-based. They conjectured that such rigorous reading instruction might mitigate the influence of problem behaviors on reading acquisition in kindergarten. They considered three types of problem behaviors: externalizing (acting out), internalizing (depressed, withdrawn or very shy), and hyperactivity (overly active and rambunctious). Their results showed that explicit, systematic, code-based instruction was more effective than was the business-as-usual control instruction for children with externalizing behavior (e.g., fighting, talking back to teachers, tantrums) and children who were hyperactive and easily distracted. Although students with problem behaviors had lower overall reading outcomes than did students with better behavior, these findings make an important contribution because students with problem behaviors who received explicit, systematic, code-based instruction were more successful than were students in less directed, more eclectic and less explicit school-directed control interventions. In considering the students with and without problem behaviors, both types of interventions raised student performance.[82] Nevertheless, the more explicit approach was particularly effective for students with the lowest pretest performance. Specifically, students in the bottom quartile scored higher across most measures when they received more explicit, systematic, code-based intervention.

Future Directions. These studies contribute to the extant literature by demonstrating that providing intensive intervention to students with low reading skills in kindergarten and first grade generally improves reading outcomes later on. Students who were English learners and students with behavioral problems also improved reading skills more than students in control groups when the interventions were systematic and included a focus on phonics. Nevertheless, these students' skills grew less during intervention compared to treated students who were native English speakers or who had no behavioral difficulties. This suggests a need to test interventions with content addressed specifically to these students experiencing these additional challenges. Also, although skills such as phonemic awareness, letter knowledge, and decoding improved, smaller gains were found for reading fluency, which is addressed in the next section.

Fluency Interventions May Increase Fluency and Comprehension

Background. Reading fluency — the rate, accuracy, and prosody of reading — is an important component of reading.[83] Researchers have demonstrated strong correlations between students' fluency and their ability to understand what they read (comprehension).[84] There is also evidence that reading interventions are frequently less effective in bringing students' fluency in line with their peers compared to their improvement in other skills, such as decoding.[85] Recently, studies have explored whether fluency might have a causal impact on reading comprehension. The assumed interrelationship can be traced back to the early automaticity model of LaBerge and Samuels

(1974), who viewed problems in reading fluency as being related to poor word decoding, which created a bottleneck in which the slow flow of thought hampered comprehension. Students with reading difficulties appeared to spend an excessive amount of time on decoding and therefore to expend valuable mental resources that could have been used for comprehension.

Contributions from IES-Supported Research

Contribution 9. Fluency interventions that focus on repeated reading or reading a range of text, along with opportunities to practice reading in the classroom may generally improve students' fluency and comprehension. In a series of IES-supported studies, Vadasy and Sanders (2008a, 2008b, 2009) randomly assigned students who were poor readers to dyads (pairs of readers) within schools, and then randomly assigned these dyads to a published repeated reading intervention called *Quick Reads* (Hiebert, 2003) or to a control group. Across studies *Quick Reads* was implemented with dyads of students in second through fifth grades in 30-minute sessions for 15 to 20 weeks. In the first study, students in fourth and fifth grade participated. In addition to *Quick Reads*, students in the intervention group also received 5 minutes of vocabulary instruction because students with reading difficulties often miss out on grade- appropriate vocabulary experience. For the fourth and fifth graders, compared to the control group students, students receiving the fluency interventions made significant gains in experimenter-designed vocabulary and comprehension tests. However, they demonstrated no advantage for fluency, which was the instructional target.[86] Given the developmental nature of reading fluency, specifically, that reading rate and accuracy improve with overall reading skills over time for typical readers, the researchers conjectured that by fourth grade, students with poor fluency were also poor in decoding and word recognition, which may have inhibited their fluency growth.

In their next experiment with second and third grade students, Vadasy and Sanders (2009) supplemented *Quick Reads* with small amounts of decoding instruction and observed significant gains in word attack (understanding letter patterns) and in reading fluency and comprehension compared to control students. Gains were strongest when students had tutors who implemented the intervention with high fidelity. In a comparison between para-educators (also called teaching assistants or instructional aides) and teacher-certificated interveners, no differences in student outcomes were found when the intervention was implemented with high fidelity, which suggests that fluency practice may be an appropriate role for well-trained para-professional educators in schools.

Vadasy and Sanders (2008b) also observed second and third grade classroom reading instruction to better understand the kinds of fluency practices that occur in general education classes. In addition to the positive effects of intervention, students with more classroom-based opportunities to practice reading made reliably greater gains during the intervention than did students who participated in the intervention but were offered fewer opportunities to practice fluency in class.

In two IES-supported randomized controlled studies, O'Connor and colleagues (2007, 2010) varied types of fluency practice for second and fourth grade students and explored the effect of rate improvement on other aspects of reading, including decoding, word recognition, vocabulary, and comprehension. In each experiment, students read aloud to an adult who provided assistance with difficult words and who corrected errors. O'Connor, White, and Swanson (2007) compared repeated versus wide reading, and O'Connor, Swanson, and Geraghty (2010) compared fluency growth when students read relatively easy or difficult levels of text. Both studies found that experimental treatments were more effective than the no-treatment control condition. There were no differences in fluency outcomes between the two types of practice conditions. Students at both grade levels made significant gains in reading rate, and their word identification and comprehension also improved significantly compared to students in the control group. However, the reading practice did not generate significant gains in decoding ability or vocabulary in either experiment. Importantly, students with learning disabilities and students who were English learners also made significant gains in reading rate and comprehension across both grades. The authors noted that opportunity to practice reading aloud in typical fourth grade classrooms is rare. In particular the fourth graders in the control condition made little gain at all in rate, which suggests that fluency practice for students with reading difficulties may be needed well past first and second grades. The trajectory of growth appeared to increase over time suggesting that fluency interventions may take longer to have an educationally important impact.

Future Directions. These studies contribute to our understanding about how to intervene to improve fluency. Two intervention practices, repeated reading and wide reading, are associated with gains in reading fluency. In addition, improving students' reading rates takes considerable practice. Both second and fourth graders' skills appear to grow significantly with practice; however, few practice opportunities were observed in the intermediate grades. Moreover, whereas gains in fluency generally improve comprehension, fluency gains do not appear to influence decoding or vocabulary, which suggests that students with reading difficulties may take less advantage of incidental learning opportunities compared to typical and strong readers. These results suggest that for students with slow reading rate, specific instruction to teach decoding and vocabulary should likely continue into the intermediate grades.

Vocabulary Interventions

Background. Children's use of spoken or oral language is a positive predictor of reading development throughout schooling. Research in preschools has documented that children who are at risk for language disabilities, which also puts them at high risk for reading disabilities,[87] appear to benefit from extensive opportunities for listening to and using complex spoken language.[88] Unfortunately, two key factors that influence the effects of language enhancements are difficult to shift. First, teachers have difficulty increasing the amount and quality of modeling and interactive talk that occurs between them and their students, as well as among students. This is likely due to insufficient training for many preschool teachers, including those teaching in Head Start and Title 1 settings.[89] Second, some children attend preschool irregularly even though regular attendance improves their opportunity to learn vocabulary.[90] The active ingredients of language stimulation (such as imitating what a child says, or extending what a child says) relate to teachers' use of high-quality language interactions, group size, and activity context.[91] Observations across preschools have indicated that teachers only used language stimulation in 36 percent of their verbal exchanges with children. In other words, the conversational responsiveness known to improve children's use of language was rarely observed in these preschools. Teachers are more likely to provide language stimulation when they respond to children during dramatic play, art, and other highly stimulating activities. The simultaneous impact of group size, activity structure, and language stimulation has important implications for training of preschool and kindergarten teachers by helping them learn to establish a positive language-learning environment, particularly when teaching children from higher poverty communities.

Contributions from IES-Supported Research

Contribution 10. Language outcomes for many preschool children at risk for language disabilities can improve if they are provided extensive opportunities to hear and use complex oral language.

In continuing efforts to understand how language and vocabulary stimulation might be increased in kindergarten settings, IES-funded researchers Coyne, McCoach, and Kapp (2007) explored ways to use storybook reading and discussion. Typically developing children frequently learn new vocabulary through exposure and incidental teaching of word meanings; children at risk for long-term vocabulary problems are likely to need more intensive and extended instruction to learn the same core of words as children who are typically developing. To test this possibility, a within-subjects design was conducted, in which students received both typical and extended instruction in random order. In the typical instruction condition where exposure to the vocabulary was more incidental, teachers read storybooks that included the target words but did not teach directly or discuss the words. The extended instruction condition included the same storybooks read aloud, but the students were encouraged to pronounce each of the words and to listen for, and raise their hands when they heard the word in the story. Teachers then provided a simple definition and reread the sentence with the target word. After the story was finished, children participated in a variety of related activities. These activities were designed to provide students with opportunities to discuss the words, to use the word in a number of different ways, and to make judgments on appropriate uses of the words. During the phase when children received extended instruction, they were generally able to provide better definitions of words than when they received typical instruction, and these gains were maintained on a delayed posttest weeks later.

In a second experiment, Coyne et al. (2007) compared extended instruction with embedded instruction. In the embedded instruction condition, teachers provided a simple definition of the target words as they were encountered in the story. Results again revealed that extended instruction was more effective, on average, than embedded instruction. These result suggest that not only did young students with weaker vocabulary skills fail to pick up meanings of words incidentally, but that providing only definitions was also insufficient for most children. When interpreting these results, the researchers conjectured that children with weaker vocabulary skills might benefit from additional review of the vocabulary because they forgot a fair number of the words they learned when they were tested two months later − although children in the extended instruction condition still remembered more words than did children in the embedded vocabulary intervention. Study designs that consider whether, over time, children actually maintain gains from interventions can provide useful information about the intervention and its effectiveness in schools.

To test classroom applications of this approach, Loftus, Coyne, McCoach, Zipoli, Kapp, and Pullen (2010) implemented vocabulary instruction in a whole-class, general education setting. Using a within-subjects design for students with below-average vocabulary, they compared the effects of whole-class instruction alone (the control) with additional extended, supplemental instruction focused on the same words in small groups (the intervention). Each student participated in whole-class instruction alone as well as the extended, supplemental intervention. The whole-class instruction followed the procedures for extended instruction described above in Coyne et al. (2007). The supplemental instruction was designed to take advantage of the small group format by providing more opportunity for children to discuss, respond to requests for elaboration, receive feedback, and say words, definitions, and target sentences aloud. Feedback and instructional support (e.g., scaffolding) was provided to students when they made errors to increase the likelihood of correct responding. Overall, the students with weaker vocabulary achieved higher scores on words they had learned through the combination of whole-class and supplemental instruction than they did when they learned words through whole-class instruction alone. Importantly, this additional layer of intervention supported students with low-skills so that they achieved vocabulary scores that were similar, on average, to those of students with stronger vocabulary skills and who received whole-class instruction on the same words.

Exploring variations of evidence-based vocabulary instruction in first grade classrooms, Maynard, Pullen, and Coyne (2010) randomly assigned teachers to three types of vocabulary instruction during storybook reading: rich instruction (called extended instruction in the earlier studies), basic instruction (providing child-friendly definitions of target words during the read-aloud), or incidental instruction (target words were not discussed). Across all groups, the same storybooks were read to students three times with general discussions following each. Results consistently favored rich instruction, which was more effective, on average, than basic instruction, which was more effective than incidental learning. A key finding was that most first grade teachers could use research-based instructional principles effectively. This demonstration is important because the teachers in the rich instruction condition received just two hours of training, and they maintained the high level of procedural fidelity generated by this training during five unannounced classroom observations.

Pullen, Tuckwiller, Maynard, Konold, and Coyne (2010) used the rich instruction approach with first graders at risk for reading difficulties and found results that were similar to Loftus et al. (2010). They found moderate positive effects favoring students with weaker skills who received additional, small-group vocabulary instruction. Unfortunately, the children did not maintain this advantage when they were tested four weeks later, which again suggests a need for periodic review of taught words. For first graders with weaker vocabulary, whole-class instruction — even when carefully managed to follow research-based recommendations — was generally insufficient to teach meanings of words in ways that students could apply in new contexts or use in conversations.

Future Directions. Across these IES-funded vocabulary studies, findings built on previous research to demonstrate that (1) enriched vocabulary instruction in whole-class settings appears to improve learning compared to less specific methods; and (2) greater instructional intensity (e.g., opportunities to respond, individualized feedback) is associated with stronger outcomes for students with weaker vocabulary skills. The most meaningful aspects of intervention for these students included increased instructional time and intensity, and decreased group size for greater opportunities to respond and explore new words across multiple contexts. Adding increasingly intensive vocabulary interventions may be a useful extension to RtI or tiered intervention approaches because small-group, supplemental, and intensive intervention may bring young children with weaker vocabulary skills into average ranges of performance on taught words, although gains appeared to be stronger for kindergarteners than for first graders. It remains to be seen whether continuing such tiered instruction might promote generalized gains in vocabulary that could be captured on standardized measures. Because of the cost associated with such intensity, research and policy attention might focus on the tiered model in which additional instruction is provided only to students with or at risk of reading difficulties, particularly students who have already fallen behind their peers and are least likely to benefit from high quality general education or Tier 1 instruction.

Importantly, these studies reveal the fragile nature of newly learned words. By a few weeks after the intervention ended, many students forgot the meanings of words learned during small- as well as large-group interventions.

Ongoing review of newly learned words is likely to be necessary for students if they are to remember the meanings of words after the intervention concludes.

Delivering Intervention through Peer-Assisted or Collaborative Learning

Background. Increasing the intensity of intervention through small group or one-to-one instruction can lead to improved reading outcomes for many students; however, it can be expensive or difficult to manage in schools with stretched resources. As an alternative to pull- out services, researchers have considered whether peers might be used as effective tutors for increasing the intensity of instruction and increasing students' opportunity to receive and to respond to appropriate feedback on reading activities.[92] In the early grades, many peer-assisted activities are focused on basic reading skills such as phonological awareness, alphabet letters, decoding, word recognition, and fluency. As students progress through school, learning how to engage with text becomes increasingly important for learning. Although isolated skills such as phonological awareness or decoding can be taught efficiently through careful instruction, reading comprehension relies on foundational reading skills in concert with strategic use of a range of cognitive processing skills. Moreover, comprehension of expository text (such as passages about history or science) is more difficult for students with reading difficulties than is reading narrative text (such as stories or novels), and the proportion of expository text students are expected to read increases tremendously in middle and high school.[93] And, as is true for learning basic reading skills, mastering skills that support comprehension takes time. Peer-assisted learning strategies have also been explored as a technique to support the acquisition of reading skill in the upper grades by providing additional opportunities to learn and practice those critical skills.

Contributions from IES-Supported Research

Contribution 11. Peer-assisted or collaborative learning is a promising method of increasing the intensity of instruction for students and improving their reading outcomes. With IES support, Saenz, McMaster, Fuchs, and Fuchs (2007) reviewed nearly 20 years of research on *Peer- Assisted Learning Strategies* (PALS), which was designed to improve the reading development of students in kindergarten through sixth grade and in high school. They found that, across studies, PALS was generally effective in improving reading outcomes, including in high poverty schools. In Grades 2-6 and high school, PALS practice activities include reading aloud to develop reading rate and accuracy, and also comprehension tasks such as recall and summarization. Results again were positive, with students in PALS classes improving in reading rate and comprehension, on average, when compared to students in control classes. Moreover, Spanish-speaking English learners showed similar gains in PALS classes.[94] A test of high school implementation also found that students who participated in PALS developed stronger reading comprehension than did students in control classrooms. However, there was no difference in their fluency. Considering all the studies, students in classes that used PALS generally outperformed students in traditional classrooms. Nevertheless, about 20 percent of low-achieving students and over 50 percent of students with disabilities did not make gains when provided tutoring by their peers. Of students who failed to benefit from peer tutoring, about 50 percent improved when the tutoring was conducted by a trained adult.

Another form of peer-assisted learning that has been tested across multiple studies is Collaborative Strategic Reading (CSR), which was designed to be used for students beyond the primary grades.[95] CSR integrates several reading processing strategies, including: previewing; monitoring understanding during reading; and summarizing after reading. To help teachers and students remember the strategies, the researchers called the strategies (a) Previewing to build background knowledge and anticipate the content, (b) Click and Clunk to monitor understanding, (c) Get the Gist to generate main ideas, and (d) Question Generation to summarize content.

In an IES-funded experimental study of CSR in 61 seventh and eighth grade classes,[96] students were randomly assigned to language arts classes, and classes were randomly assigned within teacher to CSR or a business-as-usual control condition. Teacher effects were controlled because the 17 participating teachers used CSR with some of their classes, while their other classes served as the control condition. Following four to six weeks of whole-class instruction in which teachers taught students each of the comprehension strategies, students were assigned to learning groups of four or five students to implement each of the steps in the process collaboratively. The reading content was the same across CSR and control conditions. After 18 weeks, students in the CSR groups scored higher, on average, than did students in the control group on all aspects of reading comprehension assessed.

Future Directions. Future reading intervention research might extend the duration of instruction provided through collaborative learning strategies to increase the likelihood of long-term effects. Multi-year collaborative learning interventions for students with low skill levels would also be important to explore, along with whether these types of interventions, if persistent, could improve comprehension outcomes of students at risk due to low socioeconomic status, English learner status, and other child characteristics.

Ongoing questions encompass the degree to which specific collaborative models such as PALS or CSR can be implemented by teams other than their developers, the types of support teachers will need to implement them with fidelity, conditions that influence students' responsiveness to these methods, and teachers' willingness to continue to implement them after external funding and support cease.

Differentiated (Also Called Personalized or Individualized) Instruction

Background. The interventions described thus far are often categorized as standard protocol interventions because they include specific teaching behaviors and content that are used for all of the students who are having reading difficulties at a particular grade level. Although the standardized protocol approach is sometimes preferred in intervention research because fidelity of implementation can be more rigorously assessed, evidence is growing in support of individualizing instruction.[97]

Contributions from IES-Supported Research

Contribution 12. Interventions that are differentiated to target an individual student's profile of component skills can improve reading development. In a series of randomized control studies from kindergarten through third grade, supported both by IES and NICHD, Connor, Morrison, Al Otaiba, Fishman, Schatschneider and colleagues have investigated whether the impact of reading instruction depends on the language and reading skills children bring to the classroom and whether such child characteristic by instruction (child X instruction) interactions might represent an underlying mechanism to explain why children respond to the same instruction in different ways.[98] In randomized controlled studies, in Grades K, 1, and 3, Connor and colleagues assigned schools or teachers to either a control condition or to implement a differentiated reading instruction intervention supported by *Assessment-to-Instruction* (A2i) online software, which recommends specific amounts and types of reading instruction based on students' language and reading skills. The intervention was called *Individualized Student Instruction* (ISI).[99] The comparison conditions varied across studies. In kindergarten, an alternative intervention provided training on individualizing instruction but without the A2i software.[100] In first grade students in treated classes were compared with a business as usual control.[101] In third grade, a vocabulary intervention that was not differentiated served as the alternative treatment.[102] Based on student reading profiles, recommendations were provided for four types of reading instruction, based on the *Simple View of Reading*: teacher/child-managed code-focused, teacher/child-managed meaning-focused, child-managed code-focused and child- managed meaning-focused instruction. In teacher/child-managed instruction, the teacher worked directly with students in small groups; in child-managed instruction, children worked independently or with peers. Code-focused instruction included phonological awareness, decoding, and fluency, whereas meaning-focused instruction included activities designed to improve students' comprehension of what they read. The recommendations changed over the course of the school year and as students' reading skills improved.[103]

In each study, students in the ISI classrooms demonstrated generally stronger word reading and comprehension gains than did students in control classrooms,[104] and teachers in the ISI intervention were more likely to differentiate instruction than were teachers in the control condition. Across grades, these researchers found that students with weak word reading skills appeared to require more teacher/child-managed code-focused instruction than did students with stronger reading skills. Plus, students required exponentially more time as they fell further below grade expectations. The researchers found a different pattern for vocabulary; first graders with strong entering vocabulary skills made greater gains in classrooms where teachers provided more opportunities for child-managed meaning-focused instruction, whereas children with weaker vocabulary generally made greater gains when provided smaller amounts of child- managed meaning focused instruction in the fall with steady increases in amounts over the school year. Moreover, all students demonstrated gains when they received more small-group teacher/child managed meaning-focused instruction regardless of reading skill. However, by third grade, compared to students with stronger skills, students who had weaker reading comprehension generally needed more time in such activities to reach grade level expectations. Additionally, the quality of code-focused instruction in third grade differed from that offered in kindergarten and first grade, and focused on patterns within words and morphemes (meaningful word parts, such as pre + view), rather than letter sounds.[105] The researchers also observed that, overall, teachers whose instruction for specific children most closely mirrored the A2i software recommendations for how to allot their instructional time achieved the highest literacy outcomes for their students.[106]

After third grade, word reading difficulties are often more difficult to remediate, particularly when students have already been identified as needing special education services. Gelzheiser, Scanlon, Vellutino, and Hallgren-Flynn (2011) developed and tested, using a quasi-experimental design, an interactive approach to teach students with reading disabilities in fourth grade how to read words using code-based and meaning-based approaches interactively. Students received the intervention immediately or participated in a wait-list control. The researchers combined features of two earlier approaches (*ISA: Interactive Strategies Approach* and *Reading Partners*), but tailored instruction to the needs of each student. Students in the intervention condition generally achieved stronger basic reading skills, taught vocabulary, reading comprehension, and scores on the state test of English Language Arts, but not reading rate, compared to children in the control condition. The largest effects were on reading comprehension, which is arguably the key reading outcome supporting academic learning. A meta-analysis of reading intervention for students in Grades 4 and higher[107] reported an average effect size less than 0.1 on standardized measures, whereas Gelzheiser et al. found effects greater than 1.5. The authors conclude that for students with specific strengths and weaknesses in their reading profile (those in the word emphasis or comprehension emphasis mini-lessons), targeting instruction to students' strengths and weaknesses may have accounted for the stronger reading outcomes observed for these students compared to those found in earlier studies.

Future Directions. Taken together, these findings build on previous work to indicate that one- size-fits-all approaches to reading are likely to fail many students. Instruction that is individualized to children's profiles of strengths and weaknesses, and is modified throughout the year as students' skills change, may be more effective than high quality instruction that is not differentiated. Thus what constitutes "effective instruction" appears to depend on the skills children bring with them to school. The definition of what constitutes good instruction for a particular student appears to change over time with the child's profiles of skill strengths and weaknesses. In turn, future research might investigate the timing of instructional ingredients over the first few years of school and how to better support schools and teachers' efforts to differentiate literacy instruction.

Instruction for Students with Low Incidence Disabilities

From its inception, IES funded investigations to explore literacy needs and instructional strategies for students with disabilities and who were struggling to learn to read. These populations included students with mild intellectual disabilities, moderate intellectual disabilities, deafness or who are hard of hearing, and autism spectrum disorder. This research is crucially important because children with these disabilities frequently fail to achieve even basic reading skills. Previous research has provided a limited understanding about the literacy needs of these populations of students. Overall, new IES-funded research has substantially contributed to our understanding that the developmental sequence of reading skill acquisition and theoretical descriptions of reading, such as the *Simple View of Reading*, derived from studies of typical readers may be applied effectively with these special populations of students. In this section, we discuss what we have learned from IES-funded studies focused on improving reading outcomes for children often referred to as having low incidence disabilities.

Contributions from IES-Supported Research

Contribution 13. What we are beginning to understand about how typically developing readers learn to read also appears to hold for students with low incidence disabilities, including children with mild and moderate intellectual disabilities, and children who are deaf or hard of hearing.

Children with Mild Intellectual Disabilities

Background. Students with mild intellectual disabilities have IQs in the range of 55-70 (100 is considered the average score of typically developing students). In addition to IQ scores in this range, students also must demonstrate limited adaptive behavior functioning as manifested in their social and practical skills. Students with intellectual disabilities (ID) represent approximately 1 percent of the population, and students with mild intellectual disabilities represent approximately 75 percent of those students. The majority of students with mild intellectual disabilities read at levels lower than expected for their chronological age, and comprehension appears to be the most difficult area of reading for them.[108] With current instructional models, students are reading within elementary grade levels, which provides access to simple narrative and basic functional information (e.g., labels, health and leisure directions, newspapers, vocationally-related information). Upon graduation these students will live independently and work in low-skill jobs. While living independently, many will need support from family, government, or non-profit organizations with regard to specific issues such as housing, employment, and health services).[109] IES funded research on improving the reading skills of students with mild intellectual disabilities is described below.

Contributions from IES-Supported Research

Wise, Sevcik, Romski, and Morris (2010) conducted a descriptive study of elementary students with mild intellectual disabilities who were struggling to learn to read. The purpose of this study was to examine the relationships among phonological processing skills, word, and nonword identification skills, and vocabulary knowledge for these students. Results were similar to previous findings for typically developing children. Phonological awareness was significantly correlated with reading achievement and vocabulary knowledge. As noted by the researchers, results from this study add to the limited corpus of research conducted with children with mild intellectual disabilities that provides evidence of relationships between phonological awareness and reading achievement.

Allor, Mathes, Roberts, Cheatham, and Champlin (2010) implemented and evaluated a comprehensive approach to reading instruction for students with mild to moderate intellectual disabilities. Students with IQs in the mild to moderate (40-69) range of ID were randomly assigned to an experimental curriculum group or a control group. Students in the control group received typical instruction provided by their school. The experimental group used Early Interventions in Reading, which had been validated with students without intellectual disabilities but who were struggling to read. The curriculum included multiple skill strands including concepts of print, phonological and phonemic awareness, letter knowledge, decoding, word identification, fluency, comprehension, vocabulary, and oral language development. Sixty additional lessons were developed as a foundation level for students without prerequisite skills for the curriculum.

At the end of the second and third years, results revealed that, in general, students showed significant gains in phonological awareness and oral reading fluency compared to the control group. However, there was variability in student outcomes; students with higher IQs tended to make greater gains compared to students with lower IQs. These results demonstrate that students with mild to moderate intellectual disabilities can learn basic reading skills given consistent, explicit, and comprehensive reading instruction across an extended period of time – about three years. Findings are consistent with scientifically-based reading instruction and theories of reading development for typically developing students and indicate that such research findings appear to be largely applicable for students with mild to moderate intellectual disabilities.

It is important to note, however, that the amount of time required to achieve basic literacy skills was substantially longer than the time required for typically developing students. Students required approximately three years of intensive academic instruction to achieve basic end-of-first grade reading levels. Little or no progress was seen on either standardized or progress-monitoring measures during the first year of the intervention. Many students also experienced difficulty transferring and applying skills in other contexts, and required extensive instruction and motivation to develop and maintain appropriate behavior required to participate in instruction.

Future Directions. These research findings are consistent with theories of reading development and scientifically-based reading instruction research for typically developing students. Findings support evidence of relationships between phonological awareness and reading achievement for these students. Further, based on initial results, there is support for continued investigation of explicit instruction within a comprehensive reading instruction approach. Further exploration of factors that predict and influence success in reading for students with mild intellectual disabilities is needed to inform the development of new techniques and tools specifically to address the challenges faced by these students. For example, one of the goals of future research may be to explore the reasons students with mild intellectual disabilities take longer than typically developing children to make comparable gains in areas such as phonological awareness and oral reading fluency. This will facilitate research on instructional methods that may address the time factor. Future curriculum development should build on findings that students with mild intellectual disabilities learn basic reading skills in a context that includes consistent, explicit, and comprehensive instruction. Methodologically, it is suggested that future studies include both consistent measures of intelligence as well as independent intellectual assessments to assess the validity of school classifications of mild intellectual disabilities.

Children with Moderate Intellectual Disabilities

Background. Students with moderate intellectual disabilities represent about 0.2 percent of the school population and have intelligence test scores in the range of 40-55 in conjunction with problems in adaptive behavior. Few of these students ever learn to read beyond a first grade reading level. Upon graduation they enter supported or sheltered employment opportunities when available and live in supervised group homes or with their families.[110] In school, these students are primarily the responsibility of special education professionals and spend up to 80 percent of their day in special education classes. Still, all educators in the school have a roll in their education. Although these children are provided access to the general curriculum, many are mostly taught the skills required for functioning semi-independently in various home, school, and community settings. Until recently, these students' reading instruction relied on sight-word instruction reportedly because educators and researchers operated with the assumption that students with moderate intellectual disabilities would not benefit from phonics instruction (Joseph and Seery 2004). Using the sight word approach, students are expected to memorize the look of words that they will frequently encounter at school and at home with their family as part of their daily routines (e.g., exit, stop, logos for commercial products). This approach has two serious limitations. First, students with moderate intellectual disabilities have limited memory capacities and so cannot memorize many words. Second, students are not taught any strategies for decoding and learning words that have not been explicitly taught.

Contributions from IES-Supported Research

Building on previous research, IES-funded research shows that reading instruction is generally more effective when students with moderate intellectual disabilities are taught phonological awareness and how to sound out unfamiliar words in addition to sight-word reading. Browder, Ahlgrim-Delzell, Courtade, Gibbs, and Flowers (2008) developed and evaluated a reading curriculum specifically designed for students with moderate intellectual disabilities called the *Early Literacy Skills Builder*. This curriculum is a comprehensive curriculum, which includes repeated story reading for comprehension and question answering; phonological awareness and phonics instruction including segmentation, letter-sound correspondence, phonemic awareness in identification of first and last sounds in words and pictures, pointing to letters and pictures of sounds and spoken words; and teaching sight-words to allow for vocabulary development and sentence completion. During intervention the students engaged in daily read aloud activities intended to improve their comprehension and vocabulary development).[111]

Kindergarten through fourth grade students with IQs of 55 or less were then randomly assigned to receive either *Early Literacy Skills Builder* or *Edmark*. The latter is a widely used sight-word program for this population of students. All instruction was conducted by their teachers, who received special training from the researchers. The results indicated that students in the *Early Literacy Skills Builder* intervention, compared to the control group, made significantly greater gains in phonological awareness on two researcher-designed measures of early literacy as well as on published, norm referenced measures of vocabulary and memory. This suggests that students with moderate intellectual disabilities can acquire phonological awareness and phonics skills, which are strong predictors of learning to read.

It is difficult to find standardized, norm referenced assessment instruments that provide useful data for students with moderate intellectual disabilities. This is because the test developers usually exclude these students from their test standardization sample and hence the tests do not measure the students' significantly lower levels of performance. In addition to developing the *Early Literacy Skills Builder*, this research team developed the *Nonverbal Literacy Assessment*, an instrument designed to measure emergent literacy for kindergarten through fourth grade students with IQs below 55.[112] The *Nonverbal Literacy Assessment* assesses six constructs -- phonemic awareness, phonics, comprehension, vocabulary, listening comprehension and text awareness –which, as found with typically developing students, work as a global construct of literacy.

With IES support, Alberto and colleagues developed an integrated curriculum that includes visual literacy, sight-word and phonics instruction. The visual literacy component ties meaning to pictures, picture sequences, and community logos. This may be a first step in literacy for primary aged students with severe or moderate intellectual disabilities, and may be the primary means of literacy for older students with more significant intellectual disabilities. For example, students are taught logos, such as McDonald's golden arches, in settings they and their families frequent.[113] During sight-word instruction students were taught to read simple words developed from the letters and sounds of common community words, which also were taught. The students were expected to read words individually and in connected text, and to provide motor demonstrations of comprehension.[114] Phonics instruction complemented sight-word instruction. Instruction was explicit and used simultaneous prompting, a behavioral strategy in which the correct word is supplied during instruction to provide repeated practice, but not provided during testing.

The intervention was tested in two single subject design studies. In the first study six students, three in elementary and three in middle schools were taught to read and demonstrate comprehension of a dozen commercial logos found in their communities.[115] Time delay was used as the instructional strategy and comprehension was assessed by asking students what items they could purchase in a store with that logo. In the second study, with five students ages 12-15, students were systematically taught to read individual words and connected text phrases of increasing length and complexity using simultaneous prompting. After reading an individual word or connected text phrase students were required to demonstrate comprehension by completing a motoric task. Results showed that fluency practice may help students compensate for memory difficulty when engaging extended connected text phrases. Analysis of the curriculum data indicates that many students were able to learn how to recognize the pictures and words taught and to sound out simple word. The curriculum also included storybook reading for phonemic awareness, vocabulary building, comprehension, and print awareness.

Allor, Mathes, Roberts, Jones, and Champlin (2010) also found significant gains in phonological awareness with a similar sample of early elementary students with moderate intellectual disabilities who received systematic and comprehensive reading instruction. These studies provide further evidence that explicit, systematic instruction in phonological awareness and phonics, which has shown to be generally effective for typically developing students and those in the mild range of intellectual disability, also may be effective, with some modifications, for these students. These modifications include additional time, greater intensity, highly trained teachers, and a greater number of lessons.

Future Directions. The framework for research moving forward for students with moderate to severe intellectual disabilities includes the development of curriculum that is comprehensive, and thereby provides opportunities for both sight-word and phonics instruction. Strategies might be investigated for determining appropriate placement of students within a longitudinal curriculum to account for differing ages and functioning levels.

Further curricula might allow for the accommodations that students requiring alternative communication systems and students with sensory impairments will need to be successful. Research might investigate how to (a) increase student comprehension of longer strings of information, (b) reduce the three year period for significant learning effects, and (c) develop instructional methods, to reduce the number of errors students make during probes sessions, so as to increase the degree of errorless learning. There is also a need for continued systematic investigations of various instructional strategies as has been done with time delay and simultaneous prompting. Finally, it is suggested that the final step in curriculum development should be a significant period of time of implementation by teachers in actual classrooms.

Children who are Deaf or Hard of Hearing

Background. Students who are deaf or hard of hearing (DHH) are at serious risk for reading difficulties, even though most students have typically developing cognitive skills. The typical DHH high school student will graduate with only fourth grade reading skills.[116] In the past, many severely and profoundly deaf children could not hear well enough to learn oral language skills. Whereas American Sign Language is a complete language, its grammar and vocabulary are very different from English. Fluency in American Sign Language frequently does not mean that children can read English very well. Students who do not have the opportunity to learn oral language skills frequently struggle with mastering the phonological aspects of reading. Fortunately, universal newborn infant hearing screening helps to identify DHH children much sooner so they can receive services. In addition, new technology, such as digital hearing aids and cochlear implants, are providing greater access to sound for severely and profoundly deaf children.[117]

Contributions from IES-Supported Research

IES is funding important early literacy research for this new generation of DHH children. For example, Lederberg and colleagues[118] conducted a descriptive study where they assessed emergent literacy skills and outcomes at the beginning and end of a school year for prekindergarten students (3 to 6 years old). Of these students, most relied on spoken English to communicate, but some used both speech and sign language, and others used American Sign Language and learned English through reading (a bilingual-bicultural approach). They found that 73 percent of the children were able to perceive spoken language in the fall of preschool confirming their hypothesis that this new generation of DHH children should be able to access the auditory aspects of reading, such as pairing written letters with sounds. In general, the children's early reading and vocabulary scores were not much lower than those of children with normal hearing but there was more variability. Moreover, on average, the students demonstrated developmental gains that were similar to their hearing peers in their acquisition of letter names and common written words. However, their phonological awareness and phonics scores were much lower and the children showed very little growth in phonological awareness skills. Importantly, the researchers found that DHH children with weaker phonological awareness skills tended to have weaker reading skills overall. This is what other researchers have found for children with normal hearing.[119] The researchers noted that "the development of phonological skills supports the hypothesis that, while delayed, these children have the potential to learn to appreciate the phonological structure of spoken English during preschool and kindergarten" (p. 108) and are capable of learning the skills that research suggests are foundational for literacy development.

These researchers also found that many current ways of teaching DHH children to read, such as the sight word approach, may be too limited.[120] In a study of classroom characteristics that supported the learning of emergent literacy skills of young children who were DHH, Easterbrooks, Lederberg, and Connor (2010) observed self-contained kindergarten and first-grade classrooms using a frequently used observation system, the *Early Language and Literacy Classroom Observation Tool* or ELLCO.[121] They discovered that certain classroom characteristics, such as grade and whether or not the teacher used sign language, did not predict the quality of the classroom literacy environment. However, other elements of the classroom environment did represent a significant source of influence on DHH children's emergent literacy, particularly for developing phonological awareness skills. For example, students' phonological awareness skills were stronger in classrooms where students were explicitly taught these skills. Vocabulary development was stronger when teachers and children were observed frequently interacting during reading and writing activities.

Using the information gleaned from this descriptive study, Lederberg and colleagues developed an early literacy curriculum called *Foundations for Literacy* based on the premise that research on effective literacy instruction for hearing children would apply to DHH children as long as adaptations were made to support their hearing loss. Thus, the intervention focused on teaching phonological awareness, phonics, fluency, vocabulary and language with appropriate adaptations. Their single case design studies demonstrated that DHH children who have some speech perception abilities (functional hearing) could learn specific phoneme-grapheme correspondences through explicit auditory skill instruction with language and visual support.[122] These studies are among the first to examine the instruction of phoneme-grapheme correspondences for children who are DHH at the prekindergarten age level. Results suggest that many children who are DHH, even those who have delays in language, are able to learn the foundation for the alphabetic principle during prekindergarten.

Future Directions. Future research should (1) be longitudinal to document for these students who are DHH, as is documented for typical learners, the role of alphabetic knowledge for literacy development, and (2) identify for which children auditory-based instruction to build alphabetic knowledge is appropriate, including children without speech perception abilities. It is suggested by investigators of visual phonics that it may be that, for these students, instruction using the semantic association strategy paired with visual phonics during preschool will build a foundation for reading instruction in elementary school, (3) compare approaches that build phonological awareness in children who are DHH in addition to the semantic association strategy, and (4) investigate whether processes that underlie literacy are different for children with hearing loss, depending on the nature of their representations. The IES-funded curriculum research reviewed here focuses on children with access to sound; researchers note it is equally important to develop curricula that are effective for children with little access to sound. These children may constitute a majority of the older students who are DHH in self-contained classes and resources classes, as many of the children who are DHH with access to sound become integrated into the general education setting.

Summary of Contributions for Research Question III: Intervention

Summarized below, the IES-funded research findings have contributed to knowledge regarding effective strategies to improve the reading skills of all students, including those who are at risk for reading disabilities or who have reading disabilities. Many of these interventions and strategies have been implemented in classrooms and in many cases by general education classroom teachers who received special training. Although more research is needed, in general, children who struggle with reading at all grades can make substantial reading gains when they are provided systematic and intensive interventions that may be integrated with classroom instruction or are supplemental to classroom instruction. The demands of reading change as children develop and progress through school. These changes should influence how assessments and interventions are designed, and how learning is evaluated. Effective strategies are also helpful for students who attend higher poverty schools and who are English learners.

1. There may be no need to delay reading instruction for many young children who are English learners because these beginning readers appear to make greater gains when they are taught how to read and to speak English at the same time.

2. For many students, peer-assisted learning interventions may be effective for improving reading outcomes and at the same time may save school resources. Additionally, many of the small group interventions can be implemented effectively with para-educators. Standard protocol instruction, where intensive interventions are provided to all of the students in a small group, are generally effective for many students.

3. However, accumulating research reveals that differentiated or individualized instruction -- instruction that considers the different profiles of skills students bring to the classroom, their grade and instructional needs, and that target specific amounts and types of instruction to meet students' individual needs -- may be more effective in improving reading outcomes than high quality instruction that is not differentiated.

4. Our review of the research supported by IES for students with intellectual disabilities and students who are deaf or hard of hearing suggests that there is a growing consensus on a number of issues. The findings are consistent with previously conducted scientifically based reading instruction and theories of reading development for typically developing students. Thus what we have learned about the development of reading in typically developing students may be applicable for students with intellectual disabilities and students who

are deaf or hard of hearing. Reading curricula that are comprehensive and include phonics instruction in addition to sight-word instruction appear to be more effective than sight-word instruction alone.

5. Overall, most students with intellectual disabilities required instruction over an extended period of time (2-3 years) to reach basic levels of literacy. Similar to typically developing readers, building a foundation of phonemic awareness and print knowledge, and developing vocabulary and comprehension skills using story books and oral language development strategies appears to be associated with stronger reading outcomes. For students with intellectual disabilities, explicit behaviorally-based instructional strategies (e.g., time delay, simultaneous prompting) that are consistently applied may support stronger reading skill gains.

Whereas existing measures can be used somewhat successfully for students with intellectual disabilities, there is a need for measures that will accurately detect the skills and improvements of students with the most significant disabilities and new assessments are being developed.

IV. PROFESSIONAL DEVELOPMENT: HOW DO WE BRING RESEARCH-BASED INSTRUCTIONAL PRACTICES TO THE CLASSROOM?

We cannot bring research into the classroom and improve students' reading skills if we cannot support teachers' efforts to use research-validated interventions and instructional strategies. NCLB specifically calls for students to have highly qualified teachers. Although there has been debate on defining "high quality," it has been generally agreed that high quality teachers are knowledgeable about their subject and provide effective instruction that promotes student learning.[123] Defining and identifying effective teaching using methods such as classroom observation, teacher knowledge surveys, and teacher value-added scores help to understand key aspects of effective teaching and how to support teachers better.[124] Previous and ongoing research designed to increase our understanding about how to support teachers' efforts to improve their practices has suggested that professional development should be intensive, relevant, and encourage collaboration.[125] However, many of these practices have not undergone rigorous evaluation.

Specialized Knowledge and Long-Term Support

Background. IES has funded a number of studies that investigate teacher and school characteristics that are associated with students' literacy outcomes. These include preschool teacher education, teachers' knowledge about literacy, beliefs about practice, and support from school leadership.

Contributions from IES-Supported Research

Contribution 14. We can improve many teachers' delivery of complex, evidence-based instruction and interventions through developing their specialized knowledge and supporting consistent long-term implementation of evidence-based instructional practices.

Preschool teacher education. In a correlational study, Gerde and Powell (2009) found that among Head Start teachers, formal education in the area of early childhood education was associated with greater improvements in their students' outcomes. Teachers with more education were more likely to increase their use of book-focused statements during book reading with their preschoolers. This is encouraging because in most studies with elementary, middle and high school teachers, years of education or certification did not predict students' reading outcomes.[126] However, this may not be the case for preschool. In preschool education, the state qualifications for teachers vary substantially, so improving teachers' level of education is a potentially powerful way to improve preschoolers' early reading outcomes.

Teacher knowledge. Teachers' specialized knowledge about concepts of literacy and how to teach literacy are associated with first graders' literacy outcomes, according to results from correlational studies.[127] For example, Brady and colleagues (2009) found that teachers' specialized knowledge about literacy concepts was very low (about 40 percent on a test) when tested on phonological awareness, phonics, fluency and comprehension. However, these scores improved greatly when teachers were provided professional development (to between 68 percent and 80 percent on average). Interestingly, teachers who were younger were more likely to improve their scores on the test of teacher knowledge than were older teachers. Plus teachers' attitudes generally changed as their knowledge increased, such as the belief that they could improve their students' reading skills, called self-efficacy. The researchers suggested that "teachers had acquired a better understanding of their own skill level for providing basic reading instruction" (p. 442).

Carlisle and colleagues[128] went a step farther in another correlational study. They asked whether teachers' knowledge would predict students' reading outcomes. They carefully developed and analyzed their test of teacher knowledge, which used a set of scenarios to which the teachers responded. For example, teachers might read, "Mr. Lewis' class has been learning spelling rules for adding "ing" to base words. He is looking for groups of words that illustrate the various rules to give his students a complex challenge. Which of the following groups of words would be best for this purpose?" (Appendix A). The teachers are then offered four possible answers: " (a) hopping, running, sending, getting; (b) hoping, buying, caring, baking; (c) seeing, letting, liking, carrying; (d) all of the word sets are useful for this purpose"(d is correct). They found that students whose first grade teachers had significantly higher scores on the test of teacher knowledge generally had stronger reading outcomes than did students whose teachers had lower scores but the differences were small. At the same time, second and third graders' reading outcomes were not associated with their teachers' knowledge.

Piasta, Connor, and colleagues[129] explored whether the reason teacher knowledge scores appeared to have only a small impact on student outcomes might be because teachers vary in the extent to which they actually use this knowledge to inform and implement reading instruction. Using a test that was similar to the ones used in prior research (e.g., how many phonemes in the word "box"? Answer 4, /b-a-k-s/), the researchers found that the effect of teachers' knowledge on students' reading outcomes depended on how much time in explicit instruction in basic reading skills they actually provided. If teachers had higher levels of specialized knowledge but provided very little time in explicit instruction, then their students had the same general reading outcomes as students whose teachers had lower levels of knowledge and provided little time in instruction. However, the more time high knowledge teachers provided explicit reading instruction, the greater were their students' reading outcomes. At the same time, the more time teachers with less knowledge spent providing explicit instruction, the worse their students generally did. When the researchers looked at the videotapes of these teachers' practice, they found that the teachers with less knowledge were frequently teaching the children incorrectly. Thus, although teacher knowledge may not directly predict student outcomes, it does appear to inform their practice, which in turn has implications for how well students learn to read.

Beliefs about practice. A number of IES-funded correlational studies have extended the extant research by finding that teachers' beliefs about how to teach students are associated with their response to professional development and, in turn their practice and the reading outcomes of their students. For example, when the research-based instructional strategies that teachers were learning during professional development were farther from their existing beliefs about reading instruction, it was more difficult for them to change their practice.[130] Also, the amount of time teachers had available in and out of the classroom predicted the extent to which they changed their practices; teachers who had more responsibilities outside of the school (e.g., another job) were less likely to change their practice in response to professional development. When teachers felt that professional development could help them improve their students' outcomes, they were much more likely to actually implement the new instructional strategies presented than when they perceived less benefit to their students. A particularly important belief, which was identified throughout the IES-supported and other studies, was the idea of self-efficacy. In these studies, self-efficacy was teachers' belief that they could actually make a difference in students' reading outcomes and it was their responsibility to do so.[131] In some cases, professional development was able to improve teachers' self-efficacy.[132]

Schools and leadership. An important finding across several IES-funded studies was that the contexts in which teachers provide instruction mattered, particularly in schools where teachers felt supported by their principals.[133] For example, in a study of professional development for literacy coaches, Matsumura and colleagues discovered that how frequently teachers took part in coaching activities was well below what the program hoped to achieve but this differed by school.[134] Teachers at schools where the principal and other school leaders actively supported coaching were much more likely to participate in coaching activities than were teachers at schools that did not support it. Indeed, survey results showed that principals were a key school resource in supporting coaching efforts to improve teacher practice.

Future Directions. These results point to the very real impact teachers have on their students' reading achievement and suggest several potential ways to improve teacher's effectiveness. Ideas presented that might be productive include building teachers specialized knowledge about reading while at the same time insuring that this knowledge is put into practice and better understanding teachers' beliefs about the content of professional development, how well research-based findings align with their current beliefs, and how this affects their instructional practices. This and other research also suggests that better understanding the role of educational leaders in the dynamic contexts of schools and classrooms and how to promote leadership that supports teachers effectiveness may help improve students achievement overall.

Multifaceted Teacher Professional Development

Background. Research shows that we can improve many teachers' delivery of complex evidence-based instruction through developing their specialized knowledge, changing beliefs, and supporting consistent long-term implementation.[135] However, the research just discussed shows that teachers differ in their beliefs, their knowledge, and the support they receive from school. Effective professional development likely has to consider these individual teacher differences. Additionally, teachers in kindergarten through fifth grade must generally meet basic qualifications that are fairly uniform across the United States. These include a bachelor's degree and a teaching certificate. Typically teachers must past an examination and have been provided with opportunities to teach under supervision. During the past decade, thanks in large part to federal funding of high quality research, the research evidence regarding how to teach children, including those with or at risk of reading disabilities, to read has changed substantially. Thus, previously well-trained teachers may not be well situated to teach reading using new research- based methods.

Contributions from IES-Supported Research

Contribution 15. Combining multiple professional development strategies, including coaching, linking student assessment data to instruction, using technology, and participating in communities of practice, can support teachers' learning and implementation of research-based reading instruction. There is evidence from quasi-experimental and longitudinal studies that improvements in students' reading outcomes are associated with their teachers receiving intensive professional development. Biancarosa, Bryk, and Dexter (2010) conducted a longitudinal study where kindergarten through second grade teachers received professional development, called the Literacy Collaborative. In this form of professional development, coaches work with teachers to improve their knowledge and practice. These researchers found that students made greater gains in reading when their teachers received the Literacy Collaborative professional development as compared to typical school practices. Matsumura and colleagues[136] found that professional development, which included researcher-trained but school- employed literacy coaches, was associated with improvements in fourth and fifth grade teachers' practice and their students' reading outcomes based on the state-mandated tests. In another study, when kindergarten and first grade teachers received biweekly coaching on how to implement an intervention for students who were at risk for reading disabilities, kindergarteners made significant gains in word reading when compared to students whose teachers did not receive professional development.[137] However, these researchers did not see similar gains for first graders.

But are all the components of these professional development programs, specifically workshops, communities of practice, and coaching, really necessary to improve teachers' practices and their students' reading outcomes? For example, in the studies just described, all of the teachers attended workshops and worked individually and in small groups with literacy coaches. Plus coaches observed teachers in the classroom and modeled the new strategies for them. Such professional development is very expensive and if not all components are needed; using fewer components would save school districts staff and money. In a quasi-experimental study, Carlisle and colleagues (2011) compared how well teachers improved their practice when they received different types and combinations of professional development. There were three combinations: (a) workshops designed to improve teachers' knowledge about literacy concepts and practice; (b) workshops plus learning how to evaluate their students' reading skills and then using these results to improve practice; and (c) workshops, student evaluation, plus the opportunity to work with a literacy coach and to collaborate with each other in communities of practice. Thus all of the teachers had training to improve their specialized knowledge, which holds the teacher knowledge component constant. The researchers found that the combination of all three-- workshop, student evaluation, and coaching—was associated with improvements in teacher practice compared to the other combinations. And as we saw with the research on teacher knowledge,[138] improving knowledge and improving practice are likely required to improve students' reading outcomes. Thus, although coaching is more expensive than providing workshops, it appears to be a critical component of effective professional development.

Schools are increasingly investing in technology with implications for supporting stronger implementation of research-based reading instructions.

Using longitudinal correlational studies, Connor and colleagues found that the more teachers used Assessment-to-Instruction online software, which is designed to help them interpret assessment results and plan differentiated instruction, the greater were their first graders' reading skill gains.[139] In another randomized controlled study, Al Otaiba and colleagues compared student outcomes for kindergarten teachers who were randomly assigned to receive professional development on differentiating reading instruction with treatment group teachers who received this professional development plus training and access to Assessment-to-Instruction online software.[140] They found that teachers were more likely to individualize instruction and their kindergartners made greater gains in reading when the professional development was supplemented by the technology.

Using a multi-probe single subject design, Hemmeter, Snyder and colleagues found that feedback provided to teachers based on teacher-selected video-tapes of their instruction provided via email was associated with increases in preschool teachers' interactions with students and improved student behavior. [141] When researchers provided Targeted Reading Intervention professional development to teachers at randomly assigned schools using web conferencing, laptop computers, and webcam technology, the professional development was effective and the reading skills of students with or at risk of reading disabilities improved. [142] Landry and colleagues compared four combinations of professional development with a randomly assigned control group.[143] They found that online coursework combined with coaching and instructionally-linked feedback to teachers resulted in higher quality preschool teacher practices and stronger student early reading gains.

Is technology-based coaching as effective as face-to-face coaching? That is what a team of IES- funded researchers wanted to find out.[144] Working with 88 Head Start and other preschool teachers they randomly assigned half of them to receive *Classroom Links to Early Literacy* professional development, or to wait to receive it until the next year (the control). Then teachers in each group were randomly assigned to receive the professional development face-to-face or online. All of the teachers participated in a one day face-to-face workshop. In the face-to-face condition, frequent coaching was provided in the classroom whereas in the online condition, the same amount of coaching was provided over the web. When they compared the classroom reading instruction of teachers who received professional development (either type) with control teachers, their classroom practices had improved and their students showed larger early reading gains. When they compared results for teachers who received the face-to-face version with the online version, there were no differences in classroom practice or student outcomes.[145] Thus, both types of professional development were effective. This is important because online professional development saves time and travel costs especially for rural school districts – some of the teachers were 2 hours away. Plus, teachers have access to online videos of master teachers using new strategies, which coaches can recommend to teachers as part of their feedback.[146]

Future Directions. The results of this IES-funded research suggest ways to successfully improve teachers' reading instruction in the classroom. The most effective professional development is generally fairly intensive and utilizes a combination of workshops, in-classroom support, communities of practice, and sometimes, technology. Additionally research on technologies to support teachers' practice coupled with cost-benefit analyses may provide additional key information on providing professional development that actually changes teachers instructional practices in ways that supports student learning while containing the costs of high quality professional development. This may be particularly important as more children with or at risk of reading disabilities are served in general education classrooms and classroom teachers become increasingly responsible for both Tier 1 instruction and Tier 2 interventions.

Summary of Contributions for Research Question IV: Professional Development

IES-funded research has extended our understanding about professional development as follows:

1. Teachers' specialized knowledge, their beliefs about the value of the professional development they receive, their beliefs about their ability to improve their students' learning and outcome, as well as support from educational leaders are important considerations when designing effective professional development that changes teachers' practices in ways that promote students' reading outcomes.
2. Professional development that includes multiple components and individualized feedback for teachers can be effective in supporting teachers' use of evidence-based reading instruction and interventions. These improvements in practice generally result in stronger student outcomes. It appears that effective professional development includes

a combination of strategies including workshops and coaching, where well-trained literacy coaches meet with teachers individually, observe and support them in the classroom, and help them develop communities of practice. Technology appears to enhance professional development and online coaching can be as effective as face-to-face coaching. One reason individualized professional development strategies, such as coaching, appear to be more effective is because teachers bring different attitudes, beliefs, and levels of knowledge to the classroom and individualized professional development can be tailored for each teacher.

IES CONTRIBUTIONS AND IMPLICATIONS

Contributions: What Have We Learned Thus Far from IES-Supported Research?

Across the four domains that emerged from our review of published papers describing results of IES-supported research with initial awards from 2002 through 2008, we identified 15 specific contributions to understanding how to support reading achievement for students with or at risk for reading disabilities.

I. **Assessment**: What have we learned about effective identification and assessment of students who have or are at risk for reading difficulties or disabilities?
    1. Screening all children's reading skills (i.e., universal screening) at the beginning of the school year, especially in the early grades can be a valid and efficient process to identify children who are at risk for reading difficulties and disabilities.
    2. Using assessments to monitor children's progress (i.e., progress monitoring assessment) can guide the decision making process for determining whether an intervention is improving the development of a child's reading skills.
    3. New assessments for English language learners indicate that reading comprehension can be reliably and validly assessed without overburdening word reading and oral language skills.

    4. Accommodations can be made for assessing students with disabilities that do not modify the construct being measured and therefore represent a valid measure of this construct.

II. **Basic Cognitive and Linguistic Processes**: What are the basic cognitive and linguistic processes that support successful reading and how can these skills be improved for students who have or who are at risk for reading disabilities?

    1. Several important cognitive processes such as working memory, grasp of the principles of conservation and seriation, and abstract and inferential reasoning have been found to contribute to children's reading performance.

    2. Malleable linguistic processes such as oral language skills and vocabulary positively predict children's reading performance.

    3. Although the same sets of cognitive and linguistic skills are involved in learning to read, children bring unique constellations of these skills to the classroom and this has implications for instruction.

III. **Intervention**: How do we make reading instruction more effective for students who have or are at risk for developing reading disabilities? How do we teach reading to students with low incidence disabilities?

    1. Increasing the intensity of the instruction received in kindergarten and first grade can prevent reading difficulties for many students.

    2. Fluency interventions that focus on repeated reading of text, opportunities to practice reading in the classroom, and reading a range of text generally improve students' fluency and comprehension.

    3. Language outcomes for many preschool children at risk for language delays can improve if they are provided extensive opportunities to hear and use complex oral language.

    4. Peer-assisted or collaborative learning is a promising method of increasing the intensity of instruction for some students and improving their reading outcomes.

    5. Instruction and interventions that are differentiated to target each individual student's profile of component skills improve many students' reading development.

    6. What we know about how typically developing readers learn to read also holds for students with low incidence disabilities, including children with mild and moderate intellectual disabilities, and children who are deaf or hard of hearing.

IV. **Professional Development**: How do we bring research-based instructional practices to the classroom?
  1. Developing teachers' specialized knowledge and supporting consistent long-term implementation of research-based instructional strategies can improve delivery of complex, evidence-based instruction and interventions.
  2. Combining multiple professional development strategies, including coaching, linking student assessment data to instruction, using technology, and participating in communities of practice, can support teachers' learning and implementation of effective instruction.

Implications: Where Do We Go from Here?

Throughout this document, we have highlighted specific future directions for each of the 15 recommendations and so do not repeat them here. Research in the future will build on these findings and, indeed, new and exciting research is being funded by IES and continues to inform our understanding about how best to meet the needs of students with or at risk of reading disabilities. Important new research that is not included here examines the development processes of how students develop and master reading for understanding, interventions and instructional strategies that promote this development, and better understanding of the complex and interconnected processes that underlie proficient reading for understanding. Other efforts include the creation of research centers focused on the literacy skills of deaf and hard of hearing students and on adult basic education. Other new research examines researcher-practitioner partnerships and the development and testing of intensive reading (and math) interventions for children with the most intractable learning disabilities.

The first eight years of rigorous research funded by IES has extended our knowledge about how to help students who have or are at risk for reading disabilities. The fifteen specific contributions that we identified through the published articles we reviewed reveal that IES-funded research has contributed in important ways to understanding how best to support students with or at risk for reading disabilities. During its relatively short history, IES has required rigorous standards regarding how scientific information is obtained, particularly through the use of randomized controlled field trials in schools. Through IES, research findings now inform decision-making in education in ways that were simply not considered prior to its inception and we have reason to believe that IES funded research will continue to contribute meaningful and important research findings to the professional and research fields that support the successful education of children.

APPENDIX A. IES FUNDED RESEARCH REVIEWED BY THE PANEL

Principal Investigator: Paul Alberto
Institution: Georgia State University
Project Title: *Integrated Literacy for Students with Moderate and Severe Disabilities*
Program Topic: Reading, Writing, and Language Development
Grant Award Number: R324A070144

Alberto, P. A., Waugh, R. E. & Frederick, L. D. (2010). Teaching the Reading of Connected Text Through Sight-Word Instruction to Students with Moderate Intellectual Disabilities. *Research in Developmental Disabilities, 31*, 1467-1474.

Waugh, R. E., Alberto, P. A. & Frederick, L. D. (2011). Effects of Error Correction During Assessment Probes on the Acquisition of Sight Words for Students with Moderate Intellectual Disabilities. *Research in Developmental Disabilities, 32*, 47-57.

Waugh, R. E., Alberto, P. A. & Frederick, L. D. (2011). Simultaneous Prompting: An Instructional Strategy for Skill Acquisition. *Education and Training in Autism and Other Developmental Disabilities, 46* (4), 528-543.

Principal Investigator: Jill Allor (former PI Mathes)
Institution: Southern Methodist University
Project Title: *Maximizing Literacy Learning among Children with Mild to Moderate Mental Retardation: Project Maximize*
Program Topic: Unsolicited and Other Awards: Special Education Research
Grant Award Number: H324K040011

Allor, J. H., Mathes, P. G., Champlin, T. & Cheatham, J. P. (2009). Research-Based Techniques for Teaching Early Reading Skills to Students with

Intellectual Disabilities. *Education and Training in Developmental Disabilities, 44*(3), 356-366.

Allor, J. H., Mathes, P. G., Jones, F. G., Champlin, T. M. Cheatham, J. P. (2010). Individualized Research-Based Reading Instruction for Students with Intellectual Disabilities. *Teaching Exceptional Children, 42*(3), 6-12.

Allor, J. H., Mathes, P. G., Roberts, J. K., Cheatham, J. P. & Champlin, T. M. (2010). Comprehensive Reading Instruction for Students with Intellectual Disabilities: Findings from the First Three Years of a Longitudinal Study. *Psychology in the Schools, 47*(5), 445-466.

Allor, J. H., Mathes, P. G., Roberts, J. K., Jones, F. G. & Champlin, T. M. (2010). Teaching Students with Moderate Intellectual Disabilities to Read: An Experimental Examination of a Comprehensive Reading Intervention. *Education and Training in Autism and Developmental Disabilities, 45*(1), 3-22.

Allor, J. H., Champlin, T. M., Gifford, D. B. & Mathes, P. G. (2010). Methods for Increasing Reading Instruction for Students. *Education and Training in Autism and Developmental Disabilities, 45*, 500-511.

Principal Investigator: Susan Brady
Institution: Haskins Laboratories
Project Title: *Mastering Reading Instruction: A Professional Development Project for First Grade Teachers*
Program Topic: Teacher Quality: Reading and Writing
Grant Award Number: R305M030099

Brady, S., Gillis, M., Smith, T., Lavalette, M., Liss-Bronstein, L., Lowe, E., North, W., Russo, E. & Wilder, T. D. (2009). First Grade Teachers' Knowledge of Phonological Awareness and Code Concepts: Examining Gains from an Intensive Form of Professional Development. *Reading and Writing: An Interdisciplinary Journal, 22* (4), 425–455.

Principal Investigator: Diane Browder
Institution: University of North Carolina, Charlotte
Project Title: *RAISE: Reading Accommodations and Interventions for Students with Emergent Literacy*
Program Topic: Unsolicited and Other Awards: Special Education Research
Grant Award Number: H324K040004

Browder, D. M., Mimms, P. J., Spooner, F., Ahlgrim-Delzell, L. & Lee, A. (2008). Teaching Elementary Students with Disabilities to Participate in

Shared Stories. *Research and Practice for Persons with Severe Disabilities, 33*(1-2), 3-12.

Browder, D. M., Ahlgrim-Delzell, L., Courtade, G., Gibbs, S. L. & Flowers, C. (2008). Evaluation of the Effectiveness of an Early Literacy Program for Students with Significant Developmental Disabilities. *Exceptional Children, 75*, 33-52.

Baker, J. N., Spooner, F., Ahlgrim-Delzell, L., Flowers, C. & Browder, D. M. (2010). A Measure of Emergent Literacy for Students with Severe Developmental Disabilities. *Psychology in the Schools, 47*(5), 501-513.

Principal Investigator: Anthony Bryk
Institution: University of Chicago
Project Title: *Can Literacy Professional Development be Improved with Web-based Collaborative Learning Tools: A Randomized Field Trial*
Program Topic: Teacher Quality: Reading and Writing
Grant Award Number: R305M040086

Biancarosa, G., Bryk, A. S. & Dexter, E. (2010). Assessing the Value-Added Effects of Literacy Collaborative Professional Development on Student Learning. *Elementary School Journal, 111*(1), 7–34.

Principal Investigator: Virginia Buysse
Institution: University of North Carolina, Chapel Hill
Project Title: *Improving Teacher Quality to Address the Language and Literacy Skills of Latino Children in Pre-Kindergarten Programs*
Program Topic: Teacher Quality: Reading and Writing
Grant Award Number: R305M040032

Buysse, V., Castro, D. C. & Peisner-Feinberg, E. (2010). Effects of a Professional Development Program on Classroom Practices and Outcomes for Latino Dual Language Learners. *Early Childhood Research Quarterly, 25* (1), 94–206.

Principal Investigator: Cara Cahalan-Laitusis
Institution: Educational Testing Service
Project Title: *Developing Accessible and Valid Reading Assessments: A Research Based Solution*
Program Topic: Unsolicited and Other Awards: Special Education Research
Grant Award Number: H324F040001

Cook, L., Eignor, D., Sawaki, Y., Stenberg, J. & Cline, F. (2010). Using Factor Analysis to Investigate Accommodations used by Students with Disabilities on English Language Arts Assessments. *Applied Measurement in Education, 23* (2), 187-208.

Cook, L., Eignor, D., Steinberg, J., Sawaki, Y. & Cline, F. (2009). Using Factor Analysis to Investigate the Impact of Accommodations on the Scores of Students with Disabilities on a Reading Comprehension Assessment. *Journal of Applied Testing Technology, 10*(2), 1-33.

Thurlow, M. L., Laitusis, C. C., Dillon, D. R., Cook, L. L., Moen, R. E., Abedi, J. & O'Brien, D. G. (2009). *Accessibility Principles for Reading Assessments.* Minneapolis, MN: National Accessible Reading Assessment Projects.

Principal Investigator: Cara Cahalan-Laitusis
Institution: Educational Testing Service
Project Title: *National Accessible Reading Assessment Projects: Research and Development for Students with Visual Impairments*
Program Topic: Special Education Policy, Finance, and Systems
Grant Award Number: R324A060034

Laitusis, C. C. (2010). Examining the impact of audio presentation on tests of reading comprehension. Applied Measurement in Education. *Special Issue: Testing Students with Disabilities, 23*(2), 153-167.

Stone, E., Cook, L., Laitusis, C. C. & Cline, F. (2010). Using Differential Item Functioning to Investigate the Impact of Testing Accommodations on an English Language Arts Assessment for Students who are Blind or Visually Impaired. *Applied Measurement in Education.* Special Issue: Testing Students with Disabilities. *23*(2), 132-152.

Thurlow, M. L., Laitusis, C. C., Dillon, D. R., Cook, L. L., Moen, R. E., Abedi, J. & O'Brien, D. G. (2009). *Accessibility Principles for Reading Assessments.* Minneapolis, MN: National Accessible Reading Assessment Projects.

Principal Investigator: Joanne Carlisle
Institution: The University of Michigan
Project Title: *Identifying Key Components of Effective Professional Development in Reading for First-Grade Teachers and Their Students*
Program Topic: Teacher Quality: Reading and Writing
Grant Award Number: R305M030090

Carlisle, J. F., Cortina, K. S. & Katz, L. A. (2011). First-Grade Teachers Response to Three Models of Professional Development in Reading. *Reading and Writing Quarterly, 27*, 212-238.

Principal Investigator: Joanne Carlisle
Institution: The University of Michigan
Project Title: *Assessment of Pedagogical Knowledge of Teachers of Reading*
Program Topic: Teacher Quality: Reading and Writing
Grant Award Number: R305M050087

Carlisle, J. F., Kelcey, B., Rowan, B. & Phelps, G. (2011). Teachers' Knowledge About Early Reading: Effects on Students' Gains in Reading Achievement. *Journal of Research on Educational Effectiveness, 4*(4), 289-321.

Principal Investigator: Hugh Catts
Institution: University of Kansas
Project Title: *Early Identification of Children with Reading Disabilities within an RTI Framework*
Program Topic: Special Education Policy, Finance, and Systems
Grant Award Number: R324A080118

Bridges, M. & Catts, H. W. (2011). The Use of Dynamic Assessment of Phonological Awareness for the Early Identification of Reading Disabilities in Kindergarten Children. *Journal of Learning Disabilities, 44*(4), 330-338.

Principal Investigator: Donald Compton
Institution: Vanderbilt University
Project Title: *Response-to-Intervention as an Approach to Preventing and Identifying Learning Disabilities in Reading*
Program Topic: Reading, Writing, and Language Development
Grant Award Number: R324G060036

Compton, D. L., Fuchs, D., Fuchs, L. S., Bouton, B., Gilbert, J. K., Barquero, L. A., Cho, E. & Crouch, R. C. (2010). Selecting At-Risk Readers in First Grade for Early Intervention: Eliminating False Positives and Exploring the Promise of a Two-Stage Screening Process. *Journal of Educational Psychology, 102*(2), 327-340.

Fuchs, D., Compton, D. L., Fuchs, L. S., Bouton, B. & Caffrey, E. (2011). The Construct and Predictive Validity of a Dynamic Assessment of Young

Children Learning to Read: Implications for RTI Frameworks. *Journal of Learning Disabilities, 44* (4), 339-347.

Elleman, A. M., Compton, D. L., Fuchs, D., Fuchs, L. S. & Bouton, B. (2011). Exploring Dynamic Assessment as a Means of Identifying Children at Risk of Developing Comprehension Difficulties. *Journal of Learning Disabilities, 44* (4), 348-357.

Compton, D. L., Gilbert, J. K., Jenkins, J. R., Fuchs, D., Fuchs, L. S., Cho, E., Barquero, L. A. & Bouton, B. B. (2012). Accelerating Chronically Unresponsive Children into Tier 3 Instruction: What Level of Data is Necessary to Ensure Adequate Selection Accuracy? *Journal of Learning Disabilities, 45*(3), 204-216.

Zumeta, R. O., Compton, D. L. & Fuchs, L. S. (2012). Using Word Identification Fluency to Assess First-Grade Reading Development: A Comparison of Two Word-Sampling Approaches. *Exceptional Children, 78*, 201-220.

Principal Investigator: Carol Connor
Institution: Florida State University
Project Title: *Child Instruction Interactions in Early Reading: Examining Causal Effects of Individualized Instruction*
Program Topic: Cognition and Student Learning
Grant Award Number: R305H040013

Cameron, C. E., Connor, C. M., Morrison, F. J. & Jewkes, A. M. (2008). Effects of Classroom Organization on Letter-Word Reading Iin First Grade. *Journal of School Psychology, 46*, 173-192.

Connor, C. M., Piasta, S. B., Glasney, S., Schatschneider, C., Fishman, B. & Underwood, P. (2009). Individualizing Student Instruction Precisely: Effects of Child X Instruction Interactions on First Graders' Literacy Development. *Child Development, 80*, 77-100.

Connor, C. M., Morrison, F. J., Fishman, B. J., Schatschneider, C. & Underwood, P. (2007). The EARLY YEARS: Algorithm-Guided Individualized Reading Instruction. *Science, 315*(5811), 464-465.

Connor, C. M., Morrison, F. J. & Underwood, P. (2007). A Second Chance in Second Grade? The Cumulative Impact of First and Second Grade Reading Instruction on Students' Letter-Word Reading Skills. *Scientific Studies of Reading, 11*(3), 199-233.

Piasta, S. B., Connor, C. M., Fishman, B. J. & Morrison, F. J. (2009). Teachers' Knowledge of Literacy Concepts, Classroom Practices, and Student Reading Growth. *Scientific Studies of Reading, 13*(3), 224-248.

Terry, N., Connor, C., Thomas-Tate, S. & Love, M. (2010). Examining Relationships Among Dialect Variation, Literacy Skills, and School Context in First Grade. *Journal of Speech, Language and Hearing Research, 53*(1), 126-145.

Connor, C. M. (2011). Child by Instruction Interactions: Language and Literacy Connections. In S. B. Neuman and D. K. Dickinson (Eds.), *Handbook on Early Literacy* (3rd ed., 256- 275). New York: Guilford.

Principal Investigator: Carol Connor
Institution: Florida State University
Project Title: *Child-Instruction Interactions in Reading: Examining Causal Effects of Individualized Instruction in Second and Third Grade*
Program Topic: Reading and Writing
Grant Award Number: R305B070074

Connor, C. M., Morrison, F. J., Fishman, B., Ponitz, C. C., Glasney, S., Underwood, P., et al. (2009). The ISI Classroom Observation System: Examining the Literacy Instruction Provided to Individual Students. *Educational Researcher, 38*(2), 85-99.

Connor, C. M., Ponitz, C. C., Phillips, B. M., Travis, Q. M., Glasney, S. & Morrison, F. J. (2010). First Graders' Literacy and Self-Regulation Gains: The Effect of Individualizing Student Instruction. *Journal of School Psychology, 48*, 433-455.

Al Otaiba, S., Connor, C. M., Folsom, J. S., Greulich, L., Meadows, J. & Zhi, L. (2011). Assessment Data-Informed Guidance to Individualize Kindergarten Reading Instruction: Findings from a Cluster-Randomized Control Field Trial. *Elementary School Journal, 111*(4), 535.

Terry, N. P., Connor, C. M. & Petscher, Y. (2011). Dialect Variation and Reading: Is Change in Nonmainstream American English use Related to Reading Achievement in First and Second Grade? *Journal of Speech, Language, and Hearing Research, 55*(1), 55-69.

Connor, C. M., Morrison, F. J., Schatschneider, C., Toste, J., Lundblom, E. G., Crowe, E. & Fishman, B. (2011). Effective Classroom Instruction: Implications of Child Characteristics by Reading Instruction Interactions on First Graders' Word Reading Achievement. *Journal of Research on Educational Effectiveness, 4*(3), 173-207.

Connor, C. M., Morrison, F. J., Fishman, B., Giuliani, S., Luck, M., Underwood, P., Bayraktar, A., Crowe, E. C. & Schatschneider, C. (2011). Testing the Impact of Child Characteristics X Instruction Interactions on

Third Graders' Reading Comprehension by Differentiating Literacy Instruction. *Reading Research Quarterly*, *46*, 189–221.

Connor, C. M., Morrison, F. J., Fishman, B. & Schatschneider, C. (2012). Assessment and Instruction Connections: The Impact of Teachers' Access and Use of Assessment-to- Instruction Software. In J. Sabatini, T. O'Reilly, and E.R. Albro (Eds.), *Reaching an Understanding: Innovations in How We View Reading Assessment* (81-100). Lanham, MD: R& L Education.

Principal Investigator: Michael Coyne
Institution: University of Connecticut
Project Title: *Project VITAL: Vocabulary Intervention Targeting At-Risk Learners*
Program Topic: Reading and Writing
Grant Award Number: R305G030250

Coyne, M. D., McCoach, B. & Kapp, S. (2007). Vocabulary Intervention for Kindergarten Students: Comparing Extended Instruction to Embedded Instruction and Incidental Exposure. *Learning Disabilities Quarterly*, *30*(2), 74-88.

Principal Investigator: Michael Coyne
Institution: University of Connecticut
Project Title: *Project IVI: Intensifying Vocabulary Intervention for Kindergarten Students at Risk of Learning Disabilities*
Program Topic: Reading, Writing, and Language Development
Grant Award Number: R324L060026

Loftus, S., Coyne, M. D., McCoach, D. B., Zipoli, R., Kapp, S. & Pullen, P. (2010). Effects of a Supplemental Vocabulary Intervention on the Word Knowledge of Kindergarten Students At-Risk for Language and Literacy Difficulties. *Learning Disabilities Research & Practice*, *25*(3), 124-136.

Pullen, P. C., Tuckwiller, E. D., Maynard, K., Konold, T. R. & Coyne, M. (2010). A Response to Intervention Model for Vocabulary Instruction: The Effects of Tiered Instruction for Students at Risk for Reading Disability. *Learning Disabilities Research and Practice*, *25*, 110-122.

Maynard, K. L., Pullen, P. C. & Coyne, M. (2010). Teaching Vocabulary to First Grade Students Through Repeated Shared Storybook Reading: A Comparison of Rich and Basic Instruction to Incidental Exposure. *Literacy Research and Instruction*, *49*, 209-242.

Principal Investigator: Thomas Farmer
Institution: University of North Carolina, Chapel Hill
Project Title: *National Research Center on Rural Education Support (NRCRES)*
Program Topic: National Research and Development Centers
Grant Award Number: R305A004056

Amendum, S., Vernon-Feagans, L. & Ginsberg, M. C. (2011). The Effectiveness of a Technologically Facilitated Classroom-Based Early Reading Intervention. *Elementary School Journal, 112*(1), 107-131.

Vernon-Feagans, L., Gallagher, K. C., Ginsberg, M. C., Amendum, S. J., Kainz, K., Rose, J. & Burchinal, M. (2010). A Diagnostic Teaching Intervention for Classroom Teachers: Helping Struggling Readers in Early Elementary School. *Learning Disabilities Research & Practice, 25*(4), 183-193.

Principal Investigator: David Francis
Institution: University of Houston
Project Title: *Diagnostic Assessment of Reading Comprehension: Development and Validation*
Program Topic: Reading and Writing
Grant Award Number: R305G050201

August, D., Francis, D., Hsu, H-Y. A. & Snow, C. (2006). Assessing Reading Comprehension in Bilinguals. *The Elementary School Journal, 107*(2), 221-238.

Francis, D., Snow, C., August, D., Carlson, C., Miller, J. & Iglesias, A. (2006). Measures of Reading Comprehension: A Latent Variable Analysis of the Diagnostic Assessment of Reading Comprehension. *Scientific Studies of Reading, 10*(3), 301-322.

Uccelli, P. & Páez, M. (2007). Narrative and Vocabulary Development of Bilingual Children from Kindergarten to First Grade: Developmental Changes and Associations Among English and Spanish Skills. *Language, Speech, and Hearing Services in Schools, 38*, 1-13.

Principal Investigator: Douglas Fuchs
Institution: Vanderbilt University
Project Title: *Scaling Up Peer Assisted Learning Strategies to Strengthen Reading Achievement*
Program Topic: Reading and Writing

Grant Award Number: R305G04104

McMaster, K. L., Kung, H., Han, I. & Cao, M. (2008). Peer-Assisted Learning Strategies: A Tier 1 Approach to Promoting Responsiveness to Beginning Reading Instruction for English Learners. *Exceptional Children, 74*(3), 194-214.

Saenz, L., McMaster, K., Fuchs, D. & Fuchs, L. S. (2007). Peer-Assisted Learning Strategies in Reading for Students with Different Learning Needs. *Journal of Cognitive Education and Psychology, 6*(3), 395-410.

Principal Investigator: Lynn Gelzheiser

Institution: State University of New York, Albany

Project Title: *Extending the Interactive Strategies Approach to Older Struggling Readers*

Program Topic: Reading, Writing, and Language Development

Grant Award Number: R324A070223

Gelzheiser, L. M., Scanlon, D., Vellutino, F., Hallgren-Flynn, L. & Schatschneider, C. (2011). Effects of the Interactive Strategies Approach-Extended. *The Elementary School Journal, 112*(2), 280-306.

Principal Investigator: Arthur Glenberg

Institution: University of Wisconsin, Madison

Project Title: *Training Indexing to Enhance Meaning Extraction in Young Readers*

Program Topic: Cognition and Student Learning

Grant Award Number: R305H030266

Glenberg, A. M., Brown, M. & Levin, J. R. (2007). Enhancing Comprehension in Small Reading Groups Using a Manipulation Strategy. *Contemporary Educational Psychology, 32*, 389-399.

Glenberg, A. M., Gutierrez, T., Levin, J. R., Japunitich, S. & Kaschak, M. P. (2004). Activity and Imagined Activity can Enhance Young Children's Reading Comprehension. *Journal of Educational Research, 96*(3), 424-436.

Marley, S. C. & Levin, J. R. (2006). Pictorial Illustrations, Visual Imagery, and Motor Activity: Their Instructional Implications for Native American Children with Learning Disabilities. In R.J. Morris (Ed.), *Disability Research and Policy: Current Perspectives* (103-123). Mahwah, NJ: Erlbaum.

Marley, S. C., Levin, J. R. & Glenberg, A. M. (2007). Improving Native American Children's Listening Comprehension Through Concrete Representations. *Contemporary Educational Psychology, 32*, 537-550.

Principal Investigator: Charles Greenwood
Institution: University of Kansas
Project Title: *The Infancy Preschool Early Literacy Connection: Validation Studies of the Early*
Communication (ECI) Indicator of Growth and Development
Program Topic: Early Intervention and Early Learning in Special Education
Grant Award Number: R324A070085

Buzhardt, J., Greenwood, C., Walker, D., Carta, J., Terry, B. & Garrett, M. (2010). A Web- Based Tool to Support Data-Based Early Intervention Decision Making. *Topics in Early Childhood Special Education, 29*(4), 201-213.

Principal Investigator: Michael Hock
Institution: University of Kansas
Project Title: *Improving Adolescent Reading Comprehension: a Multi-Strategy Reading Intervention*
Program Topic: Reading and Writing
Grant Award Number: R305G04011

Hock, M. F., Brasseur, I. F., Deshler, D. D., Catts, H. W., Marques, J., Mark, C.A. & Wu Stribling, J. (2009). What is the Nature of Struggling Adolescent Readers in Urban High Schools? *Learning Disability Quarterly, 32*(1), 21-38.

Principal Investigator: David Houchins
Institution: Georgia State University
Project Title: *Project LIBERATE (Literacy Instruction Based on Evidence through Research for Adjudicated Teens to Excel)*
Program Topic: Reading, Writing, and Language Development
Grant Award Number: R324A080006

Houchins, D., Jolivette, K., Shippen, M. & Lambert, R. (2010). Advancing High Quality Literacy Research in Juvenile Justice: Methodological and Practical Considerations. *Behavior Disorders, 36*(1), 61-69.

Principal Investigator: Laura Justice
Institution: University of Virginia
Project Title: *Evaluation of the Language-Focused Curriculum*
Program Topic: Preschool Curriculum Evaluation Research
Grant Award Number: R305J030084

Justice, L. M., Mashburn, A., Pence, K. & Wiggins, A. (2008). Experimental Evaluation of a Comprehensive Language-Rich Curriculum in At-Risk Preschools. *Journal of Speech, Language, and Hearing Research, 51,* 1-19.

Turnbull Pence, K., Beckman, A., Justice, L. M. & Bowles, R. (2009). Preschoolers' Exposure to Language Stimulation In Classrooms Serving At-Risk Children: The Contribution of Group Size and Activity Context. *Early Education and Development, 20,* 53-79.

Principal Investigator: Laura Justice
Institution: The Ohio State University
Project Title: *Print Referencing Efficacy*
Program Topic: Reading and Writing
Grant Award Number: R305G050005 (original award number R305G050057)

Cabell, S., Justice, L. M., Konold, T. & McGinty, A. (2011). Profiles of Emergent Literacy Skills Among Preschool Children who are at Risk for Academic Difficulties. *Early Childhood Research Quarterly, 26*(1), 1-14.

Principal Investigator: Susan Landry
Institution: University of Texas Health Science Center at Houston
Project Title: *Scaling Up a Language and Literacy Development Program at the Pre- Kindergarten Level*
Program Topic: Unsolicited and Other Awards
Grant Award Number: R305W02002

Landry, S. H., Anthony, J. L., Swank, P. R. & Monseque-Bailey, P. (2009). Effectiveness of Comprehensive Professional Development for Teachers of At-Risk Preschoolers. *Journal of Educational Psychology, 101*(2), 448-465.

Principal Investigator: Amy Lederberg
Institution: Georgia State University

Project Title: *Improving Deaf Preschoolers' Literacy Skills*
Program Topic: Early Intervention and Early Learning in Special Education
Grant Award Number: R324E060035

Easterbrooks, S. R., Lederberg, A. R. & Connor, C. M. (2010). Contributions of the Emergent Literacy Environment to Literacy Outcomes in Young Children who are Deaf. *American Annals of the Deaf*, *155*(4), 467-480.

Easterbrooks, S. R, Lederberg, A. R., Miller, E. M., Bergeron, J. P. & Connor, C.M. (2008). Emergent Literacy Skills During Early Childhood in Children with Hearing Loss: Strengths and Weaknesses. *The Volta Review*, *108*, 91-114.

Bergeron, J. P., Lederberg, A. R., Easterbrooks, S. R., Miller, E. M. & Connor, C. M. (2009). Building the Alphabetic Principle in Young Children who are Deaf or Hard of Hearing. *The Volta Review*, *109*, 87-119.

Principal Investigator: Christopher Lonigan
Institution: Florida State University
Project Title: *A Randomized Trial of Preschool Instructional Strategies to Improve School Performance and Reduce Use of Special Education*
Program Topic: Early Intervention and Early Learning in Special Education
Grant Award Number: R324E060086

Wilson, S. B. & Lonigan, C. J. (2010). Identifying Preschool Children at Risk of Later Reading Difficulties: Evaluation of Two Emergent Literacy Screening Tools. *Journal of Learning Disabilities*, *43*, 62-76.

Principal Investigator: Gayle Luze
Institution: Iowa State University
Project Title: *The Infancy Preschool Early Literacy Connection: Validation Studies of the Early Communication (ECI) Indicator of Growth and Development*
Program Topic: Early Intervention and Early Learning in Special Education
Grant Award Number: R324A070248

Luze, G. J. & Hughes, K. (2008). Using Individual Growth and Development Indicators to Assess Child and Program Outcomes. *Young Exceptional Children*, *12*, 31-41.

Principal Investigator: Patricia Mathes
Institution: Southern Methodist University
Project Title: *Scaling-up Effective Intervention for Preventing Reading Difficulties in Young Children*
Program Topic: Unsolicited and Other Awards
Grant Award Number: R305W03257

Denton, C. A., Mathes, P. G., Swanson, E., Nimon, K. & Kethley, C. (2010). Effectiveness of a Supplemental Early Reading Intervention Scaled up in Multiple Schools. *Exceptional Children, 76*(4), 394-416.

Principal Investigator: Lindsay Clare Matsumura
Institution: University of Pittsburgh
Project Title: *Content-Focused Coaching (SM) for High Quality Reading Instruction*
Program Topic: Teacher Quality: Reading and Writing
Grant Award Number: R305M060027

Matsumura, L. C., Garnier, H. & Resnick, L. B. (2010). Implementing Literacy Coaching: The Role of School Social Resources. *Educational Evaluation and Policy Analysis, 32*(2), 249-272.

Matsumura, L. C., Garnier, H. E., Correnti, R., Junker, B. & Bickel, D. D. (2010). Investigating the Effectiveness of a Comprehensive Literacy-Coaching Program in Schools with high Teacher Mobility. *Elementary School Journal, 111*(1), 35-62.

Matsumura, L. C., Sartoris, M., Bickel, D. D. & Garnier, H. E. (2009). Leadership for Literacy Coaching: The Principal's Role in Launching a New Coaching Program. *Educational Administration Quarterly, 45*(5), 655–693.

Principal Investigator: Gil Noam
Institution: McLean Hospital
Project Title: *The New 3R's – Reading, Resilience, and Relationships in After-School Programs*
Program Topic: Unsolicited and Other Awards
Grant Award Number: R305W030036

Pierce, M. E., Katzir, T., Wolf, M. & Noam, G. G. (2007). Clusters of Second and Third Grade Dysfluent Urban Readers. *Reading and Writing, 20*(9), 885-907.

Principal Investigator: Rollanda O'Connor
Institution: University of California, Riverside
Project Title: *Variations in Procedures to Improve Reading Fluency and Comprehension*
Program Topic: Reading and Writing
Grant Award Number: R305G050122

O'Connor, R. E., White, A. & Swanson, H. L. (2007). Repeated Reading Versus Continuous Reading: Influences on Reading Fluency and Comprehension. *Exceptional Children*, *74*(1), 31-46.

O'Connor, R. E., Swanson, H. L. & Geraghty, C. (2010). Improvement in Reading Rate Under Independent and Difficult Text Levels: Influences on Word and Comprehension Skills. *Journal of Educational Psychology*, *102*, 1-19.

Swanson, H. L. & O'Connor, R. E. (2009). The Role of Working Memory and Fluency Training on Reading Comprehension in Children who are Dysfluent Readers. *Journal of Learning Disabilities*, *42*, 548-575.

Principal Investigator: Robert Pasnak
Institution: George Mason University
Project Title: *An Economical Improvement in Literacy and Numeracy*
Program Topic: Cognition and Student Learning
Grant Award Number: R305B070542

Pasnak, R., Kidd, J. K., Gadzichowski, M. K., Gallington, D. A., Saracina, R. P. & Addison, K. (2008). Can Emphasizing Cognitive Development Improve Academic Achievement? *Education Research*, *50*(3), 261-276.

Pasnak, R., Kidd, J., Gadzichowski, M., Gallington, D., Saracina, R. & Addison, K. (2009). Promoting Early Abstraction to Promote Early Literacy And Numeracy. *Journal of Applied Developmental Psychology*, *30*(3), 239-249.

Pasnak, R., Maccubbin, E. & Ferral-Like, M. (2007). Using Developmental Principles to Assist at-Risk Preschoolers in Developing Numeracy and Phonemic Awareness. *Perceptual and Motor Skills*, *105*, 163-176.

Pasnak, R., Kidd, J., Gadzichowski, M., Ferral-Like, M., Gallington, D. & Saracina, R. (2007). Nurturing Developmental Processes. *Journal of Developmental Processes*, *2*, 90-115.

Principal Investigator: Douglas Powell
Institution: Purdue University
Project Title: *Professional Development in Early Reading (Classroom Links to Early Literacy)*
Program Topic: Teacher Quality: Reading and Writing
Grant Award Number: R305M040167

Powell, D. R. & Diamond, K. E. (2011). Improving the Outcomes of Coaching-Based Professional Development Interventions. In D. K. Dickinson and S. B. Neuman (Eds.), *Handbook of Early Literacy Research* (Vol. *3*, 295-307). New York, NY: Guilford.

Gerde, H. K. & Powell, D. R. (2009). Teacher Education, Book-Reading Practices, and Children's Language Growth Across one Year of Head Start. *Early Education and Development, 20* (2), 211–237.

Powell, D. R., Diamond, K. E. & Koehler, M. J. (2010). Use of a Case-Based Hypermedia Resource in an Early Literacy Coaching Intervention with Pre-Kindergarten Teachers. *Topics in Early Childhood Special Education, 29*(4), 239–249.

Powell, D., Diamond, K. E. & Burchinal, M. (2010). Effects of Early Literacy Professional Development Intervention on Head Start Teachers and Children. *Journal of Educational Psychology, 102*(2), 299-312.

Principal Investigator: Jesse Rothstein
Institution: National Bureau of Educational Research
Project Title: *Value-Added Models and the Measurement of Teacher Quality: Tracking or Causal Effects?*
Program Topic: Teacher Quality: Reading and Writing
Grant Award Number: R305A080560

Rothstein, J. (2008). Teacher Quality in Educational Production: Tracking, Decay, and Student Achievement. *National Bureau of Economic Research Working Paper* 14442.

Principal Investigator: Rose Sevcik
Institution: Georgia State University
Project Title: *Evaluating the Effectiveness of Reading Interventions for Students with Mild MR*
Program Topic: Unsolicited and Other Awards: Special Education Research
Grant Award Number: H324K040007

Wise, J. C., Sevcik, R. A., Romski, M. & Morris, R. D. (2010). The Relationship Between Phonological Processing Skills and Word and Nonword Identification Performance in Children with Mild Intellectual Disabilities. *Research in Developmental Disabilities*, *3*(6), 1170–1175.

Principal Investigator: Deborah Simmons
Institution: University of Texas at Austin
Project Title: *Project Early Reading Intervention*
Program Topic: Early Intervention and Early Learning in Special Education
Grant Award Number: R324E060067

Simmons, D. C., Coyne, M. D., Hagan-Burke, S., Kwok, O., Simmons, L. E., Johnson, C., Zou, Y., Taylor, A. B., Lentini, A., Ruby, M. F. & Crevecoeur, Y. (2011). Effects of Supplemental Reading Interventions in Authentic Contexts: A Comparison of Kindergarteners' Response. *Exceptional Children*, *77*, 207-228.

Hagan-Burke, S., Kwok, O., Zou, Y., Johnson, C., Simmons, D. & Coyne, M. D. (2010). An Examination of Problem Behaviors and Reading Outcomes in Kindergarten Students. *The Journal of Special Education*, *20*, 1-18.

Principal Investigator: Patricia Snyder
Institution: University of Florida
Project Title: *Impact of Professional Development on Preschool Teachers' Use of Embedded- Instruction Practices*
Program Topic: Early Intervention and Early Learning in Special Education
Grant Award Number: R324A070008

Hemmeter, M. L., Snyder, P. A., Kinder, K. & Artman, K. (2011). Impact of Performance Feedback Delivered via Electronic Mail on Preschool Teachers' use of Descriptive Praise. *Early Childhood Research Quarterly*, *26*(1), 96-109.

Snyder, P. A., Denny, M. K., Pasia, C., Rakap, S. & Crowe, C. (2011). Professional Development in Early Childhood Intervention. In C. Groark and L. Kaczmarek (Eds.), *Early Childhood Intervention Program Policies for Special Needs Children*, *Vol. 3: Emerging Issues*. (169-204) Santa Barbara, CA: Praeger.

Snyder, P. A., McLaughlin, T. & Denney, M. K. (2011). Program Focus in Early Intervention. In J.M. Kauffman, D.P. Hallahan, and M. Conroy

(Eds.), *Handbook of Special Education, Section XII: Early Identification and Intervention in Exceptionality*. (716-730) New York: Routledge.

Principal Investigator: Aubryn Stahmer
Institution: Rady Children's Hospital Health Center
Project Title: *Translating Pivotal Response Training Into Classroom Environments*
Program Topic: Autism Spectrum Disorders
Grant Award Number: R324B070027

Stahmer, A. C., Suhrheinrich, J., Reed, S., Bolduc, C. & Schreibman, L. (2010). Pivotal Response Teaching in the Classroom Setting. *Preventing School Failure: Alternative Education for Children and Youth, 54*(4), 265-274.

Schriebman, L., Suhrheinrich, J., Stahmer, A. & Reed, S. (2012). Translating Evidence-Based Practice from the Laboratory to the Classroom: Classroom Pivotal Response Teaching. In P. Mundy and A. Mastergeorge (Eds.), *Educational Interventions for Students with Autism* (107-130) Jossey-Bass/Wiley.

Principal Investigator: H. Lee Swanson
Institution: University of California, Riverside
Project Title: *Age-Related Changes in Word Problem Solving and Working Memory*
Program Topic: Cognition and Student Learning
Grant Award Number: R305H020055

Swanson, H. L., Howard, C. B. & Saez, L. (2006). Do Different Components of Working Memory Underlie Different Subgroups of Reading Disabilities? *Journal of Learning Disabilities, 39*(3), 252-269.

Swanson, H. L., Kehler, P. & Jerman, O. (2010). Working Memory, Strategy Knowledge, and Strategy Instruction in Children with Reading Disabilities. *Journal of Learning Disabilities, 43*(1), 24-47.

Swanson, H. L., Zheng, X. & Jerman, O. (2009). Working Memory, Short-Term Memory, and Reading Disabilities: A Selective Meta-Analysis of the Literature. *Journal of Learning Disabilities, 42*(3), 260-287.

Principal Investigator: Martha Thurlow
Institution: University of Minnesota
Project Title: *Research on Accessible Reading Assessments*

Program Topic: Unsolicited and Other Awards: Special Education Research

Grant Award Number: H324F040002

Abedi, J., Kao, J. C., Leon, S., Mastergeorge, A. M., Sullivan, L., Herman, J. & Pope, R. (2010). Accessibility of Segmented Comprehension Passages for Students with Disabilities. *Applied Measurement in Education. Special Issue: Testing Students with Disabilities*, *23*(2), 168-186.

Thurlow, M. L., Laitusis, C. C., Dillon, D. R., Cook, L. L., Moen, R. E., Abedi, J. & O'Brien, D. G. (2009). *Accessibility Principles for Reading Assessments*. Minneapolis, MN: National Accessible Reading Assessment Projects

Thurlow, M. L. (2010). Steps Toward Creating Fully Accessible Reading Assessments. *Applied Measurement in Education*, *23*(2), 121-131.

Dillon, D. R., O'Brien, D. G., Kato, K., Scharber, C., Kelly, C., Beaton, A. & Biggs, B. (2009). The Design and Validation of a Motivating Large-Scale Accessible Reading Comprehension Assessment for Students with Disabilities. *Fifty-Eighth Yearbook of The National Reading Conference* (277-293). Milwaukee, WI: The National Reading Conference.

Moen, R., Liu, K., Thurlow, M., Lekwa, A., Scullin, S. & Hausmann, K., (2009). Identifying Less Accurately Measured Students. *Journal of Applied Testing Technology*, *10*(2).

Kato, K., Moen, R. & Thurlow, M., (2009). Differentials of a State Reading Assessment: Item Functioning, Distractor Functioning, And Omission Frequency For Disability Categories. *Educational Measurement: Issues and Practice*, *28*(2), 28-40.

Principal Investigator: Patricia Vadasy

Institution: Washington Reading Institute

Project Title: *Quick Reads Supplementary Tutoring Efficacy and Replication Trials*

Program Topic: Reading and Writing

Grant Award Number: R305G040103

Vadasy, P. F. & Sanders, E. A. (2008a). Benefits of Repeated Reading Intervention for Low- Achieving Fourth- and Fifth-Grade Students. *Remedial and Special Education*, *29*, 235-249.

Vadasy, P. F. & Sanders, E. A. (2008b). Repeated Reading Intervention: Outcomes and Interactions with Readers' Skills and Classroom Instruction. *Journal of Educational Psychology*, *100*, 272-290.

Vadasy, P. F. & Sanders, E. A. (2009). Supplemental Fluency Intervention and Determinants of Reading Outcomes. *Scientific Studies of Reading*, *13*(5), 383–425.

Principal Investigator: Patricia Vadasy
Institution: Washington Reading Institute
Project Title: *Efficacy of Sound Partners Supplemental Tutoring for ELL Students, Grades K-1*
Program Topic: Reading and Writing
Grant Award Number: R305A070324

Vadasy, P. F. & Sanders, E. A. (2010). Efficacy of Supplemental Phonics Instruction for Low- Skilled Kindergarteners in the Context of Language-Minority Status and Classroom Phonics Instruction. *Journal of Educational Psychology*, *102*, 786–803.

Principal Investigator: Sharon Vaughn
Institution: University of Texas, Austin
Project Title: *Project Collaborative Strategic Reading (CSR): Interventions for Struggling Adolescent and Adult Readers and Writers*
Program Topic: Interventions for Struggling Adolescent and Adult Readers and Writers
Grant Award Number: R305A080608

Vaughn, S., Klingner, J. K., Boardman, A. G., Swanson, E. A., Roberts, G., Mohammed, S. S. & Stillman, S. J. (2011). Efficacy of Collaborative Strategic Reading with Middle School Students. *American Educational Research Journal*, *48*(3), 938-964.

Principal Investigator: Paul van den Broek
Institution: University of Minnesota
Project Title: *Improving Comprehension of Struggling Readers: Connecting Cognitive Science and Educational Practice*
Program Topic: Reading and Writing
Grant Award Number: R305G04021

van den Broek, P., White, M. J., Kendeou, P. & Carlson, S. (2009). Reading Between the Lines: Developmental and Individual Differences in Cognitive Processes in Reading Comprehension. In R. Wagner (Ed.), *Biological and Behavioral Bases of Reading Comprehension* (107-123). Mahwah, NJ: Erlbaum.

van den Broek, P., Kendeou, P. & White, M. J. (2008). Cognitive Processes During Reading: Implications for the use of Multimedia to Foster Reading Comprehension. In A.G. Bus and S.B. Neuman (Eds.), *Multimedia and Literacy Development: Improving Achievement for Young Learners* (57-74). New York, NY: Routledge.

Rapp, D. N., van den Broek, P., McMaster, K. L., Kendeou, P. & Espin, C. A. (2007). Higher- order Comprehension Processes in Struggling Readers: A Perspective for Research and Intervention. *Scientific Studies of Reading, 11*, 289-312.

Rapp, D. R. & van den Broek, P. (2005). Dynamic Text Comprehension: An Integrative View of Reading. *Current Directions in Psychological Sciences, 14*(5), 276-279.

Tilstra, J., McMaster, K., van den Broek, P., Kendeou, P. & Rapp, D. (2009). Simple but Complex: Components of the Simple View of Reading Across Grade Levels. *Journal of Research in Reading, 32*(4), 383-401.

Principal Investigator: Richard Wagner
Institution: Florida State University
Project Title: *Origins of Individual and Developmental Differences in Reading Comprehension*
Program Topic: Reading and Writing
Grant Award Number: R305G03104

Tannenbaum, K. R., Torgesen, J. K. & Wagner, R. K. (2006). Relationships Between Word Knowledge and Reading Comprehension in Third-Grade Children. *Scientific Studies of Reading, 10*(4), 381-398.

REFERENCES

Abedi, J. (2007). English Language Learners with Disabilities. In C. Cahalan Laitusis and L.L. Cook (Eds.), *Large-Scale Assessment and Accommodations: What Works?* Arlington, VA: Council of Exceptional Children.

Abedi, J., Leon, S. & Kao, J. C. (2008). Examining Differential Item Functioning in Reading Assessments for Students with Disabilities. *CRESST Report, 744*.

Adams, M. J. (1990). *Beginning to Read: Thinking and Learning about Print*. Cambridge, MA: The MIT Press.

American Educational Research Association, American Psychological Association, and National Council on Measurement in Education (1999). *Standards for Educational and Psychological Testing*. Washington, DC: AERA.

Al Otaiba, S., Connor, C. M., Folsom, J. S., Greulich, L., Meadows, J. & Li, Z. (2011). Assessment Data-Informed Guidance to Individualize Kindergarten Reading Instruction: Findings from a Cluster-Randomized Control Field Trial. *The Elementary School Journal, 111*(4), 535.

Alberto, P. A., Fredrick, L. D., Hughes, M., McIntosh, L. & Cihak, D. (2007). Components of Visual Literacy: Teaching Logos. *Focus on Autism and Other Developmental Disabilities, 22*, 234-243.

Alberto, P. A., Waugh, R. E. & Fredrick, L. D. (2010). Teaching the Reading of Connected Text Through Sight-Word Instruction to Students with Moderate Intellectual Disabilities. *Research in Developmental Disabilities, 31*, 1467-1474.

Allor, J., Mathes, P., Roberts, J., Jones, F. & Champlin, T. (2010d). Teaching Students with Moderate Intellectual Disabilities to Read: An Experimental Examination of a Comprehensive Reading Intervention. *Education and Training in Autism and Developmental Disabilities, 45*, 3-22.

Amendum, S., Vernon-Feagans, L. & Ginsberg, M. C. (2011). The Effectiveness of a Technologically-Facilitated Classroom-Based Early Reading Intervention. *The Elementary School Journal, 112*(1), 107-131.

August, D., Francis, D. J., Hsu, H. A. & Snow, C. E. (2006). Assessing Reading Comprehension in Bilinguals. *The Elementary School Journal, 107*(2), 221-238.

Badian, N. A. (1994). Preschool Prediction: Orthography and Phonological Skills & Reading. *Annals of Dyslexia, 44*, 3-25.

Baker, J., Spooner, F., Ahlgrim-Delzell, L., Florwers, C. & Browder, D. (2010). A Measure of Emergent Literacy for Students with Severe Developmental Disabilities. *Psychology in the Schools, 47*, 501-513.

Bell, L., Connor, C. M., Glasney, S. & Morrison, F. J. (2008). *The Impact of Classroom Disruptions On Literacy Skill Growth*. Paper presented at the Annual meeting of the Society for the Scientific Study of Reading, Ashville, NC.

Bergeron, J. P., Lederberg, A. R., Easterbrooks, S. R., Miller, E. M. & Connor, C.M. (2009). Building the Alphabetic Principle in Young Children who are Deaf and Hard of Hearing. *The Volta Review, 109*(2-3), 87-119.

Biancarosa, G., Bryk, A. S. & Dexter, E. R. (2010). Assessing the Value-Added Effects of Literacy Collaborative Professional Development on Student Learning. *The Elementary School Journal, 111*(1), 7-34.

Bos, C. S., Mather, N., Narr, R. F. & Babur, N. (1999). Interactive, Collaborative Professional Development in Early Literacy Instruction: Supporting the Balancing Act. *Learning Disabilities Research & Practice, 14*(4), 227-238.

Brady, S., Gillis, M., Smith, T., Lavalette, M., Liss-Bronstein, L., Lowe, E., North, W., Russo, E. & Wilder, T. D. (2009). First Grade Teaches' Knowledge of Phonological Awareness and Code Concepts: Examining Gains From an Intensive Form of Professional Development and Corresponding Teacher Attitudes. *Reading and Writing, 22*, 425-455.

Bridges, M. S. & Catts, H. W. (2011). The Use of a Dynamic Screening of Phonological Awareness to Predict Risk for Reading Disabilities in Kindergarten Children. *Journal of Learning Disabilities, 44* (4), 330-338.

Browder, D., Ahlgrim-Delzell, L., Courtade, G., Gibbs, S. & Flowers, C. (2008). Evaluation of the Effectiveness of an Early Literacy Program for Students with Significant Developmental Disabilities. *Exceptional Children, 75*, 33-52.

Browder, D., Mimms, P., Spooner, F., Ahlgrim-Delzell, L. & Lee, A. (2008). Teaching Elementary Students with Disabilities to Participate in Shared Stories. *Research and Practice for Persons with Severe Disabilities, 33*(1-2), 3-12.

Browder, D. M., Wakeman, S., Spooner, F., Ahlgrim-Delzell, L. & Algozzine, B. (2006). Research on Reading Instruction for Individuals with Significant Cognitive Disabilities. *Exceptional Children, 72*, 392-408.

Bruner, J. S. (1975). From Communication to Language: A Psychological Perspective. *Cognition, 3*, 255-287.

Buzhardt, J., Greenwood, C., Walker, D., Carta, J., Terry, B. & Garrett, M. (2010). A Web- Based Tool to Support Data-Based Early Intervention Decision Making. *Topics in Early Childhood Special Education, 29*(4), 201-213.

Cabell, S. Q., Justice, L. M., Konold, T. R. & McGinty, A. S. (2011). Profiles of Emergent Literacy Skills Among Preschool Children who are at Risk for Academic Difficulties. *Early Childhood Research Quarterly, 26*(1), 1-14

Carlisle, J. F., Cortina, K. S. & Katz, L. A. (2011). First-Grade Teachers' Response to Three Models of Professional Development in Reading. *Reading and Writing*, *27*, 212-238.

Carlisle, J. F., Kelcey, B., Rowan., B. & Phelps, G. (2011). Teachers' Knowledge About Early Reading: Effects on Students' Gains in Reading Achievement. *Journal of Research on Educational Effectiveness*, *4*(4), 289-321.

Catts, H. W. (1991). Early Identification of Dyslexia: Evidence from a Follow-Up Study of Speech-Language Impaired Children. *Annals of Dyslexia*, *41*, 163-177.

Catts, H. W. (1993). The Relationship Between Speech-Language Impairments and Reading Disabilities. *Journal of Speech, Language and Hearing Research*, *36*(5), 948.

Catts, H. W. & Kamhi, A. G. (Eds.). (2004). *Language Basis of Reading Disabilities* (2nd ed.). Needham Heights, MA: Allyn & Bacon.

Chall, J. S. (1996). *Stages of Reading Development* (2nd ed.). Orlando, FL: Harcourt Brace.

Charity, A.H., Scarborough, H.S. & Griffin, D. M. (2004). Familiarity with School English in African American Children and its Relation to Early Reading Achievement. *Child Development*, *75*(5), 1340-1356.

Compton, D. L., Fuchs, D., Fuchs, L. S. & Bryant, J. D. (2006). Selecting At-Risk Readers in First Grade for Early Intervention: A Two-Year Longitudinal Study of Decision Rules and Procedures. *Journal of Educational Psychology*, *98*, 394-409.

Compton, D. L., Fuchs, D., Fuchs, L. S., Bouton, B., Gilbert, J. K., Barquero, L. A., Cho, E. & Crouch, R. C. (2010). Selecting At-Risk Readers in First Grade for Early Intervention: Eliminating False Positives and Exploring the Promise of a Two-Stage Screening Process. *Journal of Educational Psychology*, *102*, 327-340.

Compton, D. L., Gilbert, J. K., Jenkins, J. R., Fuchs, D., Fuchs, L. S., Cho, E., Barquero, L. A. & Bouton, B. (2012). Accelerating Chronically Unresponsive Children to Tier 3 Instruction: What Level of Data is Necessary to Ensure Selection Accuracy? *Journal of Learning Disabilities*, *45*, 204-216.

Connor, C. M. (2011a). Child By Instruction Interactions: Language and Literacy Connections. In S. B. Neuman & D. K. Dickinson (Eds.), *Handbook on Early Literacy* (3rd ed., 256-275). New York: Guilford.

Connor, C. M. & Craig, H. K. (2006). African American Preschoolers' Language, Emergent Literacy Skills & Use of African American English:

A Complex Relation. *Journal of Speech, Language and Hearing Research, 49*(4), 771.

Connor, C. M., Morrison, F. J. & Katch, L. E. (2004). Beyond the Reading Wars: Exploring the Effect of Child-Instruction Interactions on Growth in Early Reading. *Scientific Studies of Reading, 8*(4), 305-336.

Connor, C. M., Morrison, F. J., Fishman, B. J., Schatschneider, C. & Underwood, P. (2007). THE EARLY YEARS: Algorithm-Guided Individualized Reading Instruction. *Science, 315*(5811), 464-465. doi: 10.1126/science.1134513

Connor, C. M., Morrison, F. J., Fishman, B. & Schatschneider, C. (2012). Assessment and Instruction Connections: The Impact of Teachers' Access and Use of Assessment-to-Instruction Software. In J. Sabatini, T. O'Reilly, and E.R. Albro (Eds.), *Reaching an Understanding: Innovations in How We View Reading Assessment* (81-100). Lanham, MD: R& L Education.

Connor, C. M., Morrison, F. J., Fishman, B., Giuliani, S., Luck, M, Underwood, P., Bayraktar, A., Crowe, E. C. & Schatschneider, C. (2011b). Testing the Impact of Child Characteristics X Instruction Interactions on Third Graders' Reading Comprehension by Differentiating Literacy Instruction. *Reading Research Quarterly, 46*, 189–221. doi: 10.1598/RRQ.46.3.1

Connor, C. M., Morrison, F. J., Schatschneider, C., Toste, J., Lundblom, E. G., Crowe, E. & Fishman, B. (2011c). Effective Classroom Instruction: Implications of Child Characteristic by Instruction Interactions on First Graders' Word Reading Achievement. *Journal for Research on Educational Effectiveness, 4*(3), 173-207.

Connor, C. M., Piasta, S. B., Fishman, B., Glasney, S., Schatschneider, C., Crowe, E., Underwood, P. & Morrison, F. J. (2009a). Individualizing Student Instruction Precisely: Effects of Child by Instruction Interactions on First Graders' Literacy Development. *Child Development, 80*(1), 77-100.

Connor, C. M., Son, S.-H., Hindman, A. H. & Morrison, F. J. (2005). Teacher Qualifications, Classroom Practices, Family Characteristics, and Preschool Experience: Complex Effects on First Graders' Vocabulary and Early Reading Outcomes. *Journal of School Psychology, 43*, 343-375.

Connor, C. M., Morrison, F. J. & Underwood, P. (2007). A Second Chance in Second Grade? The Cumulative Impact of First and Second Grade Reading Instruction on Students' Letter-Word Reading Skills. *Scientific Studies of Reading, 11*(3), 199-233.

Connor, C. M., Morrison, F. J., Fishman, B., Ponitz, C. C., Glasney, S., Underwood, P., et al. (2009b). The ISI Classroom Observation System: Examining the Literacy Instruction Provided to Individual Students. *Educational Researcher, 38*(2), 85-99.

Connor, C. M., Ponitz, C. E. C., Phillips, B., Travis, Q. M., Day, S. G. & Morrison, F. J. (2010). First Graders' Literacy and Self-Regulation Gains: The Effect of Individualizing Instruction. *Journal of School Psychology, 48*, 433-455.

Cook, L., Eignor, D., Sawaki, Y., Steinberg, J. & Cline, F. (2010). Using Factor Analysis to Investigate Accommodations Used by Students with Disabilities on an English-Language Arts Assessment. *Applied Measurement in Education. Special Issue: Testing Students with Disabilities, 23*(2), 187-208.

Cook, L. L., Eignor, D. R., Steinberg, J., Sawaki, Y. & Cline, F. (2009). Using Factor Analysis to Investigate the Impact of Accommodations on the Scores of Students with Disabilities on a Reading Comprehension Assessment. *Journal of Applied Testing Technology, 10*(2).

Coyne, M. D., Kame'enui, E. J., Simmons, D. C. & Harn, B. A. (2004). Beginning Reading Intervention as Inoculation or Insulin: First-Grade Reading Performance of Strong Responders to Kindergarten Intervention. *Journal of Learning Disabilities, 37*, 90-104.

Coyne, M. D., McCoach, B. & Kapp, S. (2007). Vocabulary Intervention for Kindergarten Students: Comparing Extended Instruction to Embedded Instruction and Incidental Exposure. *Learning Disabilities Quarterly, 30*(2), 74-88.

Craig, H. K. & Washington, J. A. (2000). An Assessment Battery for Identifying Language Impairments in African American Children. *Journal of Speech, Language and Hearing Research, 43*(2), 366.

Craig, H. K., Zhang, L., Hensel, S. L. & Quinn, E. J. (2009). African American English- Speaking Students: An Examination of the Relationship Between Dialect Shifting and Reading Outcomes. *Journal of Speech, Language, and Hearing Research, 52*, 839-855.

Denton, C. A., Mathes, P. G., Swanson, E., Nimon, K. & Kethley, C. (2010). Effectiveness of a Supplemental Early Reading Intervention Scaled Up in Multiple Schools. *Exceptional Children, 76*(4), 394-416.

Dillon, D. R., O'Brien, D. G., Kato, K., Scharber, C., Kelly, C., Beaton, A. & Biggs, B. (2009). The Design and Validation of a Motivating Large-Scale Accessible Reading Comprehension Assessment for Students with

Disabilities. *Fifty-Eighth Yearbook of the National Reading Conference* (277-293). Milwaukee, WI: The National Reading Conference.

Dingle, M. P., Brownell, M. T., Leko, M. M., Boardman, A. G. & Haager, D. (2011). Developing Effective Special Education Reading Teachers: The Influence of Professional Development, Context, and Individual Qualities. *Learning Disabilities Quarterly, 34*(1), 1-15.

Easterbrooks, S. R., et al. (2011).

Easterbrooks, S. R., Lederberg, A. R. & Connor, C. M. (2010). Contributions of the Emergent Literacy Environment to Literacy Outcomes in Young Children who are Deaf. *American Annals of the Deaf, 155*(4), 467-480.

Easterbrooks, S. R., Lederberg, A. R., Miller, E. M., Bergeron, J. P. & Connor, C. M. (2008). Emergent Literacy Skills during Early Childhood in Children with Hearing Loss: Strengths and Weaknesses. *The Volta Review, 108*(2), 91-114.

Elleman, A. M., Compton, D. L., Fuchs, D., Fuchs, L. S. & Bouton, B. (2011). Exploring Dynamic Assessment as a Means of Identifying Children At-Risk of Developing Comprehension Difficulties. *Journal of Learning Disabilities, 44* (4), 348-357.

Fletcher, J. M, Foorman, B. R., Boudousquie, A., Barnes, M. A., Schatschneider, C. & Francis, D. J. (2002). Assessment of Reading and Learning Disabilities: A Research-Based Intervention-Oriented Approach. *Journal of School Psychology, 40*, 27-63.

Foorman, B. R., Fletcher, J. M, Francis, D. J., Carlson, C. D., Chen, D., Mouzaki, A., Schatschneider, C., Wrister, K. & Taylor, R. (1998). *Technical Report Texas Primary Reading Inventory* (1998 Edition). Houston, TX: Center for Academic and Reading Skills and University of Houston.

Francis, D. J., Snow, C. E., August, D., Carlson, C. D., Miller, J. & Iglesias, A. (2006). Measures of Reading Comprehension: A Latent Variable Analysis of the Diagnostic Assessment of Reading Comprehension. *Scientific Studies of Reading, 10*(3), 301-322.

Fuchs, D. & Fuchs, L. S. (2005). Peer-assisted learning strategies: Promoting word recognition, fluency, and reading comprehension in young children. *Journal of Special Education, 39*(1), 34-44.

Fuchs, D., Compton, D. L., Fuchs, L. S., Bouton, B. & Caffrey, E. (2011). The Construct and Predictive Validity of a Dynamic Assessment of Young Children Learning to Read: Implications for RTI Frameworks. *Journal of Learning Disabilities, 44*(4), 339-347.

Fuchs, L. S., Fuchs, D. & Compton, D. L. (2004). Monitoring Early Reading Development in First Grade: Word Identification Fluency Versus Nonsense Word Fluency. *Exceptional Children, 71*, 7-21.

Garner, J. K. & Bochna, C. R. (2010). Transfer of a Listening Comprehension Strategy to Independent Reading in First-Grade Students. *Early Childhood Education Journal, 32*(2), 69-74.

Gelzheiser, L. M., Scanlon, D., Vellutino, F., Hallgren-Flynn, L. & Schatschneider, C. (2011). Effects of the Interactive Strategies Approach-Extended: A Responsive and Comprehensive Intervention for Intermediate Grade Struggling Readers. *The Elementary School Journal, 112*(2), 280-306.

Gerde, H. K. & Powell, D. (2009). Teacher Education, Book-Reading Practices, and Children's Language Growth Across One Year of Head Start. *Early Education and Development, 20*(2), 211-237.

Girolametta, L., Weitzman, E. & Greenberg, J. (2003). Training Day Care Staff to Facilitate Children's Language. *American Journal of Speech-Language Pathology, 12*, 299-311.

Glenberg, A. M., Brown, M. & Levin, J. R. (2007). Enhancing Comprehension in Small Reading Groups Using a Manipulation Strategy. *Contemporary Educational Psychology, 32*, 389-399.

Glenberg, A. M., Gutierrez, T., Levin, J. R., Japunitich, S. & Kaschak, M. P. (2004). Activity and Imagined Activity can Enhance Young Children's Reading Comprehension. *Journal of Educational Research, 96*(3), 424-436.

Glover, T. & Albers, C. (2007). Considerations for Evaluating Universal Screening Assessments. *Journal of School Psychology, 45*, 117-135.

Goldhaber, D. & Anthony, E. (2003). *Teacher Quality and Student Achievement*. Urban Diversity Series (Report: UDS-115; 153). New York: Department of Education, Washington, DC.

Goldhaber, D. D. & Brewer, D. J. (1999). *Does Teacher Certification Matter? High School Certification Status and Student Achievement*. Washington DC: Urban Institute.

Good, R. H., Simmons, D., Kame'enui, E. & Chard, D. (2001). The Importance and Decision- Making Utility of a Continuum of Fluency-Based Indicators of Foundational Reading Skills for Third-Grade High-Stakes Outcomes. *Scientific Studies of Reading, 5*, 257-288.

Hagan-Burke, S., Kwok, O., Zou, Y., Johnson, C., Simmons, D. & Coyne, M. D. (2010). An Examination of Problem Behaviors and Reading Outcomes in Kindergarten Students. *The Journal of Special Education, 20*, 1-18.

Hemmeter, M. L., Snyder, P. A., Kinder, K. & Artman, K. (2011). Impact of Performance Feedback Delivered via Electronic Mail on Preschool Teachers' Use of Descriptive Praise. *Early Childhood Research Quarterly*, *26*(1), 96-109.

Hernandez, D. J. (2011). *Double Jeopardy: How Third Grade Reading Skills and Poverty Influence High School Graduation*. New York: The Annie E. Casey Foundation. Hiebert, E. (2003). *Quick Reads*. Parsippany, NJ: Pearson Learning.

Hock, M. F., Brasseur, I. F., Deshler, D. D., Catts, H. W., Marquis, J., Mark, C. A. & Stribling, J. W. (2009). What is the Reading Component Skill Profile of Adolescent Struggling Readers in Urban Schools? *Learning Disabilities Quarterly*, *32*(1), 21-38.

Holt, J. A. (1994). Classroom Attributes and Achievement Test Scores for Deaf and Hard of Hearing Students. *American Annals of the Deaf*, *139*, 430-437.

Hoover, W. A. & Gough, P. B. (1990). The Simple View of Reading. *Reading and Writing*, *2*(2), 127-160.

Individuals with Disabilities Education Improvement Act (IDEA), 20 U.S.C. § 1400 et seq. (2004).

Jenkins, J. R. (2003, December). *Candidate Measures for Screening At-Risk Students*. Paper presented at the Conference on Response to Intervention as Learning Disabilities Identification, Sponsored by the National Research Center on Learning Disabilities, Kansas City, MO.

Jenkins, J. R. & O'Connor, R. E. (2002). Early Identification and Intervention for Young Children with Reading/Learning Disabilities. In R. Bradley, L. Danielson, & D.P. Hallahan (Eds.), *Identification of Learning Disabilities: Research to Practice* (99-149). Mahwah, NJ: Erlbaum.

Jenkins, J. R., Hudson, R. F. & Johnson, E. S. (2007). Screening for Service Delivery in a Response-To-Intervention (RTI) Framework. *School Psychology Review*, *36*, 582-600.

Joseph, L. M. & Seery, M. E. (2004). Where is the Phonics? A Review of the Literature on the use of Phonetic Analysis with Students with Mental Retardation. *Remedial and Special Education*, *25*(2), 88-94.

Juel, C. (1988). Learning to Read and Write: A Longitudinal Study of 54 Children from First Through Fourth Grades. *Journal of Educational Psychology*, *80*(4), 437-447.

Justice, L. M. & Ezell, H. K. (2002). Use of Storybook Reading to Increase Print Awareness in At-Risk Children. *American Journal of Speech-Language Pathology*, *11*, 17-29.

Justice, L. M., Mashburn, A., Pence, K. & Wiggins, A. (2008). Experimental Evaluation of a Comprehensive Language-Rich Curriculum in At-Risk Preschools. *Journal of Speech, Language, and Hearing Research, 51*, 1-19.

Kane, T., Staiger, D. O. & McCaffrey, D. (2012). Gathering feedback for teaching: Combining high-quality observations with student surveys and achievement gains. Bill and Melinda Gates Foundation. Retrieved from: http://www.metproject.org/downloads/MET_Gathering_Feedback_Practio ner_Brief.pdf

Kato, K., Moen, R. E. & Thurlow, M. L. (2009). Differentials of a State Reading Assessment: Item Functioning, Distractor Functioning, and Omission Frequency for Disability Categories. *Educational Measurement: Issues and Practice, 28*(2), 28-40.

Klingner, J. K. & Vaughn, S. (1996). Reciprocal Teaching of Reading Comprehension Strategies for Students with Learning Disabilities who use English as a Second Language. *The Elementary School Journal, 96*, 275-293.

LaBerge, D. & Samuels, S. J. (1974). Toward a Theory of Automatic Information Processing in Reading. *Cognitive Psychology, 6*, 293-323.

Laitusis, C. C. (2010). Examining the Impact of Audio Presentation on Tests of Reading Comprehension. *Applied Measurement in Education. Special Issue: Testing Students with Disabilities, 23*(2), 153-167.

Landry, S. H., Anthony, J. L., Swank, P. R. & Monseque-Bailey, P. (2010). Effectiveness of Comprehensive Professional Development for Teachers of At-Risk Preschoolers. *Journal of Educational Psychology, 101*(2), 448-465.

Loftus, S., Coyne, M. D., McCoach, D. B., Zipoli, R., Kapp, S. & Pullen, P. (2010). Effects of a Supplemental Vocabulary Intervention on the Word Knowledge of Kindergarten Students At-Risk for Language and Literacy Difficulties. *Learning Disabilities Research & Practice, 25*(3), 124-136.

Luze, G. J. & Hughes, K. (2008). Using Individual Growth and Development Indicators to Assess Child and Program Outcomes. *Young Exceptional Children, 12*, 31-40.

Marley, S. C. & Levin, J. R. (2006). Pictorial Illustrations, Visual Imagery, and Motor Activity: Their Instructional Implications for Native American Children with Learning Disabilities. In R. J. Morris (Ed.), *Disability Research and Policy: Current Perspectives* (103-123). Mahwah, NJ: Erlbaum.

Marley, S. C., Levin, J. R. & Glenberg, A. M. (2007). Improving Native American Children's Listening Comprehension Through Concrete Representations. *Contemporary Educational Psychology, 32*, 537-550.

Matsumura, L. C., Garnier, H. E. & Resnick, L. B. (2010). Implementing Literacy Coaching: The Role of School Resources. *Educational Evaluation and Policy Analysis, 32*(2), 249-272.

Matsumura, L. C., Garnier, H. E., Correnti, R., Junker, B. & Bickel, D. D. (2010). Investigating the Effectiveness of a Comprehensive Literacy Coaching Program in Schools with High Teacher Mobility. *The Elementary School Journal, 111*(1), 35-62.

Matsumura, L. C., Sartoris, M., Bickel, D. D. & Garnier, H. E. (2009). Leadership for Literacy Coaching: The Principal's Role in Launching a New Coaching Program. *Educational Administration Quarterly, 45*(5), 655-693.

Maynard, K. L., Pullen, P. C. & Coyne, M. (2010). Teaching Vocabulary to First Grade Students Through Repeated Shared Storybook Reading: A Comparison of Rich and Basic Instruction to Incidental Exposure. *Literacy Research and Instruction, 49*, 209-242.

McCardle, P., Scarborough, H. S. & Catts, H. W. (2001). Predicting, Explaining, and Preventing Children's Reading Difficulties. *Learning Disability Research and Practice, 16*, 230-239.

McConnell, S. R., McEvoy, M. A. & Priest, J. S. (2002). "Growing" Measures for Monitoring Progress in Early Childhood Education: A Research and Development Process for Individual Growth and Development Indicators. *Assessment for Effective Intervention, 27*(4), 3-14.

McMaster, K. L., Kung, H., Han, I. & Cao, M. (2008). Peer-Assisted Learning Strategies: A Tier 1 Approach to Promoting Responsiveness to Beginning Reading Instruction for English Learners. *Exceptional Children, 74*(3), 194-214.

Moats, L. C. (1994). The Missing Foundation in Teacher Education: Knowledge of the Structure of Spoken and Written Language. *Annals of Dyslexia, 44*, 81-102.

Moen, R., Liu, L., Thurlow, M. L., Lekwa, A., Scullin, S. & Hausmann, K., (2009). Identifying Less Accurately Measured Students. *Journal of Applied Testing Technology, 10*(2).

Morgan, P. L., Farkas, G., Tufis, P. A. & Sperling, R. A. (2008). Are Reading and Behavior Problems Risk Factors for Each Other? *Journal of Learning Disabilities, 41*(5), 417-436. doi: 10.1177/0022219408321123.

Morrison, F. J., Bachman, H. J. & Connor, C.M. (2005). *Improving Literacy in America: Guidelines from Research*. New Haven, CT: Yale University Press.

Muthén, B. & Muthén, L. K. (2000). Integrating Person-Centered and Variable-Centered Analyses: Growth Mixture Modeling with Latent Trajectory Classes. *Alcoholism: Clinical and Experimental Research*, *24*(6), 882-891.

National Early Literacy Panel. (2008). *Developing Early Literacy: Report of The National Early Literacy Panel*. Washington DC: National Institute for Literacy and the National Center for Family Literacy.

NAEP Reading 2011.

NICHD. (2000). National Institute of Child Health and Human Development, *National Reading Panel Report: Teaching Children to Read: An Evidence-Based Assessment of the Scientific Research Literature on Reading and its Implications for Reading Instruction*. In NIH (Ed.). Washington DC: U.S. Department of Health and Human Services, Public Health Service, National Institutes of Health, National Institute of Child Health and Human Development.

NIH (1995).

No Child Left Behind Act (NCLB), 20 U.S.C. 70 § 6301 et seq. (2002).

O'Connor, R. E. & Jenkins, J. R. (1999). The Prediction of Reading Disabilities in Kindergarten and First Grade. *Scientific Studies of Reading*, *3*, 159-197.

O'Connor, R. E., Bocian, K., Beebe-Frankenberger, M. & Linklater, D. (2010). Responsiveness of Students with Language Difficulties to Early Intervention in Reading. *Journal of Special Education*, *43*, 220-235.

O'Connor, R. E., Swanson, H. L. & Geraghty, C. (2010). Improvement in Reading Rate Under Independent and Difficult Text Levels: Influences on Word and Comprehension Skills. *Journal of Educational Psychology*, *102*, 1-19.

O'Connor, R. E., White, A. & Swanson, H. L. (2007). Repeated Reading Versus Continuous Reading: Influences on Reading Fluency and Comprehension. *Exceptional Children*, *74*(1), 31-46.

Oetting, J. B. & McDonald, J. L. (2001). Nonmainstream Dialect Use and Specific Language Impairment. *Journal of Speech, Language and Hearing Research*, *44*(1), 207.

Pasnak, R., Kidd, J. K., Ferral-Like, M., Gadzichowski, M. K., Gallington, D. A. & Saracina, R. P. (2007). Nurturing Developmental Processes in Early Abstraction. *Journal of Developmental Processes*, *2*, 90-115.

Pasnak, R., Kidd, J. K., Gadzichowski, M. K., Gallagher, J. D. & Saracina, R. P. (2008). Can Emphasizing Cognitive Development Improve Academic Achievement? *Educational Research, 50*(3), 261-276.

Pasnak, R., Kidd, J. K., Gadzichowski, M. K., Gallington, D. A., Saracina, R. P. & Addison, K. T. (2009). Promoting Early Abstraction to Promote Early Literacy and Numeracy. *Journal of Applied Developmental Psychology, 30*, 239-249.

Pasnak, R., MacCubbin, E. & Ferral-Like, M. (2007). Using Developmental Principles to Assist Preschoolers in Developing Numeracy and Literacy. *Perceptual and Motor Skills, 105*, 163-176.

Piaget, J. (1960). *The Psychology of Intelligence*. Paterson, NJ: Littlefield, Adams.

Piasta, S. B., Connor, C. M., Fishman, B. & Morrison, F. J. (2009). Teachers' Knowledge of Literacy, Classroom Practices, and Student Reading Growth. *Scientific Studies of Reading, 13*(3), 224-248.

Pierce, M. E., Katzir, T., Wolf, M. & Noam, G. G. (2007). Clusters of Second and Third Grade Dysfluent Urban Readers. *Reading and Writing, 20*, 885-907.

Polloway E., Lubin J., Smith J. D. & Patton J. R. (2010). Mild Intellectual Disabilities: Legacies and Trends in Concepts and Educational Practices. *Education and Training in Autism and Developmental Disabilities, 45*, 54–68.

Powell, D. & Diamond, K. E. (2011). Improving the Outcomes Of Coaching-Based Professional Development Interventions. In D. K. Dickinson & S. B. Neuman (Eds.), *Handbook of Early Literacy* (Vol. *3*, 295-307). New York: Guilford.

Powell, D., Diamond, K. E. & Burchinal, M. (2010). Effects of Early Literacy Professional Development Intervention on Head Start Teachers and Children. *Journal of Educational Psychology, 102*(2), 299-312.

Powell, D., Diamond, K. E. & Koehler, M. J. (2010). Use of a Case-Based Hypermedia Resource in an Early Literacy Coaching Intervention with Pre-Kindergarten Teachers. *Topics in Early Childhood Special Education, 29*(4), 239-249.

Pullen, P. C., Tuckwiller, E. D., Maynard, K., Konold, T. R. & Coyne, M. (2010). A Response to Intervention Model for Vocabulary Instruction: The Effects of Tiered Instruction For Students At Risk for Reading Disability. *Learning Disabilities Research and Practice, 25*, 110-122.

Rapp, D. N. & van den Broek, P. (2005). Dynamic Text Comprehension: An Integrative View of Reading. *Current Directions in Psychological Science, 14*(5), 276-279.

Raudenbush, S. W. (2004). What are Value-Added Models Estimating and What Does This Imply for Statistical Practice. *Journal of Educational and Behavioral Statistics, 29*(1), 121-129.

Reynolds, A. J., Temple, J. A., Robertson, D. L. & Mann, E. A. (2002). Age 21 Cost-Benefit Analysis of the Title I Chicago Child-Parent Centers. *Educational Evaluation and Policy Analysis, 24*(4), 267-303.

Rosa's Law, 20 U.S.C. § 1400 (2010).

Saenz, L., McMaster, K., Fuchs, D. & Fuchs, L. S. (2007). Peer-Assisted Learning Strategies in Reading for Students with Different Learning Needs. *Journal of Cognitive Education and Psychology, 6*(3), 395-410.

Sanders, W. & Horn, S. P. (1994). The Tennessee Value-Added Assessment System (TVAAS): Mixed-Model Methodology in Educational Assessment. *Journal of Personnel Evaluation in Education, 8*, 299-311.

Scammacca, N., Roberts, G., Vaugh, S., Edmonds, M., Wexler, J., Reutebuch, C. K. & Torgesen, J. K. (2007). *Interventions for Adolescent Struggling Readers: A Meta-Analysis with Implications for Practice*. Portsmouth, NH: RMC Research Corporation.

Scarborough, H. S. (1998). Early Identification of Children At Risk for Reading Disabilities: Phonological Awareness and Some Other Promising Predictors. In B.K. Shapiro, P.J. Accardo, and A.J. Capute (Eds.), *Specific Reading Disability: A View of the Spectrum* (75-119). Timonium, MD: York Press.

Shanahan, T. & Shanahan, C. (2008). Teaching Disciplinary Literacy to Adolescents: Rethinking Content-Area Literacy. *Harvard Educational Review, 78*(1).

Shankweiler, D., Crain, S., Brady, S. & Macaruso, P. l. (1992). Identifying the Causes of Reading Disability. In P. Gough, L. C. Ehri & R. Treiman (Eds.), *Reading Acquisition* (275-305). Hillsdale, NJ: Erlbaum.

Simmons, D. C., Coyne, M. D., Hagan-Burke, S., Kwok, O., Simmons, L. E., Johnson, C., Zou, Y., Taylor, A. B., Lentini, A., Ruby, M. F. & Crevecoeur, Y. (2011). Effects of Supplemental Reading Interventions in Authentic Contexts: A Comparison of Kindergarteners' Response. *Exceptional Children, 77*, 207-228.

Smith, M., Dickinson, D., Sangeorge, A. & Anastasopoulos, L. (2002). *Early Literacy and Language Classroom Observation Scale (ELLCO)*. Baltimore, MD: Paul Brookes.

Snell, M. E., Luckasson, R., et al. (2009). Characteristics and Needs of People with Intellectual Disability who have Higher IQs. *Intellectual and Developmental Disabilities, 47*(3), 220-233.

Snell, M. E. & Brown, F. (Eds.). (2011). *Instruction of Students with Severe Disabilities* (7th edition). Upper Saddle River, NJ: Pearson.

Snow, C. E. (1983). Literacy and Language: Relationships During the Preschool Years. *Harvard Educational Review, 53,* 165-189.

Snow, C. E. (2001). *Reading for Understanding.* Santa Monica, CA: RAND Education and the Science and Technology Policy Institute.

Snyder, L., Caccamise, D. & Wise, B. (2005). The Assessment of Reading Comprehension: Considerations and Cautions. *Topics in Language Disorders. Reading Comprehension's New Look: Influences of Theory and Technology on Practice, 25*(1), 33-50.

Snyder, P. A., Denney, M. K., Pasia, C., Rakap, S. & Crowe, C. (2011). Professional Development in Early Childhood Intervention: Emerging Issues and Promising Approaches. In C. Groark & L. Kaczmarek (Eds.), *Early Childhood Intervention Program Policies for Special Needs Children* (3rd ed.). 169-204. Santa Barbara: Praeger.

Snyder, T. D., Dillow, S. A. & Hoffman, C. M. (2007). *Digest of Education Statistics 2006.* (NCES 2007-017). Washington DC: US Government Printing Office.

Speece, D. (2005). Hitting the Moving Target Known as Reading Development: Some Thoughts on Screening Children for Secondary Interventions. *Journal of Learning Disabilities, 38,* 487-493.

Speece, D. L. & Case, L. P. (2001). Classification in Context: An Alternative Approach to Identifying Early Reading Disability. *Journal of Educational Psychology, 93,* 735-749.

Stanovich, K. E. (1980). Towards an Interactive-Compensatory Model Of Individual Differences in the Development of Reading Fluency. *Reading Research Quarterly, XVI,* 32-71.

Stone, E., Cook, L., Laitusis, C. C. & Cline, F. (2010). Using Differential Item Functioning to Investigate the Impact of Testing Accommodations on an English-Language Arts Assessment for Students who are Blind or Visually Impaired. *Applied Measurement in Education. Special Issue: Testing Students with Disabilities, 23*(2), 132-152.

Swanson, H. L. & Ashbaker, M. (2000). Working Memory, Short Term Memory, Articulation Speed, Word Recognition, and Reading Comprehension in Learning Disabled Readers: Executive and/or Articulartory System? *Intelligence, 28,* 1-30.

Swanson, H. L. & O'Connor, R. E. (2009). The Role of Working Memory and Fluency Practice on the Reading Comprehension of Students who are Dysfluent Readers. *Journal of Learning Disabilities*, *42*(6), 548-575.

Swanson, H. L., Howard, C. B. & Saez, L. (2006). Do Different Components of Working Memory Underlie Different Subgroups of Reading Disability? *Journal of Learning Disabilities*, *39*(3), 252-269.

Swanson, H. L., Kehler, P. & Jerman, O. (2010). Working Memory, Strategy Knowledge, and Strategy Instruction in Children with Reading Disabilities. *Journal of Learning Disabilities*, *43*(1), 24-47.

Swanson, H. L., Zheng, X. & Jerman, O. (2009). Working Memory, Short-Term Memory, and Reading Disabilities: A Selective Meta-Analysis of the Literature. *Journal of Learning Disabilities*, *42*(3), 260-287.

Tannenbaum, K. R., Torgesen, J. K. & Wagner, R. K. (2006). Relationships Between Word Knowledge and Reading Comprehension in Third-Grade Children. *Scientific Studies of Reading*, *10*(4), 381-398.

Terry, N. P., Connor, C. M., Petscher, Y. & Conlin, C. A. (2012). Dialect Variation and Reading: Is Change in Nonmainstream American English use Related to Reading Achievement in First and Second Grade? *Journal of Speech, Language and Hearing Research*, *55*(1), 55-69.

Terry, N. P., Connor, C. M., Thomas-Tate, S. & Love, M. (2010). Examining Relations Among Dialect Variation, Literacy Skills, and School Context in First Grade. *Journal of Speech, Language, and Hearing Research*, *53*, 126-145.

Therrien, W. J. (2004). Fluency and Comprehension Gains as a Result of Repeated Reading: A Meta-Analysis. *Remedial and Special Education*, *25*(4), 252-261.

Thurlow, M. L. (2010). Steps Toward Creating Fully Accessible Reading Assessments. *Applied Measurement in Education*, *23*, 121-131.

Thurlow, M. L., Laitusis, C. C., Dillion, D. R., Cook, L. L. Moen, R. E., Abedi, J. & O'Brien, D. G. (2009). *Accessibility Principles for Reading Assessments*. Minneapolis, MN: National Accessible Reading Assessment Projects.

Tilstra, J., McMaster, K., Van den Broek, P., Kendeou, P. & Rapp, D.N. (2009). Simple but Complex: Components of the Simple View of Reading Across Grade Levels. *Journal of Research in Reading*, *32*(4), 383-401.

Torgesen, J. K. (2002a). Empirical and Theoretical Support for Direct Diagnosis of Learning Disabilities by Assessment of Intrinsic Processing Weaknesses. In R. Bradley, L. Danielson, & D.P. Hallahan (Eds.),

Identification of Learning Disabilities: Research to Practice (565-613). Mahwah, NJ: Erlbaum.

Torgesen, J. K. (2002b). The Prevention of Reading Difficulties. *Journal of School Psychology*, *40*, 7-26.

Torgesen, J. K., Rashotte, C. A. & Alexander, A. (2001a). Principles of Fluency Instruction in Reading: Relationships with Established Empirical Outcomes. In M. Wolf (Ed.), *Dyslexia, Fluency, and the Brain* (333-355). Parkton, MD: York Press.

Torgesen, J. K., Wagner, R. K., Rashotte, C. A., Rose, E, Lindamood, P., Conway, T. & Garvan, C. (1999). Preventing Reading Failure in Young Children with Phonological Processing Disabilities: Group and Individual Responses to Instruction. *Journal of Educational Psychology*, *91*, 579-593.

Torgesen, J. K., Alexander, A. W., Wagner, R. K., Rashotte, C. A., Voeller, K. K. & Conway, T. (2001b). Intensive Remedial Instruction for Children with Severe Reading Disabilities: Immediate and Long-Term Outcomes from Two Instructional Approaches. *Journal of Learning Disabilities*, *34*, 33-58.

Turnbull Pence, K., Beckman, A., Justice, L. M. & Bowles, R. (2009). Preschoolers' Exposure to Language Stimulation in Classrooms Serving At-Risk Children: The Contribution of Group Size and Activity Context. *Early Education and Development*, *20*, 53-79.

Tymms, P. (1999). Baseline Assessment, Value-Added and the Prediction of Reading. *Journal of Research in Reading*, *22*, 27-36.

Uccelli, P. & Paez, M. M. (2007). Narrative and Vocabulary Development of Bilingual Children from Kindergarten to First Grade: Developmental Changes and Associations Among English and Spanish Skills. *Language Speech and Hearing Services in Schools*, *38*, 225-236.

Vadasy, P. F. & Sanders, E. A. (2008a). Benefits of Repeated Reading Intervention for Low- Achieving Fourth- and Fifth-Grade Students. *Remedial and Special Education*, *29*, 235-249.

Vadasy, P. F. & Sanders, E. A. (2008b). Repeated Reading Intervention: Outcomes and Interactions with Readers' Skills and Classroom Instruction. *Journal of Educational Psychology*, *100*, 272-290.

Vadasy, P. F. & Sanders, E. A. (2009). Supplemental Fluency Intervention and Determinants of Reading Outcomes. *Scientific Studies of Reading*, *13*(5), 383–425.

Vadasy, P. F. & Sanders, E. A. (2010). Efficacy of Supplemental Phonics-Based Instruction for Low-Skilled Kindergarteners in the Context of

Language Minority Status and Classroom Phonics Instruction. *Journal of Educational Psychology, 102*, 786-803.

van den Broek, P., Kendeou, P. & White, M. J. (2008). Cognitive Processes During Reading: Implications for the use of Multimedia to Foster Reading Comprehension. In A. G. Bus & S. B. Neuman (Eds.), *Multimedia and Literacy Development: Improving Achievement for Young Learners* (57-74). New York: Routledge.

van den Broek, P., White, M. J., Kendeou, P. & Carlson, S. (2009). Reading Between the Lines: Developmental and Individual Differences in Cognitive Processes in Reading Comprehension. In R.K. Wagner, C. Schatschneider and Phythian-Sence (Eds.), *Beyond Decoding: The Behavioral and Biological Foundations of Reading Comprehension* (107-123). New York: Guildford Press.

Vaughn, S., Klingner, J. K., Boardman, A. G., Swanson, E. A., Roberts, G., Mohammed, S. S. & Stillman, S. J. (2011). Efficacy of Collaborative Strategic Reading with Middle School Students. *American Educational Research Journal, 48*(3), 938-964, first published on May 31, 2011 doi:10.3102/0002831211410305.

Vellutino, F. R., Scanlon, D. M., Sipay, E. R., Small, S. G., Pratt, A., Chen, R. & Denckla, M. B. (1996). Cognitive Profiles of Difficult to Remediate and Readily Remediated Poor Readers: Early Intervention as a Vehicle for Distinguishing Between Cognitive and Experiential Deficits as Basic Causes of Specific Reading Disability. *Journal of Educational Psychology, 88*(4), 601-638.

Vernon-Feagans, L., Ginsberg, M.C., Amendum, S., Kainz, K., Rose, J. & Burchinal, M. (2010). A Diagnostic Teaching Intervention for Classroom Teachers: Helping Struggling Readers in Early Elementary School. *Learning Disabilities Research & Practice, 25*(4), 183-193.

Wagner, R. K. & Torgesen, J. K. (1987). The Nature of Phonological Processing and its Causal Role in the Acquisition of Reading Skills. *Psychological Bulletin, 101*(2), 192.

Wilson, S. B. & Lonigan, C. J. (2009). An Evaluation of Two Emergent Literacy Screening Tools for Preschool Children. *Annals of Dyslexia, 59*(2), 115-131.

Wolfram, W., Adger, C. T. & Christian, D. (1999). *Dialects in Schools and Communities*. Routledge.

Zumeta, R. O., Compton, D. L. & Fuchs, L. S. (2012). Using Word Identification Fluency to Assess First-Grade Reading Development: A

Comparison of Two Word-Sampling Approaches. *Exceptional Children*, *78*, 201-220.

End Notes

[1] Reynolds et al. (2002).

[2] Goldhaber, and Brewer (1999).

[3] Hernandez (2011); Reynolds et al. (2002).

[4] NICHD (2000); National Early Literacy Panel (2008).

[5] We use the term intellectual disability instead of the term mental retardation in response to *Rosa's Law* of 2010.

[6] NAEP (2011).

[7] Projects with initial funding dates after 2008 (i.e., 2009-2013) were not included in this review because most IES funded research projects are 3 to 4 years in length, and therefore projects funded after 2008 may not be far enough along to disseminate results through peer-reviewed articles and book chapters. This synthesis also includes discussion of five grants originally awarded through the Office of Special Education Programs (OSEP) of the U.S. Department of Education, prior to the establishment of the National Center for Special Education Research (NCSER). These five awards include funds from both OSEP and NCSER. They became the responsibility of NCSER when NCSER was established in 2006, and are considered in this review.

[8] Thurlow et al. (2009).

[9] American Educational Research Association, American Psychological Association, and National Council on Measurement in Education (1999).

[10] e.g., Compton et al. (2010); Compton et al. (2006); McCardle, Scarborough, and Catts (2001).

[11] see Glover and Albers (2007).

[12] for a review, see Jenkins, Hudson, and Johnson (2007).

[13] Torgesen (2002a, 2002b).

[14] e.g., Scarborough (1998).

[15] see Speece (2005).

[16] Fletcher et al. (2002); Tymms (1999).

[17] e.g., Badian (1994); Catts (1991); Torgesen et al. (1999).

[18] Torgesen (2002a).

[19] Catts (1991); Scarborough (1998); Torgesen (2002a, 2002b).

[20] McCardle, Scarborough, and Catts (2001).

[21] Compton et al. (2006, 2010); Fletcher et al. (2002); Foorman et al. (1998).

[22] Jenkins and O'Connor (2002); McCardle, Scarborough, and Catts (2001); O'Connor and Jenkins (1999); Scarborough (1998); Speece and Case (2001).

[23] Luze and Hughes (2008); McConnell, McEvoy and Priest (2002).

[24] Wilson and Lonigan (2009).

[25] The 2010 and 2012 articles report findings from IES-supported research.

[26] Fuchs, Fuchs, and Compton (2004).

[27] Good et al. (2001).

[28] Bridges and Catts (2011); Elleman et al. (2011); Fuchs et al. (2011).

[29] Ibid.

[30] Buzhardt et al. (2010).

[31] Abedi (2007); Abedi, Leon, and Kao (2008).

[32] August et al. (2006); Francis et al. (2006).

[33] August et al. (2006).

[34] Thurlow (2010).

[35] Thurlow et al. (2009).

[36] Two of these projects were originally awarded through the Office of Special Education Programs (OSEP), prior to the establishment of the National Center for Special Education Research (NCSER). These two awards include funds from both OSEP and NCSER. They became the responsibility of NCSER when it was established in 2006 and are considered in this review. The third project was awarded by NCSER (R324A060034).

[37] Piaget (1960).

[38] Bruner (1975).

[39] Glenberg et al. (2004); Marley and Levin (2006).

[40] Glenberg, Brown, and Levin (2007).

[41] Marley, Levin, and Glenberg (2007).

[42] Pasnak et al. (2007); Pasnak et al. (2008); Pasnak et al. (2009); Pasnak, MacCubbin, and Ferral-Like (2007).

[43] Pasnak et al. (2009).

[44] Pasnak, Kidd, et al. (2007); Pasnak, et al. (2008); Pasnak, MacCubbin, and Ferral-Like (2007).

[45] Swanson, Howard, and Saez (2006); Swanson, Zheng, and Jerman (2009).

[46] Swanson, Howard, and Saez (2006).

[47] Swanson, Kehler, and Jerman (2010).

[48] Shankweiler et al.(1992).

[49] LaBerge and Samuels (1974).

[50] Stanovich (1980).

[51] Swanson and Ashbaker (2000).

[52] Rapp and van den Broek (2005); van den Broek, Kendeou, and White (2008).

[53] van den Broek et al. (2009).

[54] Hoover and Gough (1990); Snow (2001).

[55] NICHD (2000); Torgesen, (2002).

[56] Connor et al. (2011); Snyder, Caccamise, and Wise (2005); Snyder, Dillow, & Hoffman (2007).

[57] Craig et al. (2009); Terry et al.(2012).

[58] Hoover and Gough (1990); Snow (2001); Snyder, Dillow, and Hoffman (2007).

[59] e.g., Garner and Bochna (2010).

[60] Wolfram, Adger, and Christian (1999).

[61] Craig and Washington (2000).

[62] Oetting and McDonald (2001).

[63] Charity, Scarborough, and Griffin (2004).

[64] Connor and Craig (2006).

[65] Hoover and Gough (1990).

[66] Muthén and Muthén (2000).

[67] Cabell et al. (2011).

[68] Pierce et al. (2007).

[69] Hock et al. (2009).

[70] Adams (1990).

[71] Catts and Kamhi (2004).

[72] Chall (1996); Shanahan and Shanahan (2008).

[73] Torgesen (2000); Vellutino et al. (1996).

[74] Connor, Morrison, and Katch (2004).

[75] National Early Literacy Panel (2008); NICHD (2000).

[76] Torgesen et al. (2001).

[77] Justice and Ezell (2002); Morrison, Bachman, and Connor (2005).

[78] Al Otaiba et al. (2011).

[79] e.g., Torgesen (2002b).

[80] Bell et al. (2008); Connor et al. (2010).
[81] Morgan et al. (2008).
[82] Simmons et al. (2011).
[83] Stanovich (1980); Torgesen, Rashotte, and Alexander (2001).
[84] Therrien (2004).
[85] e.g., Coyne et al. (2004); Denton et al. (2010); Torgesen et al. (2001).
[86] Vadasy & Sanders (2008a).
[87] Catts (1993).
[88] National Early Literacy Panel (2008); Snow (1983).
[89] Girolametta, Weitzman, and Greenberg (2003).
[90] Justice et al. (2008).
[91] Turnbull et al. (2009).
[92] Fuchs and Fuchs (2005).
[93] Shanahan and Shanahan (2008).
[94] see also McMaster et al. (2008).
[95] e.g., Klingner and Vaughn (1996); Vaughn et al. (2011).
[96] Vaughn et al. (2011).
[97] O'Connor et al. (2010).
[98] Al Otaiba et al. (2011); Connor (2011); Connor et al. (2007).
[99] Connor, Morrison, Fishman, et al. (2007).
[100] Al Otaiba et al. (2011).
[101] Connor et al. (2009).
[102] Connor et al. (2011).
[103] Connor et al. (2009)
[104] Al Otaiba et al. (2011); Connor et al. (2011); Connor et al. (2007); Connor, Morrison, Schatschneider, et al. (2011).
[105] Connor (2011).
[106] Ibid.
[107] Scammacca et al. (2007).
[108] Polloway et al. (2010).
[109] Polloway et al. (2010); Snell et al. (2009).
[110] Browder et al. (2006); Snell and Brown (2011).
[111] Browder et al. (2008).
[112] Baker et al. (2010).
[113] Alberto et al. (2007).
[114] Alberto, Waugh, and Fredrick (2010).
[115] Alberto et al. (2007).
[116] Holt (1994).
[117] NIH (1995).
[118] Easterbrooks et al. (2008).
[119] Wagner and Torgesen (1987).
[120] Easterbrooks et al. (2011).
[121] Smith et al. (2002).
[122] Bergeron et al. (2009).
[123] Kane, Staiger, and McCaffrey (2012).
[124] Moats (1994); Raudenbush (2004); Sanders and Horn (1994).
[125] Bos et al. (1999).
[126] Connor et al. (2005); Goldhaber and Anthony (2003).
[127] Brady et al. (2009); Carlisle et al. (2011); Piasta et al. (2009).
[128] Carlisle et al. (2011).
[129] Piasta et al. (2009).
[130] Dingle et al. (2011); Snyder et al. (2011).
[131] Brady et al. (2009); Carlisle, Kelcey et al. (2011).

[132] Brady et al. (2009).

[133] Matsumura, Garnier, and Resnick (2010); Snyder et al. (2011).

[134] Matsumura, Garnier, and Resnick (2010); Matsumura et al. (2009).

[135] Bos et al. (1999).

[136] Matsumura et al. (2010).

[137] Vernon-Feagans et al. (2010).

[138] Piasta et al. (2009).

[139] Connor et al. (2012).

[140] Al Otaiba, et al. (2011).

[141] Hemmeter et al. (2011).

[142] Amendum et al. (2011).

[143] Landry et al. (2010).

[144] Powell and Diamond (2011); Powell, Diamond, and Burchinal (2010).

[145] See also Powell, Diamond, and Koehler (2010).

[146] Powell, Diamond, and Koehler (2010).

In: Improving Outcomes for Students …   ISBN: 978-1-63321-168-1
Editor: Katrina Petrone   © 2014 Nova Science Publishers, Inc.

Chapter 2

ASSISTING STUDENTS STRUGGLING WITH READING: RESPONSE TO INTERVENTION AND MULTI-TIER INTERVENTION IN THE PRIMARY GRADES[*]

*Russell Gersten, Donald Compton, Carol M. Connor,
Joseph Dimino, Lana Santoro,
Sylvia Linan-Thompson and W. David Tilly*

INTRODUCTION

In the primary grades students with reading difficulties may need intervention to prevent future reading failure. This guide offers specific recommendations to help educators identify students in need of intervention and implement evidence-based interventions to promote their reading achievement. It also describes how to carry out each recommendation, including how to address potential roadblocks in implementing them.

We, the authors, are a small group with expertise in various dimensions of this topic. Several of us are also experts in research methodology. The recommendations in this guide reflect not only our expertise and experience

[*] This is an edited, reformatted and augmented version of a contracted report, NCEE 2009-4045, released by the National Center for Education Evaluation and Regional Assistance, Institute of Education Sciences, U.S. Department of Education, dated February 2009.

but the findings of rigorous studies of interventions to promote reading achievement.

Each recommendation received a rating that describes the strength of the research evidence that has shown its effectiveness. These ratings—"strong," "moderate," or "low"—are defined as:

Strong refers to consistent and generalizable evidence that a program causes better outcomes.[1]

Moderate refers to evidence from studies that allow strong causal conclusions but cannot be generalized with assurance to the population on which a recommendation is focused (perhaps because the findings have not been widely replicated) or to evidence from studies that are generalizable but have more causal ambiguity than offered by experimental designs (such as statistical models of correlational data or group comparison designs for which equivalence of the groups at pretest is uncertain).

Low refers to expert opinion based on reasonable extrapolations from research and theory on other topics and evidence from studies that do not meet the standards for moderate or strong evidence.

Table 1 details the criteria used to determine the level of evidence for each recommendation. For questions about what works best, high-quality experimental and quasi-experimental studies, such as those meeting the criteria of the What Works Clearinghouse (www.whatworks.ed.gov), have a privileged position. The evidence considered in developing and rating these recommendations included experimental research on providing differentiated instruction in a general education classroom and rigorous evaluations of intensive reading interventions. We also examined studies on the technical adequacy of batteries of screening measures.

The What Works Clearinghouse Standards and Their Relevance to This Guide

The panel relied on WWC Evidence Standards to assess the quality of evidence supporting educational programs and practices and apply a level of evidence rating to each recommendation. The WWC addresses evidence for the causal validity of instructional programs and practices using WWC Standards. Information about these standards is available at http://ies.ed.gov/ncee/wwc/references/standards/. The technical quality of each study is rated and placed into one of three categories:

- *Meets Evidence Standards* for randomized controlled trials and regression discontinuity studies that provide the strongest evidence of causal validity.
- *Meets Evidence Standards with Reservations* for all quasi-experimental studies with no design flaws and randomized controlled trials that have problems with randomization, attrition, or disruption.
- *Does Not Meet Evidence Screens* for studies that do not provide strong evidence of causal validity.

Based on the recommendations and suggestions for their implementation, appendix D presents more information on the research evidence supporting the recommendations.

The panel would like to thank Kelly Haymond for her contributions to the analysis, Mary Jo Taylor for her expert editorial assistance, the WWC reviewers for their contribution to the project, and Jo Ellen Kerr for her support of the intricate logistics of the project. We also would like to thank Scott Cody for his oversight of the analyses and the overall progress of the practice guide.

Dr. Russell Gersten
Dr. Donald Compton
Dr. Carol M. Connor
Dr. Joseph Dimino
Dr. Lana Santoro
Dr. Sylvia Linan-Thompson
Dr. W. David Tilly

Table 1. Institute of Education Sciences levels of evidence for practice guides

Strong	In general, characterization of the evidence for a recommendation as strong requires bothstudies with high internal validity (i.e., studies whose designs can support causal conclusions)and studies with high external validity (i.e., studies that in total include enough of the rangeof participants and settings on which the recommendation is focused to support the conclusion that the results can be generalized to those participants and settings). Strong evidencefor this practice guide is operationalized as:

Table 1. (Continued)

	• A systematic review of research that generally meets the What Works Clearinghouse (WWC)standards (see http://ies.ed.gov/ncee/wwc/) and supports the effectiveness of a program,practice, or approach, with no contradictory evidence of similar quality; OR • Several well designed, randomized controlled trials or well designed quasi-experimentsthat generally meet WWC standards and support the effectiveness of a program, practice,or approach, with no contradictory evidence of similar quality; OR • One large, well designed, randomized controlled, multisite trial that meets WWC standardsand supports the effectiveness of a program, practice, or approach, with no contradictoryevidence of similar quality; OR • For assessments, evidence of reliability and validity that meets the Standards for Educational and Psychological Testing.[a]
Moderate	In general, characterization of the evidence for a recommendation as moderate requires studieswith high internal validity but moderate external validity, or studies with high external validity but moderate internal validity. In other words, moderate evidence is derived from studiesthat support strong causal conclusions, but where generalization is uncertain, or studies thatsupport the generality of a relationship, but where the causality is uncertain. Moderate evidence for this practice guide is operationalized as: • Experiments or quasi-experiments generally meeting WWC standards and supporting theeffectiveness of a program, practice, or approach with small sample sizes and/or otherconditions of implementation or analysis that limit generalizability and no contrary evidence; OR • Comparison group studies that do not demonstrate equivalence of groups at pretest andtherefore do not meet WWC standards but that (a) consistently show enhanced outcomesfor participants experiencing a particular program, practice, or approach and (b) have nomajor flaws related to internal validity other than lack of demonstrated equivalence atpretest (e.g., only one teacher or one class per condition, unequal amounts of instructionaltime, highly biased outcome measures); OR • Correlational research with strong statistical controls for selection bias and for discerning influence of endogenous factors and no contrary evidence; OR • For assessments, evidence of reliability that meets the Standards for Educational and Psychological Testing[b] but with evidence of validity from samples not adequately representative of the population on which the recommendation is focused.

Low	In general, characterization of the evidence for a recommendation as low means that the recommendation is based on expert opinion derived from strong findings or theories in relatedareas or expert opinion buttressed by direct evidence that does not rise to the moderate orstrong levels. Low evidence is operationalized as evidence not meeting the standards for themoderate or high levels.

[a] American Educational Research Association, American Psychological Association, and National Council on Measurement in Education (1999).

[b] Ibid.

OVERVIEW

Response to Intervention (RtI) is a comprehensive early detection and prevention strategy that identifies struggling students and assists them before they fall behind. RtI systems combine universal screening and high-quality instruction for all students with interventions targeted at struggling students.

RtI strategies are used in both reading and math instruction. For reading instruction in the primary grades (K–2), schools screen students at least once a year to identify students at risk for future reading failure.[2] Students whose screening scores indicate potential difficulties with learning to read are provided with more intensive reading interventions. Student responses to the interventions are then measured to determine whether they have made adequate progress and either (1) no longer need the intervention, (2) continue to need some intervention, or (3) need even more intensive intervention.

In RtI, the levels of interventions are conventionally referred to as "tiers." RtI is typically thought of as having three tiers, with the first tier encompassing general classroom instruction.[3] Some states and school districts, however, have implemented multi-tier intervention systems with more than three tiers. Within a three-tier RtI model, each tier is defined by specific characteristics:

- Tier 1 instruction is generally defined as reading instruction provided to all students in a class. Beyond this general definition, there is no clear consensus on the meaning of the term tier 1. Instead, it is variously referred to as "evidence-based reading instruction,"[4] "high quality reading instruction,"[5] or "an instructional program...with balanced, explicit, and systematic reading instruction that fosters both code-based and text-based strategies for word identification and comprehension."[6]

- Tier 2 interventions are provided only to students who demonstrate problems based on screening measures or weak progress from regular classroom instruction. In addition to general classroom instruction, tier 2 students receive supplemental, small group reading instruction aimed at building foundational reading skills.
- Tier 3 interventions are provided to students who do not progress after a reasonable amount of time with the tier 2 intervention and require more intensive assistance. Tier 3 (or, in districts with more than three tiers, tiers 3 and above) usually entails one-on-one tutoring with a mix of instructional interventions. Ongoing analysis of student performance data is critical in tier 3. Systematically collected data are used to identify successes and failures in instruction for individual students. If students still experience difficulty after receiving intensive services, they are evaluated for possible special education services.

Though a relatively new concept, RtI and multi-tier interventions are becoming increasingly common. This is attributed in part to the 2004 reauthorization of the Individuals with Disabilities Education Act (IDEA), which encourages states to use RtI to help prevent reading difficulties and to identify students with learning disabilities.

RtI's inclusion in the 2004 reauthorization can be traced to two key reports released in 2002. First, the *President's Commission on Excellence in Special Education* (2002) report revealed that special education put too much emphasis on paperwork and too little on instruction.[7] It recommended that educators put more energy into monitoring student progress in academic areas and less into monitoring paperwork and compliance with regulations.

Second, a 2002 report from the National Academy of Sciences examined the overrepresentation of students from minority subgroups in special education.[8] This report proposed ideas for making the referral process for learning disabilities more meaningful to classroom teachers, arguing that special education "eligibility ensue when a student exhibits large differences from typical levels of performance in...[reading] *and with evidence of insufficient response to high-quality interventions...in school settings.*"[9] This encouraged schools to provide services to students struggling in reading within general education in the early grades before considering special education. Special education would be considered only for students who failed to respond to evidence-based interventions or interventions using what the field considers best practice.

There are two potential advantages of RtI and multi-tier intervention. Struggling students are provided with help in learning how to read early in their school careers. In the past many students were not provided with additional assistance in reading until they were officially diagnosed with a specific learning disability, often not until grade 2 or 3.[10] This was the practice even though longitudinal research consistently showed that students who were weak readers at the early elementary grades tended to stay weak readers in the higher grades.[11]

RtI also urges schools to use evidence-based practices in all tiers and to provide intensive services only to students who fail to benefit from a well designed, evidence-based intervention. This helps to accurately determine which students possess learning disabilities in reading since only students who do not respond to high-quality reading instruction in their general education classrooms would be considered for special education. Thus, there is the possibility— and certainly the hope—that RtI will reduce inappropriate referrals to special education, especially of ethnic minority students, low-income students, and students who received weak reading instruction.[12]

The panel also believes that RtI holds the most potential for serious ongoing collaboration between the special education community and that of general education— largely because the collaboration is based on objective data and shared understandings of the evidence.

Summary of the Recommendations

This practice guide offers five concrete recommendations for helping elementary schools implement an RtI framework to ensure that all students in the primary grades learn to read. These recommendations appear in table 2. There are many ways to orchestrate this process, and implementing this system entails involvement of school personnel at many levels: classroom teachers, special educators, school psychologists, paraprofessionals, reading coaches, specialists, and the principal. This guide provides concrete guidance on how to implement RtI; it does not describe which individuals on the team provide which services.

We begin with specific methods for setting up a universal screening system (recommendation 1). We note the specific reading and reading-related skills that should be assessed in screening and progress-monitoring measures at each grade level. We assume most educators possess some knowledge of universal screening. Therefore, we provide specific suggestions on how to ensure that the screening measures used are effective.

Table 2. Recommendations and corresponding levels of evidence

Recommendation	Level of evidence
1. *Screen all students for potential reading problems at the beginning of the year and again in the middle of the year.* Regularly monitor the progress of students at risk for developing reading disabilities.	Moderate
Tier 1 intervention/general education	
2. *Provide time for differentiated reading instruction for all students based on assessments of students' current reading level.*	Low
Tier 2 intervention	
3. *Provide intensive, systematic instruction on up to three foundational reading skills in small groups to students who score below the benchmark score on universal screening.* Typically, these groups meet between three and five times a week, for 20 to 40 minutes.	Strong
4. *Monitor the progress of tier 2 students at least once a month.* Use these data to determine whether students still require intervention. For those students still making insufficient progress, schoolwide teams should design a tier 3 intervention plan.	Low
Tier 3 intervention	
5. *Provide intensive instruction on a daily basis that promotes the development of the various components of reading proficiency to students who show minimal progress after reasonable time in tier 2 small group instruction (tier 3).*	Low

Source: Authors' compilation based on text.

As part of recommendation 1, we address the problem of false positives—students whose screening scores suggest that they need additional assistance, but who would do fine without it. This is a particular problem for measures given at the beginning of kindergarten; we explain why and what is recommended. We urge that schools seriously investigate both the degree to which a screening measure correctly identifies students at risk for reading difficulties and identifies students at low risk for such difficulties.

The second recommendation addresses how educators can use assessment data to differentiate reading instruction in tier 1. For example, classroom teachers can use assessment data to determine which students require additional instruction in decoding and vocabulary and which require additional assistance only with decoding instruction. While the concept of tier 1 instruction is amorphous, based on conventional definitions, differentiated instruction is often mentioned as a critical component of tier 1.[13]

Recommendations 3 and 4 address tier 2 interventions. In recommendation 3 we suggest that tier 2 students receive small group instruction in homogeneous groups for 20 to 40 minutes, three to five days a week. This recommendation has the most research and, most importantly, a clear convergence in findings. It is not important whether a certified teacher or a paraprofessional provides the instruction. But instruction should be systematic, highly explicit, and highly interactive. We note that interventions must not focus only on phonemic awareness, decoding, and fluent reading (depending on student proficiency level) but should also include vocabulary and comprehension components.

Recommendation 4 addresses using data to monitor progress for students in tier 2 interventions. Although no studies have experimentally tested the impact of progress monitoring on outcomes in reading, we still encourage schools to monitor the progress of these students so that personnel possess information on how a student is doing in general reading proficiency and improving in specific skills. It is important to use progress-monitoring data to regroup students after six weeks. Tier 2 students who demonstrate improvement and return to tier 1 should be carefully monitored to ensure that general classroom instruction is adequate.

Recommendation 5 addresses tier 3 interventions, and we are candid about the paucity of research on effective tier 3 intervention. Tier 3 intervention is the most ambiguous component of RtI, and we did not find research on valid programs or processes. Based on the content of small-scale intervention studies and the expert opinion of the panel, we suggest, as Vellutino et al. (2007) suggest, that tier 3 reading instruction be even more intensive than tier 2. Although student reading programs should be individualized, they should be viewed as more than one-on-one instruction. In particular, in listening and reading comprehension and vocabulary development small group instruction makes sense. We also note that districts should carefully monitor the success or failure of tier 3 programs, given the paucity of available evidence.

SCOPE OF THE PRACTICE GUIDE

Our goal is to provide evidence-based suggestions for implementing multi-tier interventions that are feasible and based on evidence from rigorous research. RtI and multi-tier interventions transgress the borders of special and general education and demand schoolwide collaboration. Thus, our target audience includes classroom teachers in the primary grades, special educators, school psychologists and counselors, as well as administrators.

This practice guide provides recommendations to schools and school districts on using RtI for primary grade students struggling with learning how to read. It is designed to guide educators on how to identify struggling students using RtI and implement interventions to improve these students' reading ability. The guide focuses on screening and interventions for struggling readers; it does not provide recommendations for general classroom reading instruction.

We limit the focus of the guide to the primary grades because the bulk of the current research has focused on these grade levels. The majority of the research on intervention and screening of students with reading difficulties was conducted in early grade levels. In addition, for the past 15 years, the country has seen a large push for early intervention to prevent reading difficulties later.[14]

Multi-tier instruction efforts like RtI can potentially prevent many struggling beginning readers from falling behind in ways that will harm their future academic success. Some aspects of RtI, however, (such as tier 1 instruction) are still poorly defined, and there is little evidence that some practices of targeted instruction will be effective. But a coordinated multi-tier instruction program that screens and monitors students accurately and addresses the core components of reading instruction can prevent struggling beginning readers from becoming struggling adolescent readers and reduce unnecessary referrals to special education.

CHECKLIST FOR CARRYING OUT
THE RECOMMENDATIONS

Recommendation 1.
Screen all students for potential reading problems at the beginning of the year and again in the middle of the year. Regularly monitor the progress of students who are at elevated risk for developing reading disabilities.

- Create a building-level team to facilitate the implementation of universal screening and progress monitoring.

- Select a set of efficient screening measures that identify children at risk for poor reading outcomes with reasonable degrees of accuracy.
- Use benchmarks or growth rates (or a combination of the two) to identify children at low, moderate, or high risk for developing reading difficulties.[15]

Recommendation 2.
Provide differentiated reading instruction for all students based on assessments of students' current reading levels (tier 1).

- Provide training for teachers on how to collect and interpret student data on reading efficiently and reliably.
- Develop data-driven decision rules for providing differentiated instruction to students at varied reading proficiency levels for part of the day.
- Differentiate instruction—including varying time, content, and degree of support and scaffolding—based on students' assessed skills.

Recommendation 3.
Provide intensive, systematic instruction on up to three foundational reading skills in small groups to students who score below the benchmark score on universal screening. Typically, these groups meet between three and five times a week for 20 to 40 minutes (tier 2).

- Use a curriculum that addresses the components of reading instruction (comprehension, fluency, phonemic awareness, phonics, and vocabulary) and relates to students' needs and developmental levels.
- Implement this program three to five times a week, for approximately 20 to 40 minutes.
- Build skills gradually and provide a high level of teacher-student interaction with opportunities for practice and feedback.

Recommendation 4.
Monitor the progress of tier 2 students at least once a month. Use these data to determine whether students still require intervention. For those students still making insufficient progress, school-wide teams should design a tier 3 intervention plan.

- Monitor progress of tier 2 students on a regular basis using grade appropriate measures. Progress monitoring should occur at least eight times during the school year.
- While providing tier 2 instruction, use progress monitoring data to identify students needing additional instruction.
- Consider using progress monitoring data to regroup tier 2 students approximately every six weeks.

Recommendation 5.
Provide intensive instruction on a daily basis that promotes the development of the various components of reading prof iciency to students who show minimal progress after reasonable time in tier 2 small group instruction (tier 3).

- Implement concentrated instruction that is focused on a small but targeted set of reading skills.
- Adjust the overall lesson pace.
- Schedule multiple and extended instructional sessions daily.
- Include opportunities for extensive practice and high-quality feedback with one-on-one instruction.
- Plan and individualize tier 3 instruction using input from a school-based RtI team.
- Ensure that tier 3 students master a reading skill or strategy before moving on.

RECOMMENDATION 1. SCREEN ALL STUDENTS FOR POTENTIAL READING PROBLEMS AT THE BEGINNING OF THE YEAR AND AGAIN IN THE MIDDLE OF THE YEAR. REGULARLY MONITOR THE PROGRESS OF STUDENTS WHO ARE AT ELEVATED RISK FOR DEVELOPING READING DISABILITIES

Universal screening is a critical first step in identifying students who are at risk for experiencing reading difficulties and who might need more instruction. Screening should take place at the beginning of each school year in kindergarten through grade 2. Schools should use measures that are efficient, reliable, and reasonably valid. For students who are at risk for reading difficulties, progress in reading and reading related-skills should be monitored on a monthly or even a weekly basis to determine whether students are making adequate progress or need additional support (see recommendation 4 for further detail). Because available screening measures, especially in kindergarten and grade 1, are imperfect, schools are encouraged to conduct a second screening mid-year.

Level of Evidence: Moderate

The panel judged the level of evidence for recommendation 1 to be *moderate*. This recommendation is based on a series of high-quality correlational studies with replicated findings that show the ability of measures of reading proficiency administered in grades 1 and 2 to predict students' reading performance in subsequent years.[16] However, it should be cautioned that few of the samples used for validation adequately represent the U.S. population as required by the Standards for Educational and Psychological Testing.[17] The evidence base in kindergarten is weaker, especially for measures administered early in the school year.[18] Thus, our recommendation for kindergarten and for grade 1 is to conduct a second screening mid-year when results tend to be more valid.[19]

Brief Summary of Evidence

The panel recommends a series of screening measures be employed to assess proficiency in several key areas (see Table 3). Five correlational studies have demonstrated that certain types of measures can be used to accurately predict future student performance.[20] Tests conducted by the Assessment Committee (2002) demonstrate that these measures meet the standards for educational and psychological testing[21] in terms of internal consistency and temporal stability.[22] While the panel is not recommending which specific measure should be adopted in each school, the panel does recommend that students are screened with measures that have properties similar to those examined in these studies.

In our review of evidence, we detected problems with commonly used measures in terms of their ability to correctly identify children at low risk for experiencing problems (known as specificity). That is, the measures tend to consistently over-identify students as needing assistance.[23] We also noted a paucity of cross-validation studies.[24] Nonetheless, the extensive body of replicated correlational research supports our conclusion that these are reasonable batteries of measures to use for early screening, particularly in grades 1 and 2.

How to Carry out This Recommendation

1. Create a Building-Level Team to Facilitate the Implementation of Universal Screening and Progress Monitoring

In the opinion of the panel, a building-level RtI team should focus on the logistics of implementing school-wide screening and subsequent progress monitoring, such as who administers the assessments, scheduling, and make-up testing, as well as substantive issues, such as determining the guidelines the school will use to determine which students require intervention and when students have demonstrated a successful response to tier 2 or tier 3 intervention. Although each school can develop its own benchmarks, it is more feasible, especially during the early phases of implementation, for schools to use guidelines from national databases (often available from publishers, from research literature, or on the Office of Special Education Programs (OSEP) Progress Monitoring and RtI websites[25]).

2. Select a Set of Efficient Screening Measures That Identify Children at Risk for Poor Reading Outcomes with Reasonable Accuracy

As children develop, different aspects of reading or reading-related skills become most appropriate to use as screening measures. Table 3 highlights the skills most appropriate for each grade level. Some controversy remains about precisely which one skill is best to assess at each grade level. For that reason, we recommend the use of two screening measures at each juncture.

Table 3 also outlines some commonly used screening measures for kindergarten through grade 2 highlighting their focus, purpose, and limitations. The limitations are based on the opinion of the panel.

Kindergarten screening batteries should include measures assessing letter knowledge, phonemic awareness, and expressive and receptive vocabulary.[27] Unfortunately, efficient screening measures for expressive and receptive vocabulary are in their infancy.

Table 3. Recommended target areas for early screening and progress monitoring

Measures	Recommended grade levels	Proficiencies assessed	Purpose	Limitations
Letter naming fluency	K–1	Letter name identification and the ability to rapidly retrieve abstract information	Screening	This measure is poor for progress monitoring since students begin to learn to associate letters with sounds. It is not valid for English learners in kindergarten, but seems valid for grade 1.
Phoneme Segmentation	K-1	Phonemic awareness	Screening and progress monitoring	This measure is problematic for measuring progress in the second semester of grade 1. As students learn to read, they seem to focus less on phonemic skills and more on decoding strategies.
Nonsense word fluency	1	Proficiency and automaticity with basic phonics rule	Screening and progress monitoring	This measure is limited to only very simple words and does not tap the ability to read irregular words or multisyllabic words.
Word identification[26]	1–2	Word reading	Screening and progress monitoring	This measure addresses many of the limitations of nonsense word fluency by including multisyllabic and irregular words.
Oral reading fluency (also called passage reading fluency)	1–2	Reading connected text accurately and fluently	Screening and progress monitoring	Although the measure has moderately strong criterion-related validity, it cannot give a full picture of students' reading proficiency. Many students will score close to zero at the beginning of grade 1. The measure still is a reasonable predictor of end of year reading performance.

Source: Authors' compilation based on Fuchs, Fuchs, Thompson, Al Otaiba, Yen, Yang, Braun, and O'Connor (2001b), Speece et al. (2003b); Schatschneider (2006); O'Connor and Jenkins (1999); and Baker and Baker (2008) for letter naming fluency. For phoneme segmentation, O'Connor and Jenkins (1999). For nonsense word fluency, Speece et al. (2003b); Good, Simmons, and Kame'enui (2001). For word identification, Fuchs, Fuchs, and Compton (2004); Compton et al. (2006). For oral reading fluency, Fuchs, Fuchs, Hosp, and Jenkins (2001a); Fuchs, Fuchs, and Maxwell (1988); Schatschneider (2006); Speece and Case (2001); Gersten, Dimino, and Jayanthi (2008); Baker, Gersten, Haager, and Dingle (2006).

As children move into grade 1, screening batteries should include measures assessing phonemic awareness, decoding, word identification, and text reading.[28] By the second semester of grade 1 the decoding, word identification, and text reading should include speed as an outcome.[29] Grade 2 batteries should include measures involving word reading and passage reading. These measures are typically timed.

Despite the importance of vocabulary, language, and comprehension development in kindergarten through grade 2, very few research-validated measures are available for efficient screening purposes. But diagnostic measures can be administered to students who appear to demonstrate problems in this area.

Technical Characteristics to Consider

The panel believes that three characteristics of screening measures should be examined when selecting which measures (and how many) will be used.

Reliability of screening measures (usually reported as internal consistency reliability or Cronbach's alpha) should be at least 0.70.[30] This information is available from the publishers' manual or website for the measure. Soon this information will be posted on the websites for National Center on Progress Monitoring and Response to Intervention.[31]

Predictive validity is an index of how well the measure provides accurate information on future reading performance of students—and thus is critical. In the opinion of the panel, predictive validity should reach an index of 0.60 or higher.

Reducing the number of false positives identified—students with scores below the cutoff who would eventually become good readers even without any additional help— is a serious concern. False positives lead to schools providing services to students who do not need them. In the view of the panel, schools should collect information on the sensitivity of screening measures and adjust benchmarks that produce too many false positives. There is a tradeoff, however, with the specificity of the measure and its ability to correctly identify 90 percent or more of students who really do require assistance.[32] Using at least two screening measures can enhance the accuracy of the screening process; however, decision rules then become more complex.

Costs in both time and personnel should also be considered when selecting screening measures. Administering additional measures requires additional staff time and may displace instruction. Moreover, interpreting multiple indices can be a complex and time-consuming task. Schools should consider these factors when selecting the number and type of screening measures.

3. Use Benchmarks or Growth Rates (or a Combination of the Two) to Identify Children at Low, Moderate, or High Risk for Developing Reading Difficulties[33]

Use cut-points to distinguish between students likely to obtain satisfactory and unsatisfactory reading proficiency at the end of the year without additional assistance. Excellent sources for cut-points are any predictive validity studies conducted by test developers or researchers based on normative samples. Although each school district can develop its own benchmarks or cut-points, guidelines from national databases (often available from publishers, from research literature, or on the OSEP, Progress Monitoring, and RtI websites[34]) may be easier to adopt, particularly in the early phases of implementation.

As schools become more sophisticated in their use of screening measures, many will want to go beyond using benchmark assessments two or three times a year and use a progress monitoring system.

Roadblocks and Suggested Approaches

Roadblock 1.1. It Is Too Hard to Establish District-Specific Benchmarks

Suggested Approach

National benchmarks can assist with this process. It often takes a significant amount of time to establish district-specific benchmarks or standards. By the time district-specific benchmarks are established, a year could pass before at-risk readers are identified and appropriate instructional interventions begin.

National standards are a reasonable alternative to establishing district-specific benchmarks.

Roadblock 1.2. Universal Screening Falsely Identifies Too Many Students

Suggested Approach

Selecting cut-points that accurately identify 100 percent of the children at risk casts a wide net—also identifying a sizeable group of children who will develop normal reading skills.

We recommend using universal screening measures to liberally identify a pool of children that, through progress monitoring methods, can be further refined to those most at risk.[35] Information on universal screening and progress monitoring measures can be found at the National Center on Student Progress Monitoring or the Iris Center at Vanderbilt University.[36]

Roadblock 1.3. Some Students Might Get "Stuck" in a Particular Tier

Suggested Approach

If schools are responding to student performance data using decision rules, students should not get stuck. A student may stay in one tier because the instructional match and learning trajectory is appropriate. To ensure students are receiving the correct amount of instruction, schools should frequently reassess—allowing fluid movement across tiers. Response to each tier of instruction will vary by student, requiring students to move across tiers as a function of their response to instruction.

The tiers are not standard, lock-step groupings of students. Decision rules should allow students showing adequate response to instruction at tier 2 or tier 3 to transition back into lower tiers with the support they need for continued success.

Roadblock 1.4. Some Teachers Place Students in Tutoring When They Are Only One Point below the Benchmark

Suggested Approach

No measure is perfectly reliable. Keep this in mind when students' scores fall slightly below or above a cutoff score on a benchmark test. The panel recommends that districts and schools review the assessment's technical manual to determine the confidence interval for each benchmark score. If a students' score falls within the confidence interval, either conduct an additional assessment of those students or monitor their progress for a period of six weeks to determine whether the student does, in fact, require additional assistance.[37]

RECOMMENDATION 2. PROVIDE DIFFERENTIATED READING INSTRUCTION FOR ALL STUDENTS BASED ON ASSESSMENTS OF STUDENTS' CURRENT READING LEVELS (TIER 1)

Ideally, classroom reading instruction would be evidence based. However, research that might provide a clear, comprehensive model of how to teach reading to students in the primary grades is lacking.[38] The purpose of this recommendation is to discuss classroom reading instruction as it relates to RtI and effective tier 1 instruction. In particular, we focus on the use of assessment data to guide differentiated reading instruction. Tier 1 provides the foundation for successful RtI overall, without which too many students would fall below benchmarks.

The panel recommends differentiating instruction in tier 1. For example, during independent work time, students weak in vocabulary can practice vocabulary with a partner or in small groups, while other students form teams to brainstorm character traits and motivations for the main characters in the story they are reading that week. Data from the various screening and progress monitoring measures in recommendation 1 should also serve a role in orchestrating differentiated instruction.

Because differentiated instruction under tier 1 requires identifying and grouping students to work on targeted skills, readers may wonder where differentiated instruction ends and tier 2 intervention begins. Differentiated instruction applies to all students, while tier 2 instruction applies only to those at risk in key areas. The panel believes that, to be effective, a multi-tier approach can blur the lines between tier 1 and tier 2, and that sensible data-driven instruction should permeate all of the tiers of reading instruction.

Level of Evidence: Low

The panel judged the level of evidence for this recommendation as *low*. A correlational study demonstrated that the more teachers used assessment information, the greater their students' reading skill growth in grade 1.[39]

Brief Summary of Evidence

One descriptive-correlational study examined how student reading growth varied by the degree to which teachers employed a specific differentiation program. This differentiation program relied on assessments to group students. Student reading growth was higher for teachers who implemented the program with greater fidelity.

How to Carry out This Recommendation

1. Provide Training for Teachers on How to Collect and Interpret Student Data on Reading Efficiently and Reliably

Provide training on how to use diagnostic measures, especially measures for those students experiencing difficulty. Informal assessments can help educators make better informed decisions. For example, listening to how a student reads a text that is slightly too difficult can yield useful information and is easily embedded within lessons. Teachers can ask a student to summarize a story they just read. This exercise will reveal how well the student comprehends what they read. Listening to the student's summary of the story can also reveal other information—for example about the student's own life or what they know of other books.[40]

2. Develop Data-Driven Decision Rules for Providing Differentiated Instruction to Students at Varied Reading Proficiency Levels for Part of the Day

According to the panel, independent silent reading activities should be gradually increased as reading skills improve. Data on student performance (a measure of word identification fluency or fluency in reading connected text) should inform this decision. For many grade 1 students, independent silent reading time would be minimal during the first few months of the year. Student-managed activities should be introduced gradually and should focus only on skills students have mastered.

3. Differentiate Instruction—Including Varying Time, Content, and Degree of Support and Scaffolding—Based on Students' Assessed Skills

The panel believes that as students fall below grade expectations, more time in explicit instruction provided by the teacher in small groups is critical to bring their skills to grade level. The panel suggests independent or group work, such as independent silent reading or buddy reading, are more effective when they are gradually increased as student reading skills improve.

Roadblocks and Suggested Approaches

Roadblock 2.1. It Is Difficult for Teachers to Interpret Assessment Results and Subsequently Use the Information for Instruction

Suggested Approach

The panel recommends providing professional development focused on how to administer assessments, interpret the results, and use the information. This should be ongoing. With proper training, teachers' instruction may be more effective.

Roadblock 2.2. Using Multiple Small Groups Is Difficult When Some Children Have Difficulty Paying Attention, Working Independently, and Interacting with Peers

Suggested Approach

Classroom management procedures should be firmly in place during reading instruction. To facilitate effective reading instruction, administrators should provide teachers with supportive efforts and motivational strategies, especially in managing independent and small group work.

RECOMMENDATION 3. PROVIDE INTENSIVE, SYSTEMATIC INSTRUCTION ON UP TO THREE FOUNDATIONAL READING SKILLS IN SMALL GROUPS TO STUDENTS WHO SCORE BELOW THE BENCHMARK ON UNIVERSAL SCREENING. TYPICALLY, THESE GROUPS MEET BETWEEN THREE AND FIVE TIMES A WEEK FOR 20 TO 40 MINUTES (TIER 2)

Tier 2 instruction should take place in small homogenous groups ranging from three to four students using curricula that address the major components of reading instruction (comprehension, fluency, phonemic awareness, phonics, and vocabulary). The areas of instruction are based on the results of students' scores on universal screening. Instruction should be systematic—building skills gradually and introducing skills first in isolation and then integrating them with other skills. Explicit instruction involves more teacher-student interaction, including frequent opportunities for student practice and comprehensible and specific feedback. Intensive instruction should occur three to five times per week for 20 to 40 minutes.

Level of Evidence: Strong

The panel judged the evidence supporting this recommendation as *strong* based on 11 studies that met WWC standards or that met WWC standards with reservations.[41] These studies on supplemental instruction in reading support tier 2 intervention as a way to improve reading performance in decoding. Six studies showed positive effects on decoding,[42] and four showed effects on both decoding and reading comprehension.[43] Six studies involved one-on-one instruction,[44] and the remainder used small groups ranging from two to five students. Given that effect sizes were not significantly higher for the one-on-one approach, small group work could be considered more practical for implementation.

Brief Summary of Evidence

The 11 studies that met WWC standards or that met WWC standards with reservations suggest that educators should emphasize the critical reading skills of phonemic awareness, decoding, reading comprehension, and fluency at appropriate grade levels. Two of five studies that measured phonemic awareness demonstrated significant effects.[45] Five of nine studies that measured decoding demonstrated significant effects, and students showed positive effects in five of seven studies[46] that measured reading comprehension. Only one study found significant effects in reading fluency. Vocabulary was the least examined outcome of the 11 studies, with only 1 study measuring and finding effects on vocabulary knowledge.[47]

Since 7 of the 11 studies that met WWC standards or that met standards with reservations produced a significant effect on at least one reading outcome, and all seven studies used explicit instruction, we concluded that explicit instruction is an effective approach to use in tier 2 intervention.[48]

How to Carry out This Recommendation

1. Use a Curriculum That Addresses the Components of Reading Instruction (Phonemic Awareness, Phonics, Vocabulary, Comprehension, and Fluency) and Relates to Students' Needs and Developmental Level

Tier 2 intervention curricula are sometimes called *standard protocols.* Standard protocols are tutoring programs taught to all students scoring below benchmark.[49] These "one size fits all" programs address foundational skills and strategies that are essential to learning to read. The panel suggests that schools should use intervention programs to provide tier 2 instruction for all students scoring below benchmark for at least five weeks to discern which students may need further intervention. After five weeks, some students may have caught up.

In choosing an intervention program for tier 2, administrators should look for programs—either commercially available intervention curricula, commercially developed supplemental curricula, or intervention programs— that are compatible with their school's core reading program and that provide intensive small group instruction in three to four foundational skills. Ideally, the intervention program has demonstrated its effectiveness through independent evaluations using rigorous experimental or quasi-experimental designs.

The intervention curriculum should teach and build foundational skills to mastery and incorporate some complex reading skills. Specific components vary by grade level and reflect the changing developmental emphasis at different stages in reading. Table 4 highlights the foundational reading skills students should develop in kindergarten through grade 2. Skills validated by research are indicated by table notes. The remaining skill areas are considered critical by the panel.

The critical skill for *kindergarteners* to master is the ability to segment phonemes, a key indicator of future success or failure in reading.[50] Also important are letter-sound identification, the alphabetic principle (the recognition of the relationship between spoken sounds and letters), and beginning decoding skills (blending written letters into words). Students who can perform these tasks understand the phonemic elements in words leading to accurate and fluent decoding.[51]

In general, during the first semester, grade 1 students who participate in tier 2 interventions will need instruction in phonics (decoding one and then two syllable words) and fluency. Since these are beginning readers, fluency instruction during the first semester is taught by first focusing on fluently and accurately reading short lists of high frequency words. During the second semester, as students move into reading connected text, interventions focusing on reading accurately, fluently, and with prosody (proper expression) should be added. Some grade 1 students will still need intensive and usually more accelerated instruction in phonemic awareness (blending and segmenting sounds) and basic phonics (letter sound correspondence) interventions to increase their understanding of the alphabetic principle.[52]

Table 4. Foundational reading skills in grades K–2

Grade	Skill
Kindergarten	Phonemic awareness[a] Letter sounds[b] Listening comprehension Vocabulary development
Grade 1	Phonemic awareness[c] Phonics[d] Fluency (high frequency words) Fluency with connected text (second half of the year)[e] Vocabulary[f] Comprehension[g]
Grade 2	Phonics[h] Fluency with connected text Vocabulary[i] Comprehension

[a] Lennon and Slesinski (1999).

[b] Lennon and Slesinski (1999).

[c] Ehri et al. (2007).

[d] Gunn et al. (2000); Jenkins et al. (2004); Ehri et al. (2007); Mathes et al. (2005); Vadasy, Sanders, and Peyton (2005).

[e] Ehri et al. (2007).

[f] Gunn et al. (2000).

[g] Jenkins et al. (2004); Ehri et al. (2007); Mathes et al. (2005); Vadasy, Sanders, and Peyton (2005); Vaughn et al. (2006).

[h] Gunn et al. (2000).

[i] Gunn et al. (2000).

Source: Authors' compilation based on information described in the text.

Phonics interventions for grade 2 students concentrate on learning more difficult skills, such as digraphs (*oa* as in boat and *ch* as in child), diphthongs (*ew* as in stew, *oi* as in soil), and controlled R (*ar* as in car, *ur* as in fur). These interventions address structural analysis skills that focus on prefixes, suffixes, forming plurals, and adding *-ed* and *-ing* to form past and progressive tenses. Students also apply phonetic skills to words with more than one syllable. Fluency should continue to be emphasized.[53]

Some intervention curricula will include what the panel believes are important activities: literal comprehension (questions whose answers are stated in the text), more sophisticated comprehension strategies (summarizing a portion of text), listening comprehension strategies, spelling, expressive writing, and read-alouds. Literal comprehension and some rudimentary comprehension instruction occur in many of the successful interventions, and so are recommended.[54] Other elements, such as inferential comprehension and vocabulary development, may be better developed with more heterogeneous groups during the reading language arts block. It is the opinion of the panel that an intervention curriculum that covers five to six skills per day may not provide the intensity necessary to improve reading achievement.

2. Implement This Program Three to Five Times a Week, for Approximately 20 to 40 Minutes

Tier 2 instruction should be implemented for 20 to 40 minutes, three to five times per week in small groups of three to four students. Student grade level and needs should determine the duration.

An intervention session can range from 20 to 30 minutes for kindergarten students to 40 to 50 minutes for grade 2 students, depending on student needs. Providing kindergarten students with 20 minutes of daily instruction has been demonstrated to have a positive impact on their acquisition of early reading skills, such as phonemic awareness and letter-sound correspondence.[55] As students move into grades 1 and 2, the time needed for interventions usually increases as the skills they need to catch up to their peers without reading difficulties broaden.

A small body of descriptive evidence suggests that the time spent on each area of instruction might be more important than the total instructional time. How time is spent and proportioned appears critical. For example, merely doubling instructional time—providing double doses of the same intervention—is not effective.[56] But according to Harn, Linan-Thompson, and Roberts (2008), doubling instructional time while changing the percentage of time allotted to each instructional area in response to students' changing needs resulted in better outcomes on timed oral reading fluency and word reading measures for students.

3. Build Skills Gradually and Provide a High Level of Teacher-Student Interaction with Opportunities for Practice and Feedback

Reading instruction should be systematic—building skills gradually and introducing skills first in isolation and then by integrating them with other skills to provide students practice and to build generalization.[57] Students should be given clear, corrective feedback, and cumulative review to ensure understanding and mastery. For example, in phonics, a critical area in grade 1 tier 2 interventions, a systematic curriculum might begin by introducing a few of the most frequently used consonants sounds (m, s, t, b) followed by a vowel, usually the short a. This allows students to integrate these newly learned sounds by blending sounds into words.

Reading instruction should also be explicit. Explicit instruction involves a high level of teacher-student interaction that includes frequent opportunities for students to practice the skill and clear, specific corrective feedback. It begins with overt and unambiguous explanations and models. An important feature of explicit instruction is making the thinking process public. Thinking aloud should occur during all instructional components of tier 2 interventions ranging from systematic skill building in phonics to teaching more complex and intricate comprehension strategies (such as summarizing or making inferences). When thinking aloud, teachers should stop, reflect, and formulate an explanation of their thinking processes.

Roadblocks and Suggested Approaches

Roadblock 3.1. Some Teachers or Reading Specialists Might Worry About Aligning the Tier 2 Intervention Program with the Core Program

Suggested Approach

Since tier 2 instruction relies on foundational (and sometimes prerequisite) skills that are determined by the students' rate of progress, it is unlikely that the same skill will be addressed in the core reading instruction at the same time. Alignment is not as critical as ensuring that instruction is systematic and explicit and focuses on the high priority reading components.

Roadblock 3.2. Finding an Additional 15 to 50 Minutes a Day for Additional Reading Instruction Can Be a Daunting Task

Suggested Approach

Schools should first determine who will provide the intervention. If the classroom teacher will provide the intervention, then small group instruction could occur when students are working independently at classroom learning centers. In grade 2 classrooms, where there is non-direct instructional time, intervention lessons can occur at times that do not conflict with other critical content areas, such as mathematics, particularly if a person other than the classroom teacher is providing the intervention. There may be situations in schools with reading blocks of two to two and a half hours where it is appropriate for students to work at learning stations or complete assignments while the classroom teacher is conducting tier 2 interventions, especially if tier 2 students are unable to complete these assignments.

RECOMMENDATION 4. MONITOR THE PROGRESS OF TIER 2 STUDENTS AT LEAST ONCE A MONTH. USE THESE DATA TO DETERMINE WHETHER STUDENTS STILL REQUIRE INTERVENTION. FOR THOSE STUDENTS STILL MAKING INSUFFICIENT PROGRESS, SCHOOL-WIDE TEAMS SHOULD DESIGN A TIER 3 INTERVENTION PLAN

Schools should establish a schedule to assess tier 2 students at least monthly—reassigning students who have met benchmarks, graphing students' progress in reading in a reliable fashion, and regrouping students who need continued instructional support.[58]

Level of Evidence: Low

Of the 11 randomized controlled trials and quasi-experimental design studies that evaluated effects of tier 2 interventions and that met WWC standards or that met WWC standards with reservations, only 3 reported using mastery checks or progress monitoring in instructional decisionmaking.[59] None of the studies demonstrate that progress monitoring is essential in tier 2 instruction. However, in the opinion of the panel, awareness of tier 2 student progress is essential for understanding whether tier 2 is helping the students and whether modifications are needed.

Brief Summary of Evidence

One study shows that progress monitoring in reading (oral reading fluency or word identification fluency in grades 1 and 2) increases teachers' awareness of students' current level of reading proficiency and has a positive effect on the instructional decisions teachers make.[60] Collecting and using progress monitoring data is sometimes a component of tier 2 instruction.

How to Carry out This Recommendation

1. Monitor Progress of Tier 2 Students on a Regular Basis Using Grade Appropriate Measures. Monitoring of Progress Should Occur at Least Eight Times during the School Year

Some researchers recommend more frequent weekly assessments for monitoring student progress.[61] However, little evidence demonstrates that weekly measures are superior to monthly ones.[62] Many tier 2 intervention programs (commercially developed, researcher developed, or district developed) contain weekly mastery tests that educators can use to guide instruction (to know which skills need to be reviewed and re-taught).

Table 5. Progress monitoring measures in grades K–2

Grade	Measure
Kindergarten	Phonemic awareness measures (especially measures of phonemesegmentation)
Grade 1	Fluent word recognition Nonword (pseudo word reading) Oral reading fluency (connected text)
Grade 2	Fluent word recognition Oral reading fluency

Source: Authors' compilation based on information described in text.

If a tier 2 program does not include mastery checks, monitor students' progress weekly, if possible, but no less than once a month. The measures should be efficient, reliable, and valid. Many progress monitoring measures are also useful as screening measures (see recommendation 1). Progress monitoring measures are the best way to assess students' retention of material taught and thus their path to reading proficiency. Table 5 indicates appropriate progress monitoring measures for kindergarten through grade 2.

2. While Providing Tier 2 Instruction, Use Progress Monitoring Data to Identify Students Needing Additional Instruction

It is important that tier 2 instruction advances at a good pace. At the same time, teaching to mastery is paramount since the skills are foundational for future success in reading. If three students are making progress and one student is lagging behind, an option to consider is to provide this student with 10 minutes of review, practice, and additional focused instruction on material previously taught. If none of the students are making progress, take a careful look at the tier 2 intervention— it may be missing critical components or moving too fast for the students in tier 2 to master the target skills.

3. Consider Using Progress Monitoring Data to Regroup Tier 2 Students Approximately Every Six Weeks

Since students' skill level changes over time and in varying degrees, use progress monitoring data to regroup students so that the groups are as homogeneous as possible. Ideally, groups may cut across more than one class, if schedules permit.

Roadblocks and Suggested Approaches

Roadblock 4.1. Students within Classes Are at Very Different Levels for Tier 2 Intervention

Suggested Approach

If students within a class are at such diverse levels as to necessitate more than two tier 2 groups, consider grouping students across classes. This will facilitate clustering children with similar needs. In such a case a reading specialist, paraprofessional, or other school personnel who have received training can conduct the intervention.

Roadblock 4.2. There Is Insufficient Time for Teachers to Implement Progress Monitoring

Suggested Approach

If teachers are too busy to assess students' progress with progress monitoring measures, consider using paraprofessionals or other school staff. Train them how to administer such measures.

RECOMMENDATION 5. PROVIDE INTENSIVE INSTRUCTION ON A DAILY BASIS THAT PROMOTES THE DEVELOPMENT OF THE VARIOUS COMPONENTS OF READING PROFICIENCY TO STUDENTS WHO SHOW MINIMAL PROGRESS AFTER REASONABLE TIME IN TIER 2 SMALL GROUP INSTRUCTION (TIER 3)

Instruction should be intensified by focusing on fewer high priority reading skills during lessons and scheduling multiple and extended instructional sessions. One-on-one or small group instruction also provides intensity as students have more opportunities to practice and respond. One-on-one instruction includes giving students feedback based on their individual responses, teaching students to mastery based on individual learning progress, and planning instruction with materials and an instructional sequence that meets individual student needs.

There is no reason to believe that a tier 3 program should consist primarily of one-on-one instruction—though such instruction should be part of a student's daily program. Student progress should be monitored regularly using progress monitoring measures to assess whether the program is on course and to determine whether a team of professionals needs to refine the instructional program to enhance achievement growth.

Level of Evidence: Low

The level of evidence for this recommendation is *low*. Although the panel found five studies on this recommendation that met the WWC standards (or met standards with reservations), no studies reported statistically significant impacts on reading outcomes.[63]

Brief Summary of Evidence

Despite over 50 years of research on special education and remedial instruction, major gaps persist in the knowledge of how to teach reading to the 3 to 5 percent of students with the most severe reading difficulties.[64] The research reveals little about students whose response to typically effective interventions is low. Therefore, the material below represents the opinion of the panel.

How to Carry out This Recommendation

1. Implement Concentrated Instruction That Is Focused on a Small but Targeted Set of Reading Skills

Focusing on a small set of reading or reading-related skills is essential to tier 3 in kindergarten through grade 2 because having too many instructional objectives for struggling readers makes it more difficult to learn the skills well enough for proficient reading. [65] In the opinion of the panel, too many instructional objectives can overwhelm students. Achieving proficiency is also difficult for students when instruction is scattered across different aspects of reading.

Diagnostic assessments can help determine why a reading problem is occurring and which reading skills or performance deficits need to be addressed to improve reading performance. Specifically, educators can ask: what aspects of reading are blocking the student from achieving reading proficiency? When these obstacles are determined, high priority skills are identified as the focus of tier 3 instruction.

For example, the panel believes that if a student is struggling with decoding, it does not make sense to use tier 3 instructional time for summary writing, comprehension monitoring instruction, or clarification strategies because the primary reading obstacle for the student is sounding out and reading words accurately. Here, decoding is considered a high priority skill because it underlies the student's overall reading difficulty.

Additionally, the panel believes that there should be depth in modeling and practice with feedback in tier 3 instruction—perhaps requiring limited breadth. Such focus provides opportunities to review, practice, and reinforce newly learned proficiencies so that students can demonstrate sustained and consistent levels of proficiency across lessons. Often a sustained 90 percent or higher criterion of correct responses on taught material is considered mastery.

Tier 3 instruction often focuses on phonemic awareness and decoding, especially for younger students or those with very limited reading proficiency. However, comprehension and vocabulary are also critical.[66] For a student receiving tier 3 instruction, several sessions each week might focus on phonemic awareness and decoding in depth. The other sessions might focus on comprehension and vocabulary in depth. To date, there are no clear-cut empirical guidelines to determine how to balance competing demands for instructional time.

2. Adjust the Overall Lesson Pace

To provide greater focus to tier 3 instruction, teachers can adjust the overall lesson pace so that it is slow and deliberate (that is, more intensive). Teachers implementing tier 3 instruction can focus the pace of lessons by focusing on a single component of a lesson. For example, teachers might focus only on introducing the new skill rather than implementing a full lesson that includes introduction, extended practice, and application. Subsequent tier 3 instruction might review the new skills (with modified or shortened instruction from the lesson's introduction) and practice the new skills. Instructional pace is slowed and focused by implementing a series of lessons concentrating only on a variety of review and practice activities. Rather than practicing how to identify the main idea in one lesson, several lessons would practice identifying the main idea.

3. Schedule Multiple and Extended Instructional Sessions Daily

While research does not suggest a specific number of intervention sessions or duration of instructional intervention (such as weeks, months, or years) for tier 3, studies do suggest that students needing tier 3 intervention require more reading instructional time than their peers without reading difficulties. On average, students participating in tier 3 interventions receive an additional 75 minutes of instruction per week. Additional instructional time ranges from about 45 minutes per week[67] to 120 minutes per week.[68]

In the opinion of the panel, schools could provide an additional 30 minutes of instruction by creating a "double dose" of reading time for struggling readers. Rather than more of the same, a double dose of instruction means a teacher might introduce skills during the first session and then re-teach with added practice during the second.

Duration, or extended implementation of tier 3 intervention, also intensifies instruction. Further research is required to examine the total hours of instruction needed and relative impact of tier 3 duration.

4. Include Opportunities for Extensive Practice and High Quality Feedback with One-on-One Instruction

To become proficient in the application of newly acquired skills and strategies, students with the most intensive instructional needs will need multiple opportunities to practice with immediate high-quality feedback. According to panel opinion, tier 3 students might require 10 or 30 times as many practice opportunities as their peers. An example considered by the panel includes the use of technology for aspects of the reading program. Technology can be a good means for students to receive the practice they need, such as practice in letter sound recognition.[69]

One-on-one instruction is an effective way to maximize practice during tier 3 instruction. If scheduling one-on-one instructional sessions is not possible, the panel suggests students be organized in small groups of homogenous reading needs. One-on-one or small-group instruction provides the greatest opportunity for continuous and active learning. For example, in whole-class instruction, individual students have few opportunities to respond, practice, and interact with the teacher. Meanwhile in one-on-one instruction, a student has many occasions to respond and practice. When working with small groups, educators can increase opportunities to respond and practice by encouraging unison group responses.

With one-on-one and small-group instruction, teachers can also provide immediate and individualized feedback.[70] A key feature of instructional feedback is error correction. By correcting student errors when they are first made, it is much less likely that errors will become internalized and therefore repeated. For example, if a student incorrectly segmented a word, the teacher could model the accurate response, give the student another opportunity to segment the word, and return to the missed word later in the lesson to reinforce the correct application of the skill. This type of ongoing, guided practice provides students with the support and feedback they need to become fluent with critical reading skills and strategies.

5. Plan and Individualize Tier 3 Instruction Using Input from a School-Based Rti Team

In the opinion of the panel, tier 3 instructional planning requires an increased level of detail because of the individualized nature of the instruction and particular student reading needs. Students with intensive reading needs require substantial supports during the initial stages of learning. As students progress in their understanding and knowledge, these supports are gradually withdrawn so that students can begin to apply skills and strategies independently.[71] For students with learning disabilities, instruction that is carefully scaffolded is essential to successful learning.[72] Teachers should introduce concepts and skills beginning with easier tasks and progressing to more difficult tasks.[73] When teaching oral segmenting, for example, it is easier for students to isolate the first sound than to completely segment the word.

Material supports also play a role in individualizing student learning. Graphic organizers, procedural facilitators (like color-coded question cards representing questions to ask before, during, and after reading), and concrete manipulatives are all visual prompts or reminders that provide support to struggling readers as they internalize skills and strategies. For example, a story map can be used to teach students how to identify a story's critical components.

As students become more adept at applying segmentation skills or using a story map to aid retelling, these material prompts are progressively faded out.

Teachers can optimize limited instructional time and instruction by teaching skills or strategies that reinforce each other. For example, emerging research suggests that teaching spelling promotes reading for struggling readers.[74] Students see spellings as maps of phonemic content rather than an arbitrary sequence of letters. Practice in using the alphabetic strategy to spell words seems to transfer to reading words.

6. Ensure That Tier 3 Students Master a Reading Skill or Strategy before Moving on

Emerging research on tier 3 instruction focuses on individualizing instruction by teaching students to mastery. Before a student moves to the next lesson, skill, or activity, they must demonstrate that a reading skill or strategy is mastered. When teaching a series of phonemic awareness activities,[75] teachers should discontinue activities when a student reaches 100 percent accuracy on all of the items in the activity.

Teachers can keep notes or records about how students perform on different reading tasks. For example, a teacher could record the exact words that a student practices reading, the student's word reading accuracy, and the number of times it takes for students to practice a word before reading it accurately.[76]

Roadblocks and Suggested Approaches

Roadblock 5.1. The Distinction between Tier 2 and Tier 3 Instructional Interventions Can Often Be Blurry

Suggested Approach

Teachers should not be too concerned about tier 2 and tier 3 differences; the tiers are merely a way to continually vary resources to match the nature and intensity of instructional need. Remember that at present, distinctions between tier 2 and tier 3 are not clear or well documented. The terms are conveniences for school personnel.

Many tier 3 students will also have tier 1 and tier 2 instruction as part of their reading program. A student receiving tier 3 instruction focused on decoding and fluency might also participate in a tier 2 heterogeneous group focused on vocabulary and comprehension. One limitation with individualized, one-on-one tier 3 instruction is that there are few opportunities for students to engage in comprehension-building discourse. Increasing comprehension through discourse requires different levels of student language, vocabulary, and comprehension skills. Small, heterogeneous groups are optimal for building student language and vocabulary because students have opportunities to hear different language examples, new vocabulary words, and content that helps connect understanding. Discourse-based vocabulary and comprehension activities are often included in tier 2 interventions.

Roadblock 5.2. Because Most Tier 3 Students Have Problems with Decoding and Fluently Reading Connected Text, Some May Have Tier 3 Interventions That Only Highlight These Areas

Suggested Approach

Targeting important comprehension proficiencies (summarizing, use of story grammar elements, vocabulary development, listening comprehension development) need to be part of any solid tier 3 intervention.

Roadblock 5.3. School and Staff Resources Are Often Too Limited to Support Individualized Instruction for Tier 3 Students

Suggested Approach

Consider creative alternatives for school and staff resources. For example, use community resources, such as parent or senior citizen volunteers, to help reinforce tier 3 instruction. While an experienced teacher or interventionist should teach new skills, volunteers can help reinforce and practice reading in focused one-on-one sessions. Community tutoring programs are also options. Technology is another resource to consider, and remember many individualized instruction activities work well with small, homogeneous group instruction.

Roadblock 5.4. Schools Tend to Give the Least Experienced Teachers the Toughest-Toteach Students

Suggested Approach

Reevaluate school schedules to ensure that the more experienced teachers or specialists are teaching tier 3 instruction. This may require some professional development and ongoing mentoring even for skilled veteran teachers.

Many teachers do not have the training to teach students with intensive reading difficulties. Given the importance of carefully planning and individualizing instruction, scaffolding skill introduction, enhancing one reading skill or strategy with another (such as adding spelling to reading instruction), structuring multiple practice opportunities, and providing high quality feedback with consistent error corrections, professional development plans and ongoing mentoring should focus on the details of instructional design and planning.

Roadblock 5.5. Adding Multiple and Extended Instructional Sessions to a Daily Schedule Can Be Overwhelming for Some Students and a Challenge for Schools in Terms of Scheduling

Suggested Approach

If a student requires an additional hour of instruction per day, teachers should consider breaking that hour into smaller instructional sessions or using several short activities to help maintain student motivation and engagement.[77]

One session could focus on decoding, and the follow-up on comprehension and vocabulary. The morning session could introduce new word reading skills, and the afternoon session practice and review.

Early reading provides critical foundational skills; such skills and strategies need to be proficient before students enter the upper elementary grades. Thus, if critical decisions need to be made about adding tier 3 instruction to a student's reading program, using time typically allocated to social studies or science may be necessary. Other less intrusive scheduling options include providing tier 3 instruction to struggling readers while other students are participating in center activities, independent projects, or the tier 1 "add-on" enrichment activities. Tier 3 instruction could also be provided during whole-class spelling instruction.

Roadblock 5.6. Some Students Who Require Tier 3 Instruction Do Not Catch-Up Despite Intensive, One-On-One Instruction

Suggested Approach

Remind school staff that a school's goal is to help each student reach proficient reading levels if at all possible. Obtaining significant progress toward reading proficiency should be the primary goal. Emphasize that the teaching process should involve more than merely providing students with an opportunity to demonstrate the reading skills that they already know. It must involve the integration of new knowledge with previously learned knowledge.

APPENDIX A. POSTSCRIPT FROM THE INSTITUTE OF EDUCATION SCIENCES

What Is a Practice Guide?

The health care professions have embraced a mechanism for assembling and communicating evidence-based advice to practitioners about care for specific clinical conditions. Variously called practice guidelines, treatment protocols, critical pathways, best practice guides, or simply practice guides, these documents are systematically developed recommendations about the course of care for frequently encountered problems, ranging from physical conditions, such as foot ulcers, to psychosocial conditions, such as adolescent development.[78]

Practice guides are similar to the products of typical expert consensus panels in reflecting the views of those serving on the panel and the social decisions that come into play as the positions of individual panel members are forged into statements that all panel members are willing to endorse. Practice guides, however, are generated under three constraints that do not typically apply to consensus panels. The first is that a practice guide consists of a list of discrete recommendations that are actionable. The second is that those recommendations taken together are intended to be a coherent approach to a multifaceted problem. The third, which is most important, is that each recommendation is explicitly connected to the level of evidence supporting it, with the level represented by a grade (high, moderate, or low).

The levels of evidence, or grades, are usually constructed around the value of particular types of studies for drawing causal conclusions about what works. Thus, one typically finds that a high level of evidence is drawn from a body of randomized controlled trials, the moderate level from well designed studies that do not involve randomization, and the low level from the opinions of respected authorities (see table 1). Levels of evidence also can be constructed around the value of particular types of studies for other goals, such as the reliability and validity of assessments.

Practice guides also can be distinguished from systematic reviews or meta-analyses such as What Works Clearinghouse (WWC) intervention reviews or statistical meta-analyses, which employ statistical methods to summarize the results of studies obtained from a rule-based search of the literature. Authors of practice guides seldom conduct the types of systematic literature searches that are the backbone of a meta-analysis, although they take advantage of such work when it is already published. Instead, authors use their expertise to identify the most important research with respect to their recommendations, augmented by a search of recent publications to ensure that the research citations are up-to-date. Furthermore, the characterization of the quality and direction of the evidence underlying a recommendation in a practice guide relies less on a tight set of rules and statistical algorithms and more on the judgment of the authors than would be the case in a high-quality meta-analysis. Another distinction is that a practice guide, because it aims for a comprehensive and coherent approach, operates with more numerous and more contextualized statements of what works than does a typical meta-analysis.

Thus, practice guides sit somewhere between consensus reports and meta-analyses in the degree to which systematic processes are used for locating relevant research and characterizing its meaning.

Practice guides are more like consensus panel reports than meta-analyses in the breadth and complexity of the topic that is addressed. Practice guides are different from both consensus reports and meta-analyses in providing advice at the level of specific action steps along a pathway that represents a more-or-less coherent and comprehensive approach to a multifaceted problem.

Practice Guides in Education at the Institute of Education Sciences

The Institute of Education Sciences (IES) publishes practice guides in education to bring the best available evidence and expertise to bear on the types of systemic challenges that cannot currently be addressed by single interventions or programs. Although IES has taken advantage of the history of practice guides in health care to provide models of how to proceed in education, education is different from health care in ways that may require a somewhat different design for practice guides in education have. Even within health care, where practice guides now number in the thousands, there is no single template in use. Rather, one finds descriptions of general design features that permit substantial variation in the realization of practice guides across subspecialties and panels of experts.[79] Accordingly, the templates for IES practice guides may vary across practice guides and change over time and with experience.

The steps involved in producing an IES– sponsored practice guide are first to select a topic, which is informed by formal surveys of practitioners and requests. Next, a panel chair is recruited who has a national reputation and up-to-date expertise in the topic. Third, the chair, working in collaboration with IES, selects a small number of panelists to coauthor the practice guide.

These are people the chair believes can work well together and have the requisite expertise to be a convincing source of recommendations. IES recommends that at least one of the panelists be a practitioner with experience relevant to the topic being addressed. The chair and the panelists are provided a general template for a practice guide along the lines of the information provided in this postscript. They are also provided with examples of practice guides. The practice guide panel works under a short deadline of six to nine months to produce a draft document. The expert panel interacts with and receives feedback from staff at IES during the development of the practice guide, but they understand that they are the authors and, thus, responsible for the final product.

One unique feature of IES-sponsored practice guides is that they are subjected to rigorous external peer review through the same office that is responsible for independent review of other IES publications. Critical tasks of the peer reviewers of a practice guide are to determine whether the evidence cited in support of particular recommendations is up-to-date and that studies of similar or better quality that point in a different direction have not been ignored. Peer reviewers also are asked to evaluate whether the evidence grade assigned to particular recommendations by the practice guide authors is appropriate. A practice guide is revised as necessary to meet the concerns of external peer reviews and gain the approval of the standards and review staff at IES. The process of external peer review is carried out independent of the office and staff within IES that instigated the practice guide.

Because practice guides depend on the expertise of their authors and their group decision-making, the content of a practice guide is not and should not be viewed as a set of recommendations that in every case depends on and flows inevitably from scientific research. It is not only possible but also likely that two teams of recognized experts working independently to produce a practice guide on the same topic would generate products that differ in important respects. Thus, consumers of practice guides need to understand that they are, in effect, getting the advice of consultants. These consultants should, on average, provide substantially better advice than an individual school district might obtain on its own because the authors are national authorities who have to reach agreement among themselves, justify their recommendations in terms of supporting evidence, and undergo rigorous independent peer review of their product.

Institute of Education Sciences

APPENDIX B. ABOUT THE AUTHORS

Panel

Russell Gersten, Ph.D., is President of RG Research Group and Executive Director of Instructional Research Group in Long Beach, California, as well as professor emeritus in the College for Education at the University of Oregon. Dr. Gersten is a nationally recognized expert on effective instructional practices to improve reading comprehension (both for narrative and expository text) and has extensive experience with the process of translating research into classroom practice. He has led the teams responsible for developing observational measures for reading comprehension and vocabulary instruction for several large-scale randomized control trials on the impact of observed practices in reading instruction on growth in reading. He is an expert in instructional strategies for improving reading comprehension, adaptations of the reading research-base for English language learner students, and longitudinal evaluation of reading programs. He has directed numerous implementation studies, large-scale evaluation projects, and randomized trial studies in the field of reading, with a focus on low-income students and English learners. Additionally, he chaired a panel of expert researchers for the National Center for Learning Disabilities in June 2005 to synthesize knowledge of best practices in early screening and intervention for students with difficulties in mathematics.

Donald L. Compton, Ph.D., is an associate professor of Special Education at Peabody College, Vanderbilt University. Before joining the faculty at Vanderbilt, Dr. Compton taught at the University of Arkansas-Fayetteville and spent a year as a postdoctoral research fellow at the Institute for Behavior Genetics at the University of Colorado-Boulder, where he worked with Dick Olson to analyze data from the twin sample of the Colorado Learning Disabilities Research Center. Dr. Compton teaches undergraduate and graduate courses in instructional principles and procedures in reading and writing for students with disabilities. His research involves modeling individual differences in the development of reading skills in children. He is currently the primary investigator on an Institute of Education Sciences (IES) project addressing the key measurement issues associated with the Response-to-Intervention (RtI) approach to identifying learning difficulties.

Carol McDonald Connor, Ph.D., is an associate professor at Florida State University and a research faculty member of the Florida Center for Reading Research. She completed her Ph.D. in Education and was an assistant research scientist in Psychology at University of Michigan prior to coming to Florida State. Dr. Connor's research interests focus on children's learning in the classroom from preschool through grade 3 and the complex relationships between children's language and literacy skills. She was recently awarded the 2006 President's Early Career Award for Scientists and Engineers and the 2007 APA Richard Snow Award. She is the principal investigator of two studies funded by the Institute of Education Sciences and the National Institute of Child Health and Human Development examining the causal effects of individualizing language arts instruction for students in grades 1–3 based on their language and reading skills.

Joseph A. Dimino, Ph.D., is a research associate at the Instructional Research Group in Long Beach, California where he is the coordinator of a national research project investigating the impact of Teacher Study Groups as a means to enhance the quality of reading instruction for first graders in high poverty schools and co-principal investigator for a study assessing the impact of collaborative strategic reading on the comprehension and vocabulary skills of English language learner and English-speaking fifth graders. Dr. Dimino has 36 years of experience as a general education teacher, special education teacher, administrator, behavior specialist, and researcher. He has extensive experience working with teachers, parents, administrators, and instructional assistants in the areas of instruction and early literacy, reading comprehension strategies, and classroom and behavior management in urban, suburban, and rural communities. He has published in numerous scholarly journals and coauthored books in reading comprehension and early reading intervention. Dr. Dimino has delivered papers at various state, national, and international conferences, including the American Educational Research Association, the National Reading Conference, and the Council for Exceptional Children and Association for Supervision and Curriculum Development. He consults nationally in the areas of early literacy and reading comprehension instruction.

Lana Edwards Santoro, Ph.D., is a research associate with the Instructional Research Group/RG Research Group and the Pacific Institutes for Research. She is a principal investigator on a series of IES–funded research on teaching reading comprehension to grade 1 students during classroom read-alouds. Of particular focus is her work to develop supplemental interventions for students at risk of early reading difficulties, students with vocabulary and language deficits, and English-language learners. She also serves as principal investigator on an IES–funded study investigating the impact of enhanced core reading instruction (tier 1) on the early literacy achievement of Spanish-speaking English language learners in transitional bilingual programs. Dr. Santoro consults with state, local, and private agencies on a variety of projects, including training presentations on effective instructional strategies, program development related to RtI and school improvement, and reading program evaluation. She has published extensively on the effects of research-based strategies on student reading. Her research has been recognized with awards from the Council for Exceptional Children and the American Educational Research Association.

Sylvia Linan-Thompson, Ph.D., is an associate professor at The University of Texas in Austin. Her research interests include development of reading interventions for struggling readers who are monolingual English speakers, English language learner and bilingual students acquiring Spanish literacy. She is co-principal investigator of several longitudinal studies funded by IES and the National Institute of Child Health and Human Development examining the language and literacy development in English and Spanish for Spanish-speaking children and the efficacy of a three-tier model of reading intervention in general education classrooms and in bilingual classrooms. She has authored curricular programs, book chapters, journal articles, and a book on reading instruction.

W. David Tilly III, Ph.D., is the Coordinator of Assessment Services at Heartland Area Education Agency. He has worked as a practicing school psychologist, a university trainer, a state department of education consultant and as an administrator in Iowa. He participated in the leadership of Iowa's transformation to using RtI practices and has extensive experience working with districts, intermediate agencies, states, and professional organizations on the implementation of RtI. His research interests include implementing system change, instructional interventions, formative assessment, and translating research into practice. He coauthored a widely used publication on RtI for the National Association of State Directors of Special Education.

Staff

Rebecca A. Newman-Gonchar, Ph.D., is a research associate with the Instructional Research Group/RG Research Group. She has experience in project management, study design and implementation, and quantitative and qualitative analysis. Dr. Newman-Gonchar has worked extensively on the development of observational measures for beginning and expository reading instruction for two major IES–funded studies of reading interventions for Title I students. She currently serves as a reviewer for the What Works Clearinghouse for reading and mathematics interventions and Response to Intervention. Her scholarly contributions include conceptual, descriptive, and quantitative publications on a range of topics. Her current interests include

Response to Intervention, observation measure development for reading and mathematics instruction, and Teacher Study Groups. She has served as the technical editor for several publications and is a reviewer for *Learning Disabilities Quarterly*.

Kristin Hallgren is a research analyst at Mathematica Policy Research and a former classroom educator. She has provided research support for several IES–sponsored practice guides, including the dropout prevention practice guide, this Response to Intervention reading and multi-tier interventions practice guide, and other forthcoming practice guides. She has conducted classroom observations and data analysis for IES–sponsored projects related to teacher quality and professional development including rigorous evaluations of teacher preparation routes and high-intensity teacher induction programs. She has also been responsible for communicating complex research design methodologies to district and school-level administrators for rigorous evaluations of supplemental educational services and mathematics curricula. Ms. Hallgren's expertise in classroom practices and background in research methodology has provided the panel with support for translating research principles into practitioner friendly text.

APPENDIX C. DISCLOSURE OF POTENTIAL CONFLICTS OF INTEREST

Practice guide panels are composed of individuals who are nationally recognized experts on the topics about which they are rendering recommendations. The Institute of Education Sciences (IES) expects that such experts will be involved professionally in a variety of matters that relate to their work as a panel. Panel members are asked to disclose their professional involvements and to institute deliberative processes that encourage critical examination of the views of panel members as they relate to the content of the practice guide. The potential influence of panel members' professional engagements is further muted by the requirement that they ground their recommendations in evidence that is documented in the practice guide. In addition, the practice guide undergoes independent external peer review prior to publication, with particular focus on whether the evidence related to the recommendations in the practice guide has been appropriately presented.

The professional engagements reported by each panel member that appear most closely associated with the panel recommendations are noted below.

Russell Gersten has no financial stake in any program or practice that is mentioned in the practice guide. He is a royalty author for what may become the Texas or national edition of the forthcoming (2010/11) Houghton Mifflin reading series, *Journeys*. At the time of publication, Houghton Mifflin has not determined whether or not they will ever release this series. Dr. Gersten provided guidance on the product as it relates to struggling and English language learner students. He excused himself from any sessions where Houghton Mifflin or any of its products were discussed. The panel never discussed the Houghton Mifflin series. Dr. Gersten also occasionally consults with universities, research agencies, and state and local education agencies on teaching English language learner students, mathematics instruction for struggling students, and various issues on bringing research findings into classroom practice.

Joseph Dimino coauthored *Interventions for Reading Success* (2007). This is not a published curriculum but a series of suggested activities for tier 2 interventions for students in the primary grades. He receives royalties from Brookes Publishing. Dr. Dimino excused himself from all discussions, reviews, and writing related to this program. This book is not referenced in this practice guide.

Lana Santoro received royalties as a consulting author for Scott Foresman Early Reading Intervention (2003). Dr. Santoro excused herself from all discussions, reviews, and writing related to this program or any other Scott Foresman products. The practice guide does not reference particular intervention or core curricula programs. It merely discusses topics that should be covered in tier 2 interventions and uses research (analyzed independently by What Works Clearinghouse) as a basis for these decisions. No specific discussion of the particular intervention program took place in panel deliberations.

Sylvia Linan-Thompson was a co-principal investigator on the research project that tested the proactive reading curriculum that is published under the name SRA's Early Interventions in Reading. Dr. LinanThompson was primarily responsible for the development of the English language learner component of the curriculum. While she is not an author on the program, SRA is considering integrating the English language learner component into some of their curricula. The proactive reading intervention was discussed in the context of two research studies, one of which met standards. However, the panel did not address specific issues in adjusting the curriculum for English learners, which is the focus of Dr. Linan-Thompson's work.

APPENDIX D. TECHNICAL INFORMATION ON THE STUDIES

Recommendation 1. Screen All Students for Potential Reading Problems at the Beginning of the Year and Again in the Middle of the Year. Regularly Monitor the Progress of Students Who Are at Elevated Risk for Developing Reading Disabilities

Level of Evidence: Moderate

The panel judged the level of evidence for recommendation 1 to be *moderate*. While a growing number of screening studies are appearing in the research literature, a majority of studies relies on correlational designs, lack cross-validation, and fail to use representative samples. In this appendix, we discuss the limited evidence base in terms of sensitivity and specificity of the measures.

Sensitivity is the degree to which a measure correctly identifies children at risk for experiencing difficulties in learning to read. In contrast, specificity is the degree to which a measure correctly identifies children at low risk for experiencing problems. These false positives refer to students who eventually become good readers but score below the cut-score on the predictive instrument and are thus falsely identified as at risk. Providing these students with extra tutoring stresses school resources, providing intervention to an inflated percentage of the population.[80]

To date, researchers have placed a premium on identification and early treatment of children at risk of future reading failure, and therefore high sensitivity rather than specificity is favored. The overall effect of demanding high sensitivity is to over-identify the risk pool of children needing tier 2 intervention. Studies predicting risk in kindergarten children have reported sensitivity rates approaching minimally acceptable level of 90 percent with specificity ranging from 56 percent to 86 percent,[81] which means that often far too many students are identified as at-risk for reading difficulties.[82]

Results are more promising for grades 1 and 2. Several studies have demonstrated sensitivity in grade 1 above 90 percent with acceptable specificity.[83] For example, Compton et al. (2006) reports sensitivity rates approaching 100 percent with specificity of 93 percent using a combination of a one-time screening battery (containing measures of word identification, phonemic awareness, and rapid naming skill) in combination with six weeks on progress monitoring. However, these results have not been cross-validated and were not obtained with a representative sample. Similar results have been reported for screening grade 2 students.[84]

Recommendation 2. Provide Differentiated Reading Instruction for All Students Based on Assessments of Students' Current Reading Levels (Tier 1)

Level of Evidence: Low

The panel rated the level of evidence for this recommendation as *low* based on one descriptive-correlational study with first and second graders that met standards with reservations and the opinion of the panel. The correlational study—Connor et al. (2008)—examines how student reading growth varied by the degree to which teachers employed a specific differentiation program. This differentiation program relied on assessments to group students. Student reading growth was higher for teachers who implemented the program with greater fidelity.

Recommendation 3. Provide Intensive, Systematic Reading Instruction on up to Three Foundational Reading Skills in Small Groups to Students Who Score below the Benchmark on Universal Screening. Typically, These Groups Meet between Three and Five Times a Week for 20 to 40 Minutes (Tier 2)

Level of Evidence: Strong

The panel judged the level of evidence supporting the recommendation to be *strong*. The panel found 11 studies conducted with students in the primary grades that met WWC standards or met standards with reservations. Table D1 provides an overview of each study's outcomes in each of the five critical aspects of beginning reading instruction as articulated in the 11 studies. The table provides an overview of the reading domains taught in each tier 2 intervention and any significant outcomes found for each of the five domains. Group size for tier 2 instruction, typical session length, and duration are also indicated. Note that many in the field consider frequency and duration as gauges of *intensity* of the intervention.[85] One study is excluded from the table but included in the accompanying text because it was a follow-up study of an intervention that produced strong effects in many reading domains.[86]

Because of the large number of high quality randomized controlled trials and quasi-experimental design studies conducted using systematic instruction in several of the critical domains of beginning reading instruction, the frequency of significant effects, and the fact that numerous research teams independently produced similar findings, the panel concluded that there is *strong* evidence to support the recommendation to provide intensive, explicit, and systematic instruction in critical reading skills stressed in National Reading Panel for tier 2 interventions.[87]

Evidence Supporting Explicit, Systematic Instruction As the Key Instructional Delivery Method for Tier 2 Tutoring on Foundational Reading Skills

All 11 studies used programs that systematically taught reading skills,[88] with seven of these studies demonstrating a positive effect on one or more reading outcomes.[89] For example, Gunn et al. (2000) conducted a randomized controlled trial involving supplementary instruction for students in kindergarten through grade 3 in phonemic awareness, sound-letter correspondence, and decoding. Instruction was highly explicit, students received many opportunities to practice each skill, and feedback was immediate and clear. Reading material consisted of decodable texts based on current reading levels. Although the emphasis was on decoding and fluency, the researchers also found an effect on reading vocabulary.

Jenkins et al. (2004) and Vadasy et al. (2005) used a virtually identical approach. Content of the intervention was similar except more time was spent on sight words and spelling. Here effects were found not only in decoding but also in comprehension. The findings suggested that, at least in kindergarten and grade 1, students with strong systematic instruction in small groups in phonemic awareness and decoding and fluent reading may also show growth in comprehension or vocabulary.

Table D1. Studies of tier 2 interventions in grades K–2 reading that met What Works Clearinghouse standards

Study	Grade level	Intervention	Reading domain assessed					Intensity		
			Phonemic awareness	Decoding	Reading comprehension	Vocabulary	Fluency	Frequency	Duration	Group size
Ebaugh, 2000	1	PA, D, E, W	*	ns				30 min./day Daily	32 weeks	5–6 students
Ehri et al. 2007	1	PA, D, E, F, C, V	*	*	*		*	30 min./day Daily	24 weeks	one-on-one
Gibbs, 2001	1	PA	ns	ns				10 min./day Daily	8 weeks	one-on-one
Gunn et al. 2000	K–3	PA, D, C, F		*	<	*	<	≥25 min./day Daily	56 weeks (over two years)	2–3 (Some one-on-one)
Jenkins et al. 2004	1	D, E		*	*		<	30 min. four times a week	25 weeks	one-on-one
Lennon and Slesinski, 1999	K	PA, D, C	*	*				30 min./day Daily	10 weeks	2 students
Mathes et al. 2005	1	Both: PA, D, C Responsive: E, F, V, W		*	* (responsive intervention) < (proactive intervention)		ns	40 min./day Daily	32 weeks	3 students

Table D1. (Continued)

Study	Grade level	Intervention	Reading domain assessed					Intensity		
			Phonemic awareness	Decoding	Reading comprehension	Vocabulary	Fluency	Frequency	Duration	Group size
Ebaugh, 2000	1	PA, D, E, W		ns				30 min./day Daily	32 weeks	5–6 students
McMaster et al. 2005	1	PA, D	ns	ns	Ns	ns	ns	35 min./day three times a week	7 months	one-on-one
Vadasy et al., 1997	1	PA, D, E	ns	ns				30 min/day four times a week	28 weeks	one-on-one
Vadasy et al., 2005	1	PA, D, E		*	*		ns	30 min/day four times a week	32 weeks	one-on-one
Vaughn et al., 2006	1	PA, D, E, C, F, V		*	*		ns	50 min./day Daily	28 weeks	3–5 students

Note: Studies in bold showed statistically significant effects in at least one domain of reading instruction.

PA = phonemic awareness, D = decoding, E = encoding (Spelling related to phonics instruction), C = Comprehension, V=Vocabulary, F=Fluency, W = writing

ns = not statistically significant (p > .10).

^ = approached significance (p = .05–.10).

* = statistically significant (p < .05).

Source: Authors' analysis based on studies in table.

Both Ehri et al. (2007) and Vaughn et al. (2006) offered the widest menu of reading domains, including comprehension and vocabulary instruction along with the core foundational skills for learning how to read. Vaughn et al. found effects in comprehension as well as decoding, whereas Ebaugh's effects were limited to decoding. Ehri included phonemic awareness, decoding, reading comprehension, and fluency.

In summary, this highly explicit, highly systematic mode of small group instruction consistently produces positive effects, often significant effects in the area of decoding and often in comprehension and vocabulary as well. What remains uncertain is the balance of "learning to read" skills and comprehension, vocabulary, and language development in tier 2 interventions. Most important, the field needs to systematically study which domain areas make the most sense for students at various levels of reading proficiency. Our hypothesis is that the balance increases to more complex reading comprehension activities once students learn to read. However, for those still struggling to learn to read, it is unclear how much instruction in vocabulary and listening comprehension is necessary.

In understanding the nature of this body of evidence, the reader should keep in mind that instruction was often one-on-one (6 out of 11 of the WWC-rated studies) or in very small groups of two to three students.

In the remainder of the section, we review impacts on specific domains of tier 2 reading instruction.

Evidence Supporting Instruction of Critical Reading Skills

Phonemic Awareness

Five studies measured phonemic awareness—a student's understanding that words consist of individual phonemes. Phonemic awareness is a potent predictor of future success in reading and a critical foundational skill for becoming a reader.[90] Significant outcomes were found for only two studies although most of the tier 2 interventions did have a phonemic awareness component.[91]

Three of the five studies showed no significant effects for phonemic awareness. In some cases, ceiling effects may have played a role in the lack of significant findings. Meanwhile, lack of significant effects in the Gibbs (2001) study may be due to the short intensity and duration of the intervention. In this investigation students received 10 minutes of phonemic awareness instruction five times per week for only eight weeks. In addition, it is common for students' phonological skills to decrease as they begin to understand letter-sound correspondence. In other words, by the time students were post-tested their understanding of the relationship between letters and the sounds they make may have influenced their performance on the phonemic awareness assessments.

Decoding

Students' ability to read real words and individual sentences (not connected text), was measured in all nine studies.[92] Significant effects were reported in five of these studies.[93] The fact that this finding is replicated frequently indicates that the various approaches to systematic explicit instruction all seem to produce growth in this domain.

Reading Comprehension

Reading comprehension assessments were used as outcome measures in 7 of the 11 studies,[94] and significant outcomes were reported in five studies.[95] This also is a sizeable proportion and indicates that one can expect effects in this domain. This is especially interesting because of the five studies that demonstrated significant effects; only three had a comprehension component. For example, Vadasy et al. (2005) and Jenkins et al. (2004) included a good deal of oral reading of decodable texts[96] but no explicit comprehension instruction. Yet effects on comprehension were significant. The reader should keep in mind that although this is an important finding, the level of comprehension tapped in most of these measures for grade 1 and 2 students is usually not very complex.

Vaughn et al's (2006) intervention included a good deal of work with oral reading of connected text but also small group instruction in a variety of comprehension strategies (using K-W-L, summarization, and retelling). This intervention led to significant effects.

Vocabulary

Students' vocabulary knowledge was rarely assessed. Of the three studies that assessed this domain,[97] significance was reported in only one.[98] Reading vocabulary is thus unlikely to improve unless the intervention contains a vocabulary component. But the small number of studies that assessed this phenomenon means that results are simply inconclusive.

Fluency

Students' ability to read connected text fluently and accurately was assessed in 7 of the 11 studies,[99] and treatment students performed significantly better in one study and approached significance (p was between .5 and .10) in two studies.[100] Students' performance on these measures resulted in a few intriguing findings. In the follow up study conducted a year after the supplemental tier 2 intervention, Gunn et al. (2002) found that fluency outcomes were significant, but the original study (Gunn et al. 2000) did not demonstrate significant fluency outcomes. In other words, it may take time before a fluency intervention demonstrates impact.

As primary grade students practice reading fluently, they seem to improve their word reading accuracy. When considered together, results suggest that fluency interventions are a promising practice, as opposed to a clear evidence-based practice for tier 2 interventions at this point in time.

Research Supporting Intensity: Frequency and Duration of Sessions and Group Size

Tier 2 instruction varied from three to five times a week. Six of the studies with significant outcomes on decoding, reading comprehension, or fluency provided daily instruction.[101] But data suggesting that daily interventions lead to better effects than those administered four days a week or even three is insufficient.

In terms of length of intervention sessions, nine studies provided at least 25 minutes of instruction,[102] with one study reporting 50 minutes of instruction per session:[103] the seven studies that had an effect on decoding, reading comprehension, or fluency provided instruction for at least 25 minutes,[104] while the three studies that had no significant effects varied in the length of sessions from 10 to 35 minutes.[105]

It is not possible to determine the role the number of days of intervention played in the studies in which no significant findings were found despite the intensity of the intervention. Although one study provided intervention five times a week, it did so for only ten minutes a day,[106] and one study provided instruction for 35 minutes but only three times a week.[107] Based on the evidence from these studies, it would be advisable to provide intervention four to five times a week and for at least 30 minutes.

In 6 of the 11 studies students were instructed on one-on-one.[108] Configurations for the remaining studies[109] consisted of small groups ranging from two to six students. The panel suggests that the combination of intensity (the amount of time per session) and duration (number of weeks) rather than the grouping configuration may be the critical variable contributing to positive outcomes for students. However, this is only speculative at this point.

The only inference that can be clearly drawn is that the 10-minute phonemic awareness lessons conducted daily for eight weeks were not intense enough to produce significant effects in reading-related skills. The one-on-one sessions tended to be reasonably lengthy (30 minutes) and of long duration. Three of the four produced significant effects.[110]

In the four investigations where students were taught in small groups[111] significant outcomes were reported for interventions that ranged between 10 weeks and 1.5 years and were conducted for 25 to 50 minutes daily. Only Mathes et al. (2005) and Vaughn et al. (2006) reported significant effects in reading comprehension. Significant outcomes in decoding and fluency were reported by Gunn (2000), while Lennon and Slesinski (1999) reported significant effects in phonemic awareness and decoding. Decoding was the only outcome measure in the Ebaugh (2000). Unfortunately, after 30 minutes of instruction per day for 32 weeks, there were no significant effects.

A Study of Intensive, Explicit, and Systematic Small Group Instruction— Vaughn, Mathes, Linan-Thompson, Cirino, Carlson, Pollard-Durodola, et al. 2006

This intervention study was conducted in two sites in Texas that were selected because they were representative of the population areas where large numbers of bilingual students go to school and because students were receiving reading instruction in English. Four schools within these districts that were considered effective for bilingual students were selected using a priori criteria: schools were providing English intervention for reading to at least two classes of grade 1 English language learner students, at least 60 percent of the student population was Latino, and schools' state-level reading achievement tests at grade 3 indicated that 80 percent or more of students passed the test.

The research team screened all students in 14 bilingual, grade 1 classrooms in the four schools. Criteria for selecting students for the intervention were determined as being those who scored below the 25th percentile in grade 1 on the Letter Word Identification subtest in both Spanish and English, and who were unable to read more than one word from the simple word list. Two-hundred sixteen students were administered both the Spanish and English screen at the four target schools. One-hundred eleven students (51 percent) met the Spanish intervention inclusion criteria, 69 students (32 percent) met the English intervention inclusion criteria, and 58 students (27 percent) met both criteria. Eleven students met the English cutoff but not the Spanish cutoff, and these students were not eligible for the intervention.

The study was initiated with 24 intervention students and 24 contrast students and due to ordinary attrition (students' families moving or students transferring to other schools), the study ended with 22 intervention and 19 contrast students (8 percent attrition for intervention and 21 percent attrition for contrast); data were not obtainable on one student (contrast) at either testing time point. The mean age of the 47 students with pretest data was 6.59 years (SD = 0.54). All students were Hispanic, and female students comprised 50 percent of the sample (n = 23).

Eligible students received daily supplemental instruction from October to April. Each session was 50 minutes long. Forty minutes were spent on literacy instruction.

The literacy strands varied in time from 5 to 12 minutes. More time was dedicated to a strand when new elements were introduced, and less time when it was review. The read aloud was always 10 minutes.

Daily lesson plans were comprised of six to ten short activities representing five content strands: phonemic awareness, letter knowledge, word recognition, connected text fluency, and comprehension strategies. Daily lessons were fully specified and provided exact wording to ensure teachers' language was clear and kept to a minimum. To ensure student engagement, there was constant interaction between the instructor and students. The lesson cycle included modeling, group response, and individual turns. Pacing was another characteristic of the intervention. A rapid pace was maintained both in the exchange in each strand and in moving from activity to activity within each lesson. Tutors also consistently monitored students' responses, provided positive praise for correct responses, and scaffolded errors as they occurred. Finally, mastery checks were conducted after every five lessons.

Given that students were assigned to intervention and contrast groups randomly, there were no significant group mean differences in performance on either of the skills (Woodcock Language Proficiency Battery-Revised (WLPB-R), letter word identification, and experimental word reading list) used in the intervention screen, in English[112] or Spanish.[113] Furthermore, mean comparison of skill performance on the larger battery administered prior to the onset of treatment indicated that students in the intervention and contrast groups performed at comparable levels on all English and Spanish skills assessed, with no significant differences between students on any measure. Reading and language performances were approximately 1 to 3 standard deviations below normative levels for both groups, with performances nearing the average range only for English Word Attack scores (for both groups).

Intervention students' performance on English measures indicate that they outperformed control students on measures that ranged from rapid letter naming to reading comprehension as measured by WLPB-R passage comprehension subtest. Intervention students' were able to match sounds, blend sounds to form words, segment words into phonemes, and delete sounds better than control students. They also outperformed intervention students on the WLPB-R Word Attack subtest, indicating that intervention students demonstrated a greater ability to apply phonic and structural analysis skills to pronounce phonetically regular nonsense words in English.

Recommendation 4. Monitor the Progress of Tier 2 Students at Least Once a Month. Use These Data to Determine Whether Students Still Require Intervention. For Those Students Still Making Insufficient Progress, School-Wide Teams Should Design a Tier 3 Intervention Plan

Level of Evidence: Low

The panel rated the level of evidence as *low*. Only three studies[114] of tier 2 interventions that met WWC standards or that met standards with reservations included a weekly progress monitoring or unit mastery component. However, neither of the studies evaluated progress monitoring as an independent variable. Thus, no inferences can be drawn about its effectiveness based on the research reviewed.

In the Mathes et al. (2005) study, teachers used data from student assessments to identify needs and strengths, and planned instruction from that analysis. In the Gibbs (2001) study, tutors collected data weekly using mastery tests. After each mastery test, tutors were directed to proceed to the next lesson or to repeat lessons based on number of correct responses.[115]

A few studies of tier 2 interventions that met WWC standards or that met standards with reservations reported using data at certain points during the intervention, but did not report on how often data was collected or if students were regrouped based on progress. Two studies used data to inform student pairings for practice within tier 2 instruction.[116] Pairs were rearranged when one participant was making more progress than the other.[117] Three additional studies used data on student progress to determine the type of instruction that students received, such as echo, partner, or independent reading.[118]

Despite the lack of evidence supporting use of progress monitoring, the panel decided to recommend this practice for students in tier 2 interventions. In our experience, progress monitoring data are used to determine students' response to tier 2 instruction and to inform instructional decisions in two ways.[119] First, data are used to identify students who need additional instruction to benefit from tier 2 instruction. This additional support, usually an additional 10 to 15 minutes, is provided to accelerate the learning of a student who is lagging behind the other students in the group.[120] It also identifies students who no longer require tier 2 instruction. It can be used to regroup students who continue to need tier 2 instruction so that tier 2 groups remain homogenous.[121] An advantage of using progress monitoring measures for these decisions (as opposed to daily or weekly mastery tests) is that they provide a more valid picture of overall growth in reading proficiency.

Recommendation 5. Provide Intensive Instruction on a Daily Basis That Promotes the Development of the Various Components of Reading Proficiency to Students Who Show Minimal Progress after Reasonable Time in Tier 2 Small Group Instruction (Tier 3)

Level of Evidence: Low
The level of evidence for this recommendation is rated as *low*. Although the panel found five studies that met the What Works Clearinghouse standards (or met standards with reservations) relating to this recommendation, no studies reported statistically significant impacts on reading outcomes.[122]

For the purposes of this document, tier 3 is defined as a layer of instructional intervention for any student in kindergarten through grade 2 who requires something substantially more intensive or substantially different than tier 2 instruction. However, tier 2 instruction is not the same as special education for students with learning disabilities. Thus, we did not include the literature base for special education for students with learning disabilities in our review, though undoubtedly some ideas about promising practice might be gleaned from this body of research.

Distinctions between tier 2 and tier 3 interventions are far from clear. In our search of the literature, we found two studies[123] on interventions that *simultaneously* targeted tier 2 and tier 3 students.[124] We, therefore, included these two studies since they provided adequate information to draw inferences about the impact on tier 3 students; three studies clearly addressed a tier 3 population.[125]

Although we found no evidence of significant effects, we believe that several of the studies suggest promising practices for tier 3 intervention. The reader should keep in mind, though, that these are merely potentially promising practices.

Although all five studies focused on a small number of high priority reading-related skills, only one included actual work on reading of words or pseudowords.[126] A trend across interventions was the use of multiple and extended instructional sessions ranging from a month[127] to a full school year.[128]

A key trait of all five studies was the use of extensive practice on the targeted reading-related skills. In all but one (Foorman et al. 1998), if a student made an error, the teaching guide or script provided explicit procedures for teachers to correct student responses. Another key trait of all but Foorman et al. (1998) was to use mastery criteria. Before a student could progress to the next skill level or new activity, they had to perform a task correctly. For example, Blumsack (1996) required that students master segmenting three phoneme items and letter-sound associations before moving forward to the next activity level.

All five studies included instruction that was designed to systematically move from easy to more difficult skills. Three of the five studies included specific material supports and manipulatives to make student learning more concrete.[129] In summary, all involved systematic instruction with extensive practice, clear feedback, teaching to mastery, and carefully thought out progression from easy to hard learning activities—all elements of direct instruction.[130]

A Study of Carefully Planned Individualized Instruction— O'Connor and Jenkins, 1995

O'Connor and Jenkins (1995) wanted to know whether teaching spelling to kindergarteners experiencing extreme difficulty learning to read would accelerate their reading growth. The intervention included ten students who had been identified as developmentally delayed and eligible for special education services while in kindergarten. The students had previously participated in 60 hours of code-emphasis, decoding-based reading instruction as part of SRA's *Reading Mastery I* series,[131] which explicitly teaches phonics and blending of phonemes.

Ten students were paired and then randomly assigned to experimental and control conditions. Students in the experimental group received 20 minutes of daily individual spelling instruction during May of their kindergarten year in addition to their daily small group code-emphasis reading instruction provided in small groups. In their spelling lessons, students pointed to and wrote letters that made a particular sound, started a particular word, or ended a particular word. Lessons at the end of the instructional sequence required students to use magnetic letters to spell words from a selected word list, as well as write two or three of the same words on paper. As students mastered words on a particular word list, new words were introduced. The teacher tracked the exact words presented during a session, the student's accuracy, and the number of times the student practiced the word before mastering the word's spelling.

Spelling instruction included systematic routines. For example, a teacher would ask students to show (point to) a letter that makes a particular sound, then write the letter that makes that particular sound. Next, students would show a letter that starts a word and then write the letter that starts the word. These routines were repeated across lessons. Instruction was also scaffolded from easier tasks to more difficult tasks. Instruction began with an individual letter and sound, then moved to first sounds, and then last sounds. Student feedback was also individualized. If a student had difficulty with a word, teachers would first ask the child to orally segment the word (a scaffold or support strategy to help the student identify the sounds in the word) and then present earlier tasks as prompts to help guide the student's response. Students in the control group received no spelling instruction at all. They spent their time practicing reading words.

Results from O'Connor and Jenkins indicate that the intensive spelling instruction component resulted in promising, although non-significant, effects in many aspects of reading and spelling. A measure of decoding approached significance with a p level of .09. Despite outcomes on spelling and word reading measures, there were no differences between groups on a phonemic segmentation task.

In addition to careful instructional planning that included individualized student feedback and error correction, mastery criteria, and lessons that moved systematically from easier tasks for more difficult tasks, O'Connor and Jenkins' results may suggest a promising practice for students who require tier 3 intervention. Specifically, the students who received spelling had a clearer and more direct presentation of how the alphabetic principle (words include letters and letters are linked to sounds) works in reading. Spelling may be a more accessible way to apply phonological skills to reading. Potentially, spelling could help demonstrate how word reading works.

REFERENCES

American Educational Research Association, American Psychological Association, and National Council on Measurement in Education. (1999). *Standards for educational and psychological testing*. Washington, DC: AERA Publications.

American Psychological Association. (2002). Criteria for practice guideline development and evaluation. *American Psychologist, 57*(12), 1048–1051.

Assessment Committee. (2002). Analysis of reading assessment measures, coding form for Dynamic Indicators of Basic Early Literacy Skills. Retrieved from the University of Oregon, DIBELS data system website: https://dibels.uoregon. edu/techreports/dibels_5th_ed.pdf.

Badian, N. A. (1994). Preschool prediction: orthographic and phonological skills, and reading. *Annals of Dyslexia, 44*(1), 3–25.

Baker, S., Gersten R., Haager, D., & Dingle, M. (2006). Teaching practice and the reading growth of first-grade English learners: Validation of an observation instrument. *Elementary School Journal, 107*(2), 199–219.

Baker, S. K., & Baker, D. L. (2008). English learners and response to intervention: Improving quality of instruction in general and special education. In E. L. Grigorenko (Ed.), *Educating individuals with disabilities: IDEA 2004 and beyond*. New York: Springer.

Barker, A. B., & Torgesen, J. K. (1995). An evaluation of computer-assisted instruction in phonological awareness with below average readers. *Journal of Educational Computing Research, 13*(1), 89–103.

Blumsack, J. B. (1996). Teaching phonological awareness to children with language impairments. (Doctoral dissertation, Syracuse University, 1996). *Dissertation Abstracts International, 58*(07A), 74–2587.

Catts, H. (1991). Early identification of dyslexia: Evidence from a follow-up study of speech-language impaired children. *Annals of Dyslexia, 41*(1), 163–177.

Chambless, J., & Chambless, M. (1994). The impact of instructional technology on reading/writing skills of 2nd grade students. *Reading Improvement, 31*(3), 151–155.

Compton, D. L., Fuchs, D., Fuchs, L. S., & Bryant, J. D. (2006). Selecting at-risk readers in first grade for early intervention: a two-year longitudinal study of decision rules and procedures. *Journal of Educational Psychology, 98*(2), 394–409.

Connor, C. M., Morrison, F. J., Fishman, B. J., Schatschneider, C., & Underwood, P. (2007). The early years: Algorithm-guided individualized reading instruction. *Science, 315*(5811), 464–465.

Connor, C. M., Piasta, S. B., Fishman, B., Glasney, S., Schatschneider, C., Crowe, E., Underwood, P., & Morrison, F. J. (2009). Individualizing student instruction precisely: Effects of child by instruction interactions on first graders' literacy development. *Child Development, 80*(1), 77–100.

Cunningham, A. E., & Stanovich, K. E. (1997). Early reading acquisition and its relation to reading experience and ability ten years later. *Developmental Psychology, 33*(6), 934–945.

Division for Learning Disabilities. (2007). *Thinking about response to intervention and learning disabilities: A teacher's guide.* Arlington, VA: Author.

Donovan, S., & Cross, C. T. (Eds.). (2002). *Minority students in special and gifted education.* Washington, DC: National Academies Press.

Ebaugh, J. C. (2000). The effects of fluency instruction on the literacy development of at-risk first graders. (Doctoral dissertation, Fordham University, 2000). *Dissertation Abstracts International, 61*(06A), 0072.

Ehri, L. C., Dreyer, L. G., Flugman, B., & Gross, A. (2007). Reading rescue: An effective tutoring intervention model for language-minority students who are struggling readers in first grade. *American Educational Research Journal, 44*(2), 414–48.

Englemann, S., & Bruner, E. (1988). *Reading Mastery.* Chicago: Science Research Associates.

Engelmann, S., & Carnine, D. (1982) *Theory of instruction: principles and practice.* New York: Irvington.

Felton, R. H. (1992). Early identification of children at risk of reading disabilities. *Topics in Early Childhood Special Education, 12*(2), 212–229.

Felton, R. H., & Pepper, P. P. (1995). Early identification and intervention of phonological deficits in kindergarten and early elementary children at risk for reading disability. *School Psychology Review, 24*(3), 405–414.

Field, M. J. & Lohr, K. N. (Eds). (1990). *Clinical practice guidelines: Directions for a new program.* Washington, DC: National Academy Press.

Foorman, B. R., Fletcher, J. M., Francis, D. J., Schatschneider, C., & Mehta, P. (1998). The role of instruction in learning to read: Preventing reading failure in at-risk children. *Journal of Educational Psychology, 90*(1), 37–55.

Francis, D. J., Fletcher, J. M., Stuebing, K. K., Lyon, G. R., Shaywitz, B. A., & Shaywitz, S. E. (2005). Psychometric approaches to the identification of LD: IQ and achievement scores are not sufficient. *Journal of Learning Disabilities, 38*, 98–108.

Francis, D. J., Shaywitz, S. E., Stuebing, K. K., Shaywitz, B. A., & Fletcher, J. M. (1996). Developmental lag versus deficit models of reading disability: A longitudinal, individual growth curve analysis. *Journal of Educational Psychology, 88*(1), 3–17.

Fuchs, L. S., Deno, S. L. & Mirkin, P. K. (1984). Effects of frequent curriculum-based measurement on pedagogy, student achievement, and student awareness of learning. *American Educational Research Journal, 21*(2), 449–450

Fuchs, L. S., Fuchs, D., & Compton, D. L. (2004). Monitoring early reading development in first grade: Word identification fluency versus nonsense word fluency. *Exceptional Children, 71*(1), 7–21.

Fuchs, L S., Fuchs, D., & Hamlett, C. L. (1989a). Effects of alternative goal structures within curriculum-based measurement. *Exceptional Children, 55*(5), 429–438.

Fuchs, L. S., Fuchs, D., & Maxwell, L. (1988). The validity of informal reading comprehension measures. *Remedial and Special Education, 9*(2), 20–29.

Fuchs, L. S., Fuchs, D., Hosp, M., & Jenkins, J. R. (2001a). Oral reading fluency as an indicator of reading competence: A theoretical, empirical, and historical analysis. *Scientific Studies of Reading, 5*(3), 239–256.

Fuchs, D., Fuchs, L. S., Thompson, A., Al Otaiba, S., Yen, L., Yang, N., Braun, M., & O'Connor, R. (2001b). Is reading important in reading-readiness programs? A randomized field trial with teachers as program implementers. *Journal of Educational Psychology, 93*(2), 251–267.

Fuchs, D., Fuchs, L. S., & Vaughn, S. (Eds.). (2008). *Response to intervention.* Newark, DE: International Reading Association.

Gersten, R., Dimino, J., & Jayanthi, M. (2008). *Reading comprehension and vocabulary instruction: Results of an observation study of first grade classrooms.* Paper presented at the annual meeting of the Society for the Scientific Study of Reading, Asheville, NC, July 10–12, 2008.

Gibbs, S. E. L. (2001). Effects of a one-to-one phonological awareness intervention on first grade students identified as at risk for the acquisition of beginning reading. (Doctoral dissertation, University of South Carolina, 2001). *Dissertation Abstracts International, 62*(07A), 0202.

Gillon, G. T. (2000). The efficacy of phonological awareness intervention for children with spoken language impairment. *Language, Speech and Hearing Services in Schools, 31*(2), 126–141.

Good, R. H., & Kaminski, R. (2003). *Dynamic indicators of basic early literacy skills.* Longmont, CO: Sopris West Educational Services.

Good, R. H., Simmons, D. C., & Kame'enui, E. J. (2001). The importance of decision-making utility of a continuum of fluency-based indicators of foundational reading skills for third grade high-stakes outcomes. *Scientific Studies of Reading, 5*(3), 257–288.

Gunn, B., Biglan, A., Smolkowski, K., & Ary, D. (2000). The efficacy of supplemental instruction in decoding skills for Hispanic and non-Hispanic students in early elementary school. *The Journal of Special Education, 34*(2), 90–103.

Gunn, B., Smolkowski, K., Biglan, A., & Black, C. (2002). Supplemental instruction in decoding skills for Hispanic and non-Hispanic students in early elementary school: a follow-up. *The Journal of Special Education, 36*(2), 69–79.

Haager, D., Klingner, J., & Vaughn, S. (Eds.). (2007). *Evidence-based reading practices for response to intervention.* Baltimore, MD: Paul Brooks Publishing Co.

Harn, B. A., Linan-Thompson, S., & Roberts, G. (2008). Intensifying instruction. *Journal of Learning Disabilities, 41*(2), 115–125.

Heller, K. A., Holtzman, W. H., & Messick, S. (Eds.). (1982). *Placing children in special education: A strategy for equity.* Washington, DC: National Academy Press.

Individuals with Disabilities Education Improvement Act, Pub. L. No. 108–446 (2004).

Jenkins, J. R. (2003, December). *Candidate measures for screening at-risk students.* Paper presented at the Conference on Response to Intervention as Learning Disabilities Identification, sponsored by the National Research Center on Learning Disabilities, Kansas City, MO.

Jenkins, J. R., Hudson, R. F., & Johnson, E. S. (2007). Screening for at-risk readers in a response to intervention framework. *School Psychology Review, 36*(4), 582–600.

Jenkins, J. R., & O'Connor, R. E. (2002). Early identification and intervention for young children with reading/learning disabilities. In R. Bradley, L. Danielson, and D. P. Hallahan (Eds.), *Identification of learning disabilities: Research to practice* (pp. 99–149). Mahwah, NJ: Erlbaum.

Jenkins, J. R., Peyton, J. A., Sanders, E. A., & Vadasy, P. F. (2004). Effects of reading decodable texts in supplemental first-grade tutoring. *Scientific Studies of Reading*, *8*(1), 53–85.

Johnson, E., Jenkins, J., Petscher, Y., & Catts, H. (in press). How can we improve the accuracy of screening instruments? *Learning Disabilities Research & Practice*.

Juel, C. (1988). Learning to read and write: A longitudinal study of 54 children from first through fourth grades. *Journal of Educational Psychology*, *80*(4), 437–447.

Lennon, J. E., & Slesinski, C. (1999). Early intervention in reading: Results of a screening and intervention program for kindergarten students. *School Psychology Review*, *28*(3), 353–364.

Mathes, P. G., Denton, C., Fletcher, J., Anthony, J., Francis, D., & Schatschneider, C. (2005). The effects of theoretically different instruction and student characteristics on the skills of struggling readers. *Reading Research Quarterly*, *40*(2), 148–182.

McCardle, P., Scarborough, H. S., & Catts, H. W. (2001). Predicting, explaining, and preventing children's reading difficulties. *Learning Disabilities Research & Practice,* *16*(4), 230–239.

McMaster, K. L., Fuchs, D., Fuchs, L. S., & Compton, D. L. (2005). Responding to nonresponders: An experimental field trial of identification and intervention methods. *Exceptional Children*, *71*(4), 445–463.

National Association of State Directors of Special Education. (2005). *Response to intervention: Policy considerations and implementation.* Alexandria, VA: Author.

National Reading Panel. (2000). *Teaching children to read: An evidence-based assessment of the scientific research literature on reading and its implications for reading instruction* (National Institute of Health Pub. No. 00-4769). Washington, DC: National Institute of Child Health and Human Development.

Nunnally, J. (1978). *Psychometric theory*. New York, NY: McGraw–Hill.

O'Connor, R. E., & Jenkins, J. R. (1995). Improving the generalization of sound/ symbol knowledge: Teaching spelling to kindergarten children with disabilities. *Journal of Special Education*, *29*(3), 255–275.

O'Connor, R. E., & Jenkins, J. R. (1999). The prediction of reading disabilities in kindergarten and first grade. *Scientific Studies of Reading*, *3*(2), 159–197.

Phillips, L. M., Norris, S. P., Osmond, W. C., & Maynard, A. M. (2002). Relative reading achievement: A longitudinal study of 187 children from first through sixth grades. *Journal of Educational Psychology, 94*(1), 3–13.

President's Commission on Excellence in Special Education. (2002). *A new era: Revitalizing special education for children and their families. Washington, DC:* Author.

Scarborough, H. S. (1998a). Early identification of children at risk for reading disabilities: Phonological awareness and some other promising predictors. In B. K. Shapiro, P. J. Accardo, & A. J. Capute (Eds.), *Specific reading disability: A view of the spectrum* (pp. 75–119). Timonium, MD: York Press.

Schatschneider, C. (2006). *Reading difficulties: Classification and issues of prediction.* Paper presented at the Pacific Coast Regional Conference, San Diego, CA.

Snow, C. E. (2001). *Reading for understanding.* Santa Monica, CA: RAND Education and the Science and Technology Policy Institute.

Snow, C. S., Burns, S. M., & Griffin, P. (1998). *Preventing reading difficulties in young children.* Washington, DC: National Academy Press.

Speece, D., & Case, L. (2001). Classification in context: an alternative approach to identifying early reading disability. *Journal of Educational Psychology, 93*(4), 735–749.

Speece, D., Mills, C., Ritchey, K., & Hillman, E. (2003b). Initial evidence that letter fluency tasks are valid indicators of early reading skill. *Journal of Special Education, 36*(4), 223–233.

Swanson, H. L., Hoskyn, M., & Lee, C. (1999). *Interventions for students with learning disabilities: A meta-analysis of treatment outcomes.* New York, NY: Guilford Press.

Technical report: Texas primary reading inventory (1999 Edition). Retrieved from: http://www.tpri.org/Documents/ 19981999TechnicalReport.pdf.

Torgesen, J. K. (2002). The prevention of reading difficulties. *Journal of School Psychology, 40*(1), 7–26.

Torgesen, J. K., & Burgess, S. R. (1998). Consistency of reading-related phonological processes throughout early childhood: Evidence from longitudinal-correlational and instructional studies. In J. Metsala, & L. Ehri (Eds.), *Word recognition in beginning reading* (pp. 161–188). Hillsdale, NJ: Lawrence Erlbaum Associates.

Torgesen, J. K., Rashotte, C. A., & Alexander, A. (2001). Principles of fluency instruction in reading: Relationships with established empirical outcomes. In M. Wolf (Ed.), *Time, fluency, and developmental dyslexia.* Parkton, MD: York Press.

Torgesen, J. K., Wagner, R. K., & Rashotte, C. A. (1997). Prevention and remediation of severe reading disabilities: Keeping the end in mind. *Scientific Studies of Reading, 1*(3), 217–234.

Vadasy, P. F., Jenkins, J. R., Antil, L. R., Wayne, S. K., & O'Connor, R. E. (1997). The effectiveness of one-to-one tutoring by community tutors for at-risk beginning readers. *Learning Disability Quarterly, 20*(2), 126–139.

Vadasy, P. F., Sanders, E. A., & Peyton, J. A. (2005). Relative effectiveness of reading practice or word-level instruction in supplemental tutoring: How text matters. *Journal of Learning Disabilities, 38*(4), 364–380.

Vaughn, S., & Fuchs, L.S. (2006). A response to "Competing views: A dialogue on response to intervention." *Assessment for Effective Intervention, 32*(1), 58–61.

Vaughn, S., Linan-Thompson, S., & Hickman, P. (2003). Response to instruction as a means of identifying students with reading/learning disabilities. *Exceptional Children, 69*(4), 391–409.

Vaughn, S., Mathes, P., Linan-Thompson, S., Cirino, P., Carlson, C., Pollard-Durodola, S., Cardenas-Hagan, E., & Francis, D. (2006). Effectiveness of an English intervention for first-grade English language learners at risk for reading problems. *Elementary School Journal, 107*(2), 153–180.

Vellutino, F. R., Scanlon, D. M., Small, S. G., Fanuele, D. P., & Sweeney, J. (2007). Preventing early reading difficulties through kindergarten and first grade intervention: A variant of the three-tier model. In D. Haager, S. Vaughn, & J. K. Klinger (Eds.), *Validated practices for three tiers of reading intervention* (pp. 186). Baltimore, MD: Paul H. Brookes Publishing Co.

Wagner, R. K., Torgesen, J. K., & Rashotte, C. A. (1999). *Comprehensive test of phonological processing.* Austin, TX: PRO-ED.

Wanzek, J., & Vaughn, S. (2007). Research-based implications from extensive early reading interventions. *School Psychology Review, 36*(4), 541–562.

Woodcock, R. W. (1991). *Woodcock language proficiency battery—revised.* Chicago, IL: Riverside.

Woodcock, R. W., & Muñoz-Sandoval, A. F. (1995). *Woodcock language proficiency battery—revised: Spanish form.* Itasca, IL: Riverside.

End Notes

[1] Following WWC guidelines, we consider a positive, statistically significant effect, or an effect size greater than 0.25, as an indicator of positive effects.

[2] Johnson, Jenkins, Petscher, and Catts (in press, pp. 3–4).

[3] Fuchs, Fuchs, and Vaughn (2008) make the case for a three-tier RtI model.

[4] Vaughn and Fuchs (2006).

[5] Division for Learning Disabilities (2007).

[6] Vellutino, Scanlon, Small, Fanuele, and Sweeney (2007).

[7] Haager, Klingner, and Vaughn (2007).

[8] Donovan and Cross (2002).

[9] Cited in Haager et al. (2007, p. 5, emphasis added).

[10] Donovan and Cross (2002); Heller, Holtzman, and Messick (1982).

[11] See Cunningham and Stanovich (1997); Felton and Pepper (1995); Phillips, Norris, Osmond, and Maynard (2002); Francis, Shaywitz, Stuebing, Shaywitz, and Fletcher (1996); Juel (1988); Torgesen and Burgess (1998); Torgesen, Rashotte, and Alexander (2001).

[12] Donovan and Cross (2002); Heller, Holtzman, and Messick (1982).

[13] Connor, Morrison, Fishman, Schatschneider, and Underwood (2007).

[14] Burns, Snow and Griffin (1996).

[15] Schatschneider (2006).

[16] Compton, Fuchs, Fuchs, and Bryant (2006); McCardle, Scarborough, and Catts (2001); O'Connor and Jenkins (1999); Scarborough (1998a); Fuchs, Fuchs, and Compton (2004); Speece, Mills, Ritchey, and Hillman (2003b).

[17] American Education Research Association, American Psychological Association, and National Council on Measurement in Education (1999).

[18] Jenkins and O'Connor (2002); O'Connor and Jenkins (1999); Scarborough (1998a); Torgesen (2002); Badian (1994); Catts (1991); Felton (1992).

[19] Compton et al. (2006); Jenkins, Hudson, and Johnson (2007).

[20] Compton et al. (2006); McCardle, Scarborough, and Catts (2001); O'Connor and Jenkins (1999); Scarborough (1998a); Fuchs, Fuchs, and Compton (2004); Speece et al. (2003b).

[21] American Education Research Association, American Psychological Association, and National Council on Measurement in Education (1999).

[22] Coefficient alpha estimates are .84 for grade 1 letter sound knowledge, .80 for grade 1 phoneme blending, and .85 and .83 for grade 1 and 2 word reading on the Texas Primary Reading Inventory (1999). Coefficient alpha estimates are .92 and .91 for 6 and 7 year old children on the elision measure and .89 and .86 for 6 and 7 year old children on the sound matching measure on the Comprehensive Test of Phonological Processing (Wagner, Torgeson, and Rashotte 1999). Alternate test-form and stability coefficients exceed .90 in grade 1 for the word identification fluency task (Compton et al. 2006). For the DIBELS measures alternative-form reliability estimate for grade 1 letter naming fluency, .86 for grade 1 non-word fluency it is .83, and .90 for grade 2 oral reading fluency (Good and Kaminski 2003).

[23] Foorman, Fletcher, Francis, Schatschneider, and Mehta (1998); O'Connor and Jenkins (1999); Jenkins and O'Connor (2002); McCardle, Scarborough, and Catts (2001).

[24] Compton et al. (2006); O'Connor and Jenkins (1999); Foorman et al. (1998).

[25] See http://www.rti4success.org/ or http:// www.studentprogress.org/.

[26] Fuchs et al. (2004); Compton et al. (2006)

[27] Jenkins and O'Connor (2002); McCardle, Scarborough, and Catts (2001); O'Connor and Jenkins (1999); Scarborough (1998a); Torgesen (2002).

[28] Foorman et al. (1998).

[29] Compton et al. (2006); Fuchs et al. (2004).

[30] Nunnally (1978).

[31] See http://www.rti4success.org/ or http:// www.studentprogress.org/.

[32] Jenkins (2003).

[33] Schatschneider (2006).

[34] See http://www.rti4success.org/ or http:// www.studentprogress.org/.

[35] Compton et al. (2006).

[36] See http://www.studentprogress.org/ or http://iris

[37] Francis et al. (2005).

[38] National Reading Panel (2000).

[39] Connor, Piasta, Fishman, Glasney, Schat- schneider, Crowe, Underwood, and Morrison (2009).

[40] Snow (2001).

[41] Ebaugh (2000); Gunn, Biglan, Smolkowski, and Ary (2000); Mathes, Denton, Fletcher, Anthony, Francis, and Schatschneider (2005); Jenkins, Peyton, Sanders, and Vadasy (2004); Lennon and Slesinski (1999); Vaughn, Mathes, LinanThompson, Cirino, Carlson, Pollard-Durodola, Cardenas-Hagan, and Francis (2006); Vadasy, Sanders, and Peyton (2005); Ehri, Dreyer, Flugman, and Gross (2007); Gibbs (2001); McMaster, Fuchs, Fuchs, and Compton (2005); Vadasy, Jenkins, Antil, Wayne, and O'Connor (1997).

[42] Ebaugh (2000); Gunn et al. (2000); Jenkins et al. (2004); Lennon and Slesinski (1999); Vadasy, Sanders, and Peyton (2005); Vaughn et al. (2006).

[43] Gunn et al. (2000); Jenkins et al. (2004); Vadasy, Sanders, and Peyton (2005); Vaughn et al. (2006).

[44] Gunn et al. (2000); McMaster et al. (2005); Vadasy et al. (1997); Vadasy, Sanders, and Peyton (2005); Jenkins et al. (2004); Gibbs (2001).

[45] Ehri et al. (2007); Lennon and Slesinski (1999).

[46] Vadasy, Sanders, and Peyton (2005); Jenkins et al. (2004); Vaughn et al. (2006); Ehri et al. (2007).

[47] Gunn et al. (2000).

[48] Gunn et al. (2000); Jenkins et al. (2004); Ehri et al. (2007); Ebaugh (2000); Vadasy, Sanders, and Peyton (2005); Vaughn et al. (2006).

[49] There are some obvious exceptions, such as students already identified as students with significant cognitive disabilities, students who already have Individualized Education Programs in reading or language involving a much more basic curriculum.

[50] Lennon and Slesinski (1999).

[51] Gunn et al. (2000).

[52] Gunn et al. (2000); McMaster et al. (2005); Jenkins et al. (2004); Vaughn et al. (2006); Ehri et al. (2007).

[53] Gunn et al. (2000).

[54] Vaughn et al. (2006); Gunn et al. (2000).

[55] Gunn et al. (2000); Gunn, Smolkowski, Biglan, and Black (2002); Lennon and Slesinski (1999).

[56] Wanzek and Vaughn (2007).

[57] Gunn et al. (2002); Vadasy, Sanders, and Peyton (2005); Vaughn et al. (2006); Mathes et al. (2005); Jenkins et al. (2004); McMaster et al. (2005).

[58] Vaughn, Linan-Thompson, and Hickman (2003).

[59] McMaster et al. (2005); Vaughn et al. (2006); Mathes et al. (2005).

[60] Fuchs, Deno, and Mirkin (1984).

[61] Fuchs, Deno, and Mirkin (1984).

[62] Johnson et al. (in press).

[63] McMaster et al. (2005); Foorman et al. (1998); Blumsack (1996); Gillon (2000); O'Connor and Jenkins (1995).

[64] Torgesen, Wagner, and Rashotte (1997).

[65] Blumsack (1996); Foorman et al. (1998); Gillon (2000).

[66] National Reading Panel (2000).

[67] Blumsack (1996).

[68] Gillon (2000).

[69] Barker and Torgesen (1995); Chambless and Chambless (1994); National Reading Panel (2000).

[70] Blumsack (1996); Gillon (2000); McMaster et al. (2005); O'Connor and Jenkins (1995).

[71] Blumsack (1996); Foorman et al. (1998); Gillon (2000); O'Connor and Jenkins (1995).

[72] Swanson, Hoskyn, and Lee (1999).

[73] Blumsack (1996); Foorman et al. (1998); Gillon (2000); McMaster et al. (2005); O'Connor and Jenkins (1995).

[74] O'Connor and Jenkins (1995).

[75] Gillon (2000).

[76] O'Connor and Jenkins (1995).

[77] Gillon (2000).

[78] Field and Lohr (1990).

[79] American Psychological Association (2002).

[80] Jenkins and O'Connor (2002).

[81] Foorman et al. (1998); O'Connor and Jenkins (1999).

[82] See Jenkins and O'Connor (2002) for a discussion of the issue and for designing a manageable and acceptable risk pool for use within an RtI framework.

[83] Compton et al. (2006); O'Connor and Jenkins (1999).

[84] Foorman et al. (1998).

[85] National Association of State Directors of Special Education (2005).

[86] Gunn et al. (2002).

[87] National Reading Panel (2000).

[88] Gunn et al. (2000); McMaster et al. (2005); Vadasy et al. (1997); Vadasy, Sanders, and Peyton (2005); Jenkins et al. (2004); Gibbs (2001); Vaughn et al. (2006); Ebaugh (2000); Ehri et al. (2007); Mathes et al. (2005).

[89] Gunn et al. (2000); Jenkins et al. (2004); Ehri et al. (2007); Ebaugh (2000); Vadasy, Sanders, and Peyton (2005); Vaughn et al. (2006).

[90] Vaughn et al. (2006); Gunn et al. (2000); Vadasy, Sanders, and Peyton (2005); Ebaugh (2000); Lennon and Slesinski (1999).

[91] Vadasy, Sanders, and Peyton (2005); Lennon and Slesinksi (1999).

[92] Gunn et al. (2000); McMaster et al. (2005); Vadasy et al. (1997); Vadasy, Sanders, and Peyton (2005); Jenkins et al. (2004); Gibbs (2001); Lennon and Slesinski (1999); Ebaugh, (2000); Ehri et al. (2007).

[93] Ehri et al. (2007); Gunn et al. (2000); Jenkins et al. (2004); Lennon and Slesinski (1999); Vadasy, Sanders, and Peyton (2005).

[94] Gunn et al. (2000); McMaster et al. (2005); Vadasy, Sanders, and Peyton (2005); Jenkins et al. (2004); Vaughn et al. (2006); Ehri et al. (2007); Mathes et al. (2005).

[95] Vadasy, Sanders, and Peyton (2005); Jenkins et al. (2004); Vaughn et al. (2006); Ehri et al. (2007); Mathes et al. (2005).

[96] Jenkins et al. (2004) also contained a condition where students read books that were not necessarily decodable. This condition, too, led to significant effects in comprehension.

[97] Gunn et al. (2000); Gunn et al. (2002); McMaster et al. (2005).

[98] Gunn et al. (2000).

[99] Gunn et al. (2000); Mathes et al. (2005); Jenkins et al. (2004); Ehri et al. (2007); McMaster et al. (2005); Vadasy, Sanders, and Peyton (2005); Vaughn et al. (2006).

[100] Gunn et al. (2002); Vadasy, Sanders, and Peyton (2005); Ehri et al. (2007).

[101] Ebaugh (2000); Gibbs (2001); Gunn et al. (2000); Lennon and Slesinski (1999); Vaughn et al. (2006); Mathes et al. (2005).

[102] Ebaugh (2000); Gibbs (2001); Gunn et al. (2000); Mathes et al. (2005); Jenkins et al. (2004); Lennon and Slesinski (1999); McMaster et al. (2005); Vadasy et al. (1997); Vadasy, Sanders, and Peyton (2005).

[103] Vaughn et al. (2006).

[104] Ebaugh (2000); Gunn et al. (2000); Gunn et al. (2002); Jenkins et al. (2004); Lennon and Slesinski (1999); Vadasy, Sanders, and Peyton (2005); Vaughn et al. (2006).

[105] McMaster et al. (2005); Vadasy et al. (1997); Gibbs (2001).

[106] Gibbs (2001).

[107] McMaster et al. (2005).

[108] McMaster et al. (2005); Vadasy et al. (1997); Vadasy, Sanders, and Peyton (2005); Jenkins et al. (2004); Gibbs (2001); Erhi et al. (2007).

[109] Lennon and Slesinski (1999); Ebaugh (2000); Gunn et al. (2000); Vaughn et al. (2006).

[110] Vadasy, Sanders, and Peyton (2005); Jenkins et al. (2004); Ehri et al. (2007).

[111] Lennon and Slesinski (1999); Ebaugh (2000); Gunn et al. (2000); Vaughn et al. (2006).

[112] Woodcock (1991).

[113] Woodcock and Muñoz-Sandoval (1995).

[114] Mathes et al. (2005); McMaster et al. (2005); Gibbs (2001).

[115] Gibbs (2001).

[116] Lennon and Slesinski (1999); Gunn et al. (2000).

[117] Lennon and Slesinski (1999).

[118] Jenkins et al. (2004); Vadasy, Sanders, and Peyton (2005); Ehri et al. (2007).

[119] McMaster et al. (2005).

[120] Vaughn, Linan-Thompson, and Hickman (2003).

[121] Vaughn, Linan-Thompson, and Hickman (2003).

[122] McMaster et al. (2005); Foorman et al. (1998); Blumsack (1996); Gillon (2000); O'Connor and Jenkins (1995).

[123] Foorman et al. (1998); McMaster et al. (2005).

[124] Both tier 2 and tier 3 studies were conducted with students in the primary grades with reading difficulties or significant delays in reading (for example, students were considered "nonresponders" due to reading performance and growth rates substantially below average achieving peers).

[125] Blumsack (1996); Gillon (2000); O'Connor and Jenkins (1995).

[126] Foorman et al. (1998).

[127] O'Connor and Jenkins (1995).

[128] McMaster et al. (2005); Foorman et al. (1998).

[129] Blumsack (1996); Gillon (2000); O'Connor and Jenkins (1996).

[130] Engelmann and Carnine (1981).

[131] Engelmann and Bruner (1988).

INDEX

D

M

N

O

P

Q

R